ADAPTIVE HYPERTEXT AND HYPERMEDIA

ADAPTIVE HYPERTEXT
AND
HYPERMEDIA

Edited by

Peter Brusilovsky
Carnegie Mellon University

Alfred Kobsa
GMD FIT
German National Research Centre for Information Technology

and

Julita Vassileva
University of Saskatchewan

KLUWER ACADEMIC PUBLISHERS
DORDRECHT / BOSTON / LONDON

A C.I.P. Catalogue record for this book is available from the Library of Congress.

ISBN 978-90-481-4944-5

Published by Kluwer Academic Publishers,
P.O. Box 17, 3300 AA Dordrecht, The Netherlands.

Sold and distributed in the U.S.A. and Canada
by Kluwer Academic Publishers,
101 Philip Drive, Norwell, MA 02061, U.S.A.

In all other countries, sold and distributed
by Kluwer Academic Publishers,
P.O. Box 322, 3300 AH Dordrecht, The Netherlands.

Printed on acid-free paper

PREFACE

Hypertext/hypermedia systems and user-model based adaptive systems in the areas of learning and information retrieval have for a long time been considered as two mutually exclusive approaches to information access. Adaptive systems cater information to the user and may guide the user in the information space to present the most relevant material, taking into account a model of the user's goals, interests and preferences. Hypermedia systems, on the other hand, are "user neutral"; they provide the user with the tools and the freedom to explore an information space by browsing through a complex network of information nodes. Adaptive hypertext and hypermedia systems attempt to bridge the gap between these two approaches.

Adaptation of hypermedia systems to each individual user is increasingly needed. With the growing size, complexity and heterogeneity of current hypermedia systems, such as the World Wide Web, it becomes virtually impossible to impose guidelines on authors concerning the overall organization of hypermedia information. The networks therefore become so complex and unstructured that the existing navigational tools are no longer powerful enough to provide orientation on where to search for the needed information. It is also not possible to identify appropriate pre-defined paths or subnets for users with certain goals and knowledge backgrounds since the user community of hypermedia systems is usually quite inhomogeneous. This is particularly true for Web-based applications which are expected to be used by a much greater variety of users than any earlier standalone application. A Web-based hypertext application which is designed with a particular class of users in mind may not suit users of other classes.

A possible remedy for the negative effects of the traditional "one-size-fits-all" approach in the development of hypermedia systems is to equip them with the ability *to adapt to the needs of their individual users*. A possible way for achieving adaptivity is by modeling the users and tailoring the system's interactions to their goals, tasks and interests. In this sense, the notion of adaptive hypertext/hypermedia comes natural to denote *a hypertext or hypermedia system which reflects some features of the user and/or characteristics of his system usage in a user model, and utilizes this model in order to adapt various behavioral aspects of the system to the user.*

Adaptive hypertext and hypermedia (for brevity, we will henceforth use the acronym AH) are a very new kind of user-model-based adaptive systems. Though they are well grounded in research on Intelligent Tutoring Systems, Help Systems and Information Retrieval Systems, real adaptive hypertext systems appeared less than 5 years ago. However, quite a few have been developed during the past four years. AH systems become increasingly important with the growing commercial availability of hypermedia applications. More and more users who have access to such systems are unfamiliar with them and/or

v

their domains, and face difficulties in navigation and query formulation. The need for AH systems has also been recently recognized by the industry, and this field promises to become one of great commercial interest in the near future.

This book is the first comprehensive publication on adaptive hypertext and hypermedia. It is oriented towards researchers and practitioners in the fields of hypertext and hypermedia, information systems, and personalized systems. It is also an important resource for the numerous developers of Web-based applications. The design decisions, adaptation methods, and experience presented in this book are a unique source of ideas and techniques for developing more usable and more intelligent Web-based systems suitable for a great variety of users. The practitioners will find it important that many of the adaptation techniques presented in this book proved to be efficient and are ready to be used in various applications. From a research point of view it is important that the papers in this book provide a topical state-of-the-art picture of adaptive hypertext and hypermedia problems and solutions.

This book has its origin in the recently published special issue of *User Modeling and User Adapted Interaction: An International Journal [1]*. Since its publication, this special issue has become a source of creative ideas for many researchers on hypermedia and adaptive systems. The five papers which constitute the special issue are highly cited in many recent publications. User Modeling and User Adapted Interaction is a journal known as the primary source of high-quality papers on adaptive systems. It is not surprising that three earlier important full-size papers on adaptive hypertext were also published in this journal. The goal of this book is to make all these excellent papers available to a broader audience under a single cover.

Altogether, this book is a collection of the currently most influential papers on adaptive hypertext and hypermedia.

Brusilovsky's article provides a comprehensive state-of-the-art review of adaptive hypertext and hypermedia. This highly cited survey is centered around methods and techniques used in existing AH systems. The other papers go deeply into the characteristics of a particular AH system, attempt to generalize the major concerns that define adaptivity, or describe in detail a particular application.

The paper by Kaplan, Fenwick and Chen is one of the first and most often referenced papers on adaptive navigation support.. It describes an on-line information system, HYPERFLEX, which can suggest an adaptively sorted list of relevant links, taking into account users' search goals and preferences. The results of two experiments with HYPERFLEX presented in the paper show that this kind of adaptive navigation support leads to more efficient navigation.

Boyle and Encarnacion discuss the problems of *expertise-adapted presentation* in hypermedia systems. They present MetaDoc, one of the earliest and most influential adaptive hypermedia systems. MetaDoc uses the stretchtext technique to adapt the content of hypermedia manual pages to the experience level of the user. Experiments with MetaDoc described in the paper show that adaptive stretchtext can increase reading comprehension without increasing document reading time.

The paper by Hohl, Böcker and Gunzenhäuser is the first archive publication of Hypadapter, an early adaptive hypertext system that gives individualized support in exploratory learning and programming in the domain of Common Lisp. The system employs domain and user modeling techniques to provide two principled types of assistance: *individualized presentations of topic nodes and individualized navigation help.*

Beaumont's paper provides an example of an intelligent tutoring systems (ITS) with an adaptive hypermedia component. The system Anatom-Tutor presented in the paper demonstrates how a traditional ITS student model can be used to support *hypermedia adaptation on the content level.*

Höök et al. discuss principles for *adaptive interface design using a hypertext help* system as an example, which is able to infer users' tasks and plans, and to provide appropriate help.

Mathé and Chen describe an *adaptive hypermedia information retrieval system* which maintains an individual model of users' tasks, preferences, history, queries etc., in order to provide a complex secondary indexing scheme called "Adaptive Relevance Network". This network provides long-term adaptation based both on system usage and on explicit user input. Without any *a priori* specialized structure or statistical knowledge, the system evolves its dynamic indexing structure over time and allows users to quickly access information relevant to specific tasks.

Vassileva takes the opposite approach of Mathé and Chen. She describes a deployed application of an adaptive hypermedia system for hospital information (namely a large loosely-coupled office documentation systems with underlying databases). The *system limits the browsing space based on the current task* performed by the user (tasks are defined *a-priori* by task-analysis), thus achieving higher efficiency in task performance. It also *adapts the size of the browsing space and the direct search options available to the user's level of experience* by gradually allowing the use of alternative indexing schemes.

The editors hope that this book will shed new light on adaptation and user modeling in AH systems and will become a landmark on the road towards more user-friendly hypertext and hypermedia systems.

Peter Brusilovsky

Alfred Kobsa

Julita Vassileva

TABLE OF CONTENTS

Methods and Techniques of Adaptive Hypermedia

PETER BRUSILOVSKY

HCII, School of Computer Science, Carnegie Mellon University, Pittsburgh, PA 15213, U.S.A.
E-mail: plb@cs.cmu.edu

(Received 8 November 1995; in final form 17 March 1995)

Abstract. Adaptive hypermedia is a new direction of research within the area of adaptive and user model-based interfaces. Adaptive hypermedia (AH) systems build a model of the individual user and apply it for adaptation to that user, for example, to adapt the content of a hypermedia page to the user's knowledge and goals, or to suggest the most relevant links to follow. AH systems are used now in several application areas where the hyperspace is reasonably large and where a hypermedia application is expected to be used by individuals with different goals, knowledge and backgrounds. This paper is a review of existing work on adaptive hypermedia. The paper is centered around a set of identified methods and techniques of AH. It introduces several dimensions of classification of AH systems, methods and techniques and describes the most important of them.

Key words: Adaptive hypermedia, navigation support, collaborative user modeling, adaptive text presentation, intelligent tutoring systems, student models.

1. Introduction

Hypermedia systems have become increasingly popular in the last five years as tools for user-driven access to information. Adaptive hypermedia is a new direction of research within the area of user-adaptive systems. The goal of this research is to increase the functionality of hypermedia by making it personalized. Adaptive hypermedia (AH) systems build a model of the goals, preferences and knowledge of the individual user and use this throughout the interaction for adaptation to the needs of that user.

AH systems can be useful in any application area where the system is expected to be used by people with different goals and knowledge and where the hyperspace is reasonably big. Users with different goals and knowledge may be interested in different pieces of information presented on a hypermedia page and may use different links for navigation. AH tries to overcome this problem by using knowledge represented in the user model to adapt the information and links being presented to the given user. Adaptation can also assist the user in a navigational sense, which is particularly relevant for a large hyperspace. Knowing user goals and knowledge, AH systems can support users in their navigation by limiting browsing space, suggesting most relevant links to follow, or providing adaptive comments to visible links. The goal of this paper is to provide an overview of recent work on the development of adaptive hypermedia systems.

1

P. Brusilovsky et al. (eds.), Adaptive Hypertext and Hypermedia, 1–43.
© 1998 *Kluwer Academic Publishers.*

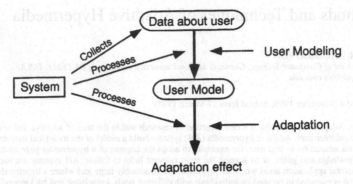

Figure 1. Classic loop "user modeling – adaptation" in adaptive systems.

Since this area of research is very new, the concept of adaptive hypermedia systems has not been clearly defined yet. To make the scope of the review more clear we use in this paper the following working definition:

> by adaptive hypermedia systems we mean all hypertext and hypermedia systems which reflect some features of the user in the user model and apply this model to adapt various visible aspects of the system to the user.

In other words, the system should satisfy three criteria: it should be a hypertext or hypermedia system, it should have a user model, and it should be able to adapt the hypermedia using this model (i.e. the same system can look different to the users with different models). We have identified more than 20 systems which can be named as adaptive hypermedia systems according to our criteria (Appendix 1). The analysis of these systems is the main content of our review. Note that not all known systems which are named or referred to as adaptive hypermedia satisfy our definition. Some of them are not full-fledged hypermedia systems (Brusilovsky, 1992b; Yetim, 1993; André & Rist, 1996); some of them are not really adaptive, but rather adaptable (Waterworth, 1996) (this distinction will be made clearer later). There are also some projects which suggest interesting relevant ideas but have not yet reached the implementation stage (Tomek, Maurer & Nassar, 1993; Zyryanov, 1996). All these works, however, contain interesting ideas and we refer to them when it is relevant to the main line of presentation.

In this paper, the critical feature of adaptive hypermedia systems is the possibility of providing hypermedia adaptation on the basis of the user model. Therefore, the paper is centered around the problems of *adaptation*, the second part of the overall adaptation process in adaptive computer systems (Figure 1). The main content of the paper (Sections 2–6) is a review of existing *methods and techniques* of adaptation in AH systems. The problems of *user modeling*, i.e. building and updating the user model in AH systems, are not a focus of the paper because they are not as critical for AH systems as a subclass of adaptive computer systems. Specific problems of user modeling in AH systems are discussed in Section 7 which provides a comparative review of several methods of user modeling in AH systems. Special attention is paid to collaborative user modeling which is especially important for AH systems. The conclusion summarizes the content of the paper and discusses the prospects for research in the area of adaptive hypermedia.

2. Methods and Techniques of Adaptive Hypermedia

Adaptation techniques refers to methods of providing adaptation in existing AH systems. These techniques are a part of the implementation level of an AH system. Each technique can be characterized by a specific kind of knowledge representation and by a specific adaptation algorithm. Adaptive hypermedia is a new area of research and most of the adaptation techniques are still unique in the sense that each of them was suggested in conjunction with the development of an AH system. However, some popular techniques were already implemented with minor variants in several earlier systems.

Adaptation methods are defined as generalizations of existing adaptation techniques. Each method is based on a clear adaptation idea which can be presented at the conceptual level. For example, " ... insert the comparison of the current concept with another concept if this other concept is already known to the user", or " ... hide the links to the concepts which are not yet ready to be learned". The same conceptual method can be implemented by different techniques. At the same time, some techniques are used to implement several methods using the same knowledge representation.

The set of methods and techniques forms a tool kit or an "arsenal" of adaptive hypermedia and can be used as a source of ideas for the designers and developers of adaptive hypermedia systems.

To review AH systems it is first necessary to establish the basis for the classification of adaptive hypermedia methods and techniques (Figure 2). The identified dimensions are quite typical for the analysis of adaptive systems in general (Dieterich et al., 1993).

- The first dimension considered is *where adaptive hypermedia systems can be helpful*. The review identifies several application areas for AH systems (see Table I) and for each area points the problems which can be partly solved by applying adaptive hypermedia techniques (Section 3).
- The second dimension is *what features of the user are used as a source of the adaptation*, i.e. to what features of the user the system can adapt its behavior. The review identifies several user features which are considered important by existing AH systems and discusses the common ways to represent them (Section 4).
- The third dimension is *what can be adapted* by a particular technique. Which features of the system can be different for different users. Along this dimension the review identifies seven ways to adapt hypermedia (see Figure 4). They can

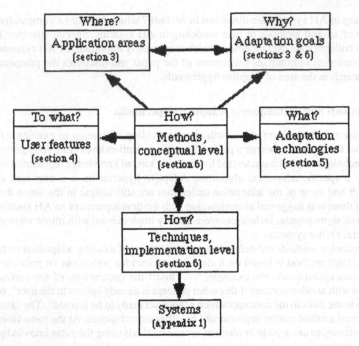

Figure 2. Possible classifications for AH methods and techniques.

be divided into two essentially different groups – content adaptation and link adaptation (Section 5). I call different ways to adapt hypermedia *technologies of adaptation.*

- The fourth dimension of classification is the *adaptation goals* achieved by different methods and techniques: why these methods and techniques are applied, and which problems of the users they can solve. The adaptation goals are dependent on application areas. Each application area has its own set of problems and each goal is important in some range of application areas (Section 3). The adaptation goals are considered in parallel with reviewing of relevant adaptation methods and techniques which implement these methods (Section 6).

The four identified dimensions are very suitable to classify various application methods. Usually, each method is an application of a particular adaptation technology (such as text adaptation or hiding of links) to achieve one of possible adaptation goals using one of the users features as a source for adaptation (as an exception, methods can achieve more than one goal or use more than one feature of the user).

Table I. Existing adaptive hypermedia systems classified according their application areas. Second entries for the systems that fit two categories are shown in *italics*. Bibliographic references are provided in Appendix 1.

Educational Hypermedia Systems	Anatom-Tutor, C-Book, [Clibbon], ELM-ART, ISIS-Tutor, ITEM/PG, HyperTutor, Land Use Tutor, Manuel Excel, SHIVA, SYPROS, ELM-PE, *Hypadapter, HYPERCASE*
On-line Information Systems	Hypadapter, HYPERCASE, KN-AHS, MetaDoc, PUSH, *HYPERFLEX, CID, Adaptive HyperMan*
On-line Help Systems	EPIAIM, HyPLAN, Lisp-Critic, ORIMUHS, WING-MIT, *SYPROS*
Information Retrieval Hypermedia	CID, DHS, Adaptive HyperMan, HYPERFLEX, WebWatcher
Institutional Hypermedia	Hynecosum
Personalized Views	Basar, Information Islands

According to its goals and used features a particular method can be useful in a subset of application areas.

3. Where and Why Adaptive Hypermedia Can Be Helpful

Unlike other kinds of application systems, any hypermedia system is adaptive in some sense: using free browsing different users can adapt the system to their information needs. Many researchers hold that it is the user who should bring the adaptivity to the man-machine hypermedia system. Why do we need any other kind of adaptation? Why do we need that a hypermedia system adapts itself to the particular user? The answer depends on an application area perspective. Analysis of existing AH systems allow us to name six kinds of hypermedia systems which are used at present as application areas in most of research projects on adaptive hypermedia. These are: educational hypermedia, on-line information systems, on-line help systems, information retrieval hypermedia systems, institutional information systems, and systems for managing personalized views (Table I). In each of these areas adaptive hypermedia techniques can be helpful because they help solve the identified problems. This section characterizes all these application areas, pointing out their specific features and identifying problems.

The most popular area for adaptive hypermedia research is *educational hypermedia*. Existing educational hypermedia systems have relatively small hyperspaces representing a particular course or section of learning material on a particular subject. The goal of the student is usually to learn all this material or a reasonable part of it. The hypermedia form supports student-driven acquisition of the learning material. The most important user feature in educational hypermedia is user knowledge of the subject being taught. Adaptive hypermedia techniques can be useful to solve a number of the problems associated with the use of educational hypermedia. Firstly, the knowledge of different users can vary greatly and the knowledge of a particular user can grow quite fast. The same page can be unclear for a novice and at the same time trivial and boring for an advanced learner. Second, novices enter the hyperspace of educational material knowing almost nothing about the subject. Most of the offered links from any node lead to the material which is completely new for them. They need navigational help to find their way through the hyperspace. Without such a help they can "get lost" even in reasonably small hyperspaces, or use very inefficient browsing strategies (Hammond, 1989).

Another popular application for adaptive hypermedia is the area of various *on-line information systems* from on-line documentation to electronic encyclopedias. The goal of these systems is to provide reference access to information (rather then a systematic introduction as in educational hypermedia) for the users with different knowledge level of the subject. Each node of the hyperspace usually represents one concept of the subject and contains several pages of information. Depending on the subject, the size of the hyperspace can range from reasonably small to very large. Similar to educational hypermedia, on-line information systems have problems with satisfying the needs of very different users. Those with different knowledge and background need different information about a concept and at different levels of detail. They usually have no time to browse all the information about the concept to look for the required portion of information. Users also have different goals when accessing an information system. In some cases they know which concepts to access to achieve their goals and do not need any navigational support (Boyle & Encarnacion, 1994; Kobsa et al., 1994). However, when the goal cannot be directly mapped to the structure of the hyperspace or when the hyperspace is large, users need help in navigation and in finding relevant pieces of information. To provide such help, the system has to know the user's goal (Höök et al., 1996; Micarelli & Sciarrone, 1996). As we will see later (Section 7) inferring the user's goal is a difficult problem in on-line information systems unless the goal is provided directly by the user (Höök et al., 1996).

Very close to on-line information systems are *on-line help systems*. These systems serve on-line information about computer applications (such as a spreadsheet, programming environment, or expert system) which is required to help the users of this system. The difference from the former category is that on-line help systems are not independent as on-line information systems but are attached to their application system. Another difference is that the hyperspace in existing on-line help systems is reasonably small. As we will see later, the distinction between small and large hyperspace is important from adaptation point of view, and that gives a reason to distinguish these application areas. On-line help systems and on-line information systems share the problem of serving different information to different users. At the same time, the problem of helping users to find relevant pieces of information is less important for on-line help systems because the hyperspace is not large and because the system knows the context from which the user called for on-line help (context-sensitive help). The context of work in an application system provides a reliable source of information for an adaptive on-line help system to determine the user's goal and to offer the most relevant help items (Encarnação, 1995b; Grunst, 1993; Kim, 1995).

The three application areas listed above belong to traditional application areas for hypermedia. The majority of existing hypermedia systems belong to one of these three areas. It is not surprising that most adaptive hypermedia systems also belong to these areas. The three areas listed below are more recent application areas for hypermedia.

Information retrieval (IR) hypermedia systems is a new class of IR systems which combine traditional information retrieval techniques with a hypertext-like access from the index terms to documents and provide the possibility of browsing the hyperspace of documents using similarity links between documents (Agosti et al., 1995; Helmes et al., 1995). It is known that browsing can help users to find the required documents when they have problems with constructing a proper formal query. The size of hyperspace in regular IR hypermedia is usually very large and cannot be structured "by hand". It means that the links in this hyperspace are not provided by a designer as in on-line information systems, but are calculated by the system (for example, using similarity measurements). Another difference from on-line information systems is that users of IR hypermedia are more often professionals in different areas who use the system in their everyday work with different IR goals. A very new special kind of IR hypermedia is IR systems on Word Wide Web which have slightly different nature in their links and a potentially unlimited hyperspace. Existing adaptive IR systems (Kok, 1991) show some ways to help the user in pure IR settings. Adaptive IR hypermedia systems can offer some additional help by limiting the navigation choice (Boy, 1991; Mathé & Chen, 1996) and by suggesting the most relevant links to follow (Armstrong et al., 1995; Kaplan et al., 1993; Katsumoto et al., 1996; Mathé & Chen, 1996).

Another new area of application for adaptive hypermedia is *institutional information systems* which serves on-line all the information required to support the work of some institution, for example, a hospital (Vassileva, 1996). Originally, these kinds of systems were developed as a set of loosely related databases, but in some recent systems such databases are joined into a single hyperspace which can be reasonably large. A specific feature of these systems is that they are a medium for everyday work of many institution employees. According to their profession they may always use only a specific area of hyperspace, and according to the current working goal they may need an access to a very small subset of it. Most of users never need to access the parts of the hyperspace outside their working area, moreover, too many navigation opportunities somewhat distract them from their primary work. In this respect *work-oriented* institutional information systems significantly differs from *search-oriented* IR hypermedia and on-line information systems where the "working area" of a user is the entire hyperspace. At the same time users of institutional information systems may need assistance in organizing a more convenient personalized access to their working areas (Vassileva, 1996). Another problem of institutional information systems which is similar to one of the problems of educational hypermedia is related to new employees who are not familiar with the structure of the hyperspace (though they can be familiar with the application domain itself) and can get lost even in their small professional subarea.

The last of the new application areas is *systems for managing personalized views in information spaces* such as Information Islands (Waterworth, 1996) and Basar (Thomas, 1995). Existing telecommunication systems such as World-Wide Web (WWW) offer huge amount of different information and on-line services which form a really unlimited hyperspace. Many users need to have an access too one or more subsets of all the hyperspace for their everyday work. To protect themselves from the complexity of the overall hyperspace, they maybe interested to define *personalized views* on the entire hyperspace. Each view can be devoted to one of the goals or interests related with the work of the user. Partly, this application area is similar to institutional hypermedia and other kinds of information systems where users need a convenient access to a subset of an information space for everyday work. A new factor which affects systems dealing with wide (and *world-wide*) information spaces is the dynamic character of hyperspace where items can appear, disappear, or evolve. Personalized views in world-wide information spaces require permanent management: searching for new and relevant items and identifying expired or changed items (in this sense, this application area is similar to IR hypermedia). Adaptation to the user goals, interests, and background can help to solve the identified problems (Thomas, 1995; Thomas & Fischer, 1996).

It is worthwhile to stress again that all six listed application areas are not mutually exclusive. Some of them are pairwise similar and share the same problems. These pairs are: IR hypermedia and on-line information systems, on-line information/help systems and educational hypermedia, educational hypermedia and institutional hypermedia, institutional hypermedia and information space management systems. Also, the difference between neighboring areas is not always clear-cut and some systems belong to both areas, for example, Hypadapter (Hohl et al., 1996) and HYPERCASE (Micarelli & Sciarrone, 1996) share features of educational hypermedia and on-line information systems, and HYPERFLEX shares features of on-line information systems and IR hypermedia. In fact, all mentioned application areas can be ordered along a continuum (Figure 3) where similar areas are placed together. This diagram offers us some interesting insights to the order and structure of hypermedia.

More traditional educational hypermedia and on-line help are located in the center. These systems are "real hypermedia," and can demonstrate all classic hypermedia features: all kinds of links including contextual links, indexes, local and global maps, guided tours, etc. The systems located at the ends of the continuum use only some of the traditional hypermedia features. The size of the hyperspace grows from reasonably small in the center to huge on both ends. It is not surprising that the systems standing on both the ends of the continuum are also similar, because they share the problems related with large hyperspace. The systems above the center are more search-oriented while the systems below are more work-oriented. According

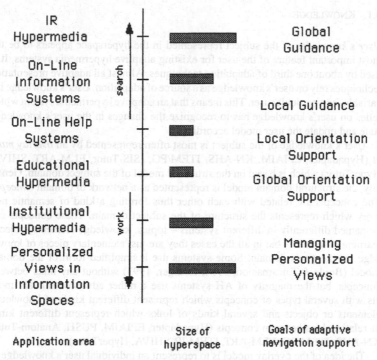

Figure 3. The continuum of adaptive hypermedia systems.

to that, the relative size of *working subset* decreases gradually from top to bottom from the entire hyperspace in IR hypermedia to a very small personalized subset of it in Basar-like systems.

4. Adapting to What?

The second question to pose when speaking about a particular kind of adaptive system is: What aspects of the user working with the system can be taken into account when providing adaptation? To which features – that can be different for different users (and may be different for the same user at different time) – can the system adapt? Generally, there are many features related to the current context of the user work and to the user as an individual which can be taken into account by an adaptive system. So far, this paper identifies five features which are used by existing adaptive hypermedia systems: users' goals, knowledge, background, hyperspace experience, and preferences.

4.1. KNOWLEDGE

User's knowledge of the subject represented in the hyperspace appears to be the most important feature of the user for existing adaptive hypermedia systems. It is used by about one third of adaptation techniques. Almost all adaptive presentation techniques rely on user's knowledge as a source of adaptation. User's knowledge is a variable for a particular user. This means that an adaptive hypermedia system which relies on user's knowledge has to recognize the changes in the user's knowledge state and update the user model accordingly.

User's knowledge of the subject is most often represented by an *overlay model* (Hypadapter, EPIAIM, KN-AHS, ITEM/PG, ISIS-Tutor, ELM-ART, SHIVA, HyperTutor) which is based on the structural model of the subject domain. Generally, the structural domain model is represented as a network of domain *concepts*. The concepts are related with each other thus forming a kind of semantic network which represents the structure of the subject domain. These concepts can be named differently in different systems – topics, knowledge elements, objects, learning outcomes – but in all the cases they are just elementary pieces of knowledge for the given domain. Some systems use a simplified form of the domain model (Boyle & Encarnacion, 1994; Zeiliger, 1993) without any links between concepts, but the majority of AH systems use a rather advanced domain models with several types of concepts which represent different kinds of knowledge elements or objects and several kinds of links which represent different kinds of relationships between concepts (Hypadapter, EPIAIM, PUSH, Anatom-Tutor, KN-AHS, ITEM/PG, ELM-ART, ITEM/IP, SHIVA, HyperTutor).

The idea of the overlay model is to represent an individual user's knowledge of the subject as an "overlay" of the domain model. For each domain model concept, an individual overlay model stores some value which is an estimation of the user knowledge level of this concept. This can be just a binary value (known–not known), a qualitative measure (good–average–poor), or a quantitative measure, such as a probability that the user knows the concept. An overlay model of user knowledge can be represented as a set of pairs "concept-value", one pair for each domain concept. Overlay models are powerful and flexible, they can independently measure user knowledge of different topics. Overlay models were originally developed in the area of intelligent tutoring systems and *student* modeling (Greer & McCalla, 1993). In many ITS the student model is just the overlay model of student knowledge. As a result, in the area of adaptive interfaces, an overlay model of user's knowledge (which is a part of the overall user model) is sometimes called the student model (Benyon & Murray, 1993).

Sometimes a simpler stereotype user model is used to represent the user's knowledge (Beaumont, 1994; Boyle & Encarnacion, 1994; Hohl et al., 1996). A stereotype user model distinguishes several typical or "stereotype" users. For each dimension of user modeling the system can have a set of possible stereotypes. For example, MetaDoc uses two dimensions of classification and two sets of stereotypes (novice – beginner – intermediate – expert): one to represent user's knowledge of general computer concepts, another to represent user's knowledge of UNIX (which is the domain of the system). A particular user is usually modelled by assigning this user to one of stereotypes for each dimension of classification (for example, intermediate for general computer concepts, novice for UNIX).

A stereotype user model can also be represented as a set of pairs "stereotype-value", where the value can be not only "true" or "false" (what means that the user belongs or does not belong to the stereotype) but also some probabilistic value (what represents the probability that the user belongs to the stereotype). Stereotype model is simpler and less powerful then overlay model but it is also more general and much easier to initialize and to maintain.

A problem with the stereotype model of knowledge is that many efficient adaptation techniques require a more fine-grained overlay model. One way to solve this problem is to provide a mapping from stereotype to overlay model. This can be done by associating a fixed set of pairs concept-value with each stereotype (Boyle & Encarnacion, 1994; de Rosis et al., 1993), or by a more flexible way which is based on the "difficulty" of concepts (Hohl et al., 1996). In turn, an overlay user model has the problem of initialization – it is very hard to set all its values after a short interview with a new user. Good results can be achieved by combining stereotype and overlay modeling (Anatom-Tutor, EPIAIM, KN-AHS, Hypadapter). They can be combined in the following way (de Rosis et al., 1993; Hohl et al., 1996): stereotype modeling is used at the beginning of work to classify a new user and to set initial values for overlay model, then a regular overlay model is used.

4.2. GOALS

User's goal or user's task is a feature related with the context of a user's work in hypermedia rather than with the user as an individual. Depending on the kind of system, it can be the goal of the work (in application systems), a search goal (in information retrieval systems), and a problem-solving or learning goal (in educational systems). In all of these cases the goal is an answer to the question "Why is the user using the hypermedia system and what does the user actually want to achieve?" User's goal is the most changeable user feature: almost always it changes from session to session and often can change several times within one session of work. In some systems it is reasonable to distinguish local or low-level goals which can change quite often and general or high level goals and tasks which are more stable. For example, in educational systems the learning goal is a high-level goal, while the problem-solving goal is a low-level goal which changes from one educational problem to another several times within a session. The user's goal can be considered as a very important feature of the user for adaptive hypermedia systems. Almost one third of existing adaptation techniques rely on it. Interestingly, nearly all of these techniques are adaptive navigation support techniques.

The user current goal is usually modeled by a way which is somewhat similar to overlay knowledge modeling. As a rule, each system supports a set of possible user goals or tasks which it can recognize (HyPLAN, ORIMUHS, PUSH, HYPER-CASE, Hynecosum, HYPERFLEX). In some cases, the set of goals is very small and the goals are not related to each other (Höök et al., 1996; Kaplan et al., 1993). To model the current user goal, the system includes one of these goals into the user model. More advanced goal-based systems (Encarnação, 1995; Grunst, 1993; Vassileva, 1996) use a more advanced representation of possible goals and current user goals. The most advanced representation of possible user goals is a hierarchy (a tree) of tasks (Vassileva, 1996). The most advanced representation of user current goals is a set of pairs "goal-value" where the value is usually the probability that the corresponding goal is the current goal of the user (Encarnação, 1995; Grunst, 1993; Micarelli & Sciarrone, 1996).

4.3. BACKGROUND AND EXPERIENCE

Two features of the user which are similar to user's knowledge of the subject but functionally differ from it are user's background and user's experience in the given hyperspace. By *user's background* we mean all the information related to the user's previous experience outside the subject of the hypermedia system, which is relevant enough to be considered. This includes the user's profession, experience of work in related areas, as well as the user's point of view and perspective. The systems EPIAIM, C-Book, and Anatom-Tutor include user's background feature in the user model and apply it to adaptive presentation and Adaptive HyperMan applies it to adaptive navigation support.

By *user's experience in the given hyperspace* we mean how familiar is the user with the structure of the hyperspace and how easy can the user navigate in it. This is not the same as user's knowledge of the subject (Vassileva, 1996). Sometimes, the user who is generally quite familiar with the subject itself is not familiar at all with the hyperspace structure. Vice versa, the user can be quite familiar with the structure of the hyperspace without deep knowledge of the subject. One more reason to distinguish hyperspace experience from knowledge level is the existence of an adaptive navigation technique (Pérez et al., 1995a; Vassileva, 1996) which relies on this feature of the user (see Section 6.4).

Such individual features of a user as background or experience are usually also modeled by a stereotype user model (MetaDoc, Anatom-Tutor, EPIAIM, C-Book). The stereotype can be an experience stereotype (Pérez et al., 1995a; Vassileva, 1996), or a background stereotype for such dimensions as profession (de Rosis et al., 1993), prospect (Beaumont, 1994), or native language (Kay & Kummerfeld, 1994b).

4.4. PREFERENCES

The last, but not the least important feature of the user considered by adaptive hypermedia systems is *user's preferences*. For different reasons the user can prefer some nodes and links over others and some parts of a page over others. These preferences can be absolute (Hypadapter, Information Islands) or relative, i.e., dependent from the current node, goal (PUSH, HYPERFLEX) and current context in general (WebWatcher, CID, DHS, Adaptive HyperMan). Preferences are used most heavily in IR hypermedia and, at the same time, in most adaptive IR hypermedia systems preferences are the only stored information about the user.

User's preferences differ from other user model components in several aspects. Unlike other components, the preferences cannot be deduced by the system. The user has to inform the system directly or indirectly (by a simple feedback) about such preferences. It looks more close to adaptability then to adaptivity. The difference is that adaptive hypermedia systems can generalize the user's preferences and apply it for adaptation in new contexts (Armstrong et al., 1995; Boy, 1991; Höök et al., 1996; Kaplan et al., 1993; Katsumoto et al., 1996; Mathé & Chen, 1996). Another specific feature of preference modeling is the way of representation. While other parts of the user model are usually represented symbolically, preferences are often represented and calculated numerically by very special ways (Kaplan et al., 1993; Katsumoto et al., 1996; Mathé & Chen, 1996). The numeric way of presentation has some preferences over the symbolic way: it opens the possibility to combine several user models and to accumulate a *group user model* (Kaplan et al., 1993; Mathé & Chen, 1996). Group models accumulate preferences of a specific group of users (such as a research laboratory). A group model is a nice starting model for a new member of the group. Group models are important also for collaborative work (it is very hard to collaborate when collaborators use individual user models and thus have different adapted views on the same subject).

5. What Can Be Adapted in Adaptive Hypermedia?

An important question to ask when speaking about any kind of adaptive systems is: what can be adapted in this system? Which features of the system can differ for different users? What is the space of possible adaptations? In adaptive hypermedia, the adaptation space is quite limited: there are not so many features which can be altered. At some level of generalization, hypermedia consist of a set of nodes or *hyperdocuments* (for the purpose of brevity we will call them "pages") connected by links. Each page contains some local information and a number of links to related pages. Hypermedia systems can also include an index and a global map which provide links to all accessible pages. What can be adapted in adaptive hypermedia are the content of regular pages (content-level adaptation) and the links from regular pages, index pages, and maps (link-level adaptation). We distinguish content-level and link-level adaptation as two different classes of hypermedia adaptation and call

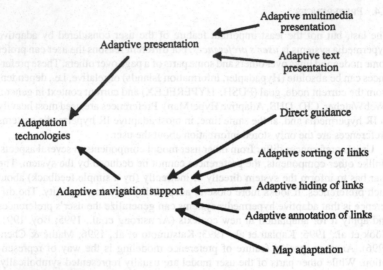

Figure 4. Adaptation technologies in adaptive hypermedia.

the first one adaptive presentation and the second one adaptive navigation support (Figure 4).

5.1. ADAPTIVE PRESENTATION

The idea of various adaptive presentation techniques is to adapt the content of a page accessed by a particular user to current knowledge, goals, and other characteristics of the user. For example, a qualified user can be provided with more detailed and deep information while a novice can receive additional explanations. In hypermedia systems, the content of a regular page may be not only a text as in classic hypertext systems but also a set of various multimedia items. From this point of view, we could distinguish adaptive text presentation and adaptive multimedia presentation in hypermedia systems. However, at present all work on adaptive presentation in hypermedia are really the works on adaptive text presentation. Some existing adaptive hypermedia systems do contain non-textual items (Brusilovsky & Zyryanov, 1993; de Rosis et al., 1993; Kobsa et al., 1994), but cannot present these items adaptively. At the same time, there are a number of good techniques for adaptive multimedia presentation (Maybury, 1993; André & Rist, 1996) but these techniques have never been used in full-fledged hypermedia systems.

As for adaptive text presentation, it is the most studied technology of hypermedia adaptation. Most part of the early works on adaptive hypermedia was centered around adaptive text presentation (Beaumont, 1994; Böcker et al., 1990; Boyle &

Encarnacion, 1994; Brusilovsky, 1992b; de Rosis et al., 1993; Fischer et al., 1990). This direction of research was influenced by the research on adaptive explanation and adaptive presentation in intelligent systems (Moore & Swartout, 1989; Paris, 1988; Zukerman & McConachy, 1993). As we will show in the following sections, there are a number of different techniques for adaptive text presentation. We group these techniques into one single technology because they look very similar from a "what can be adapted" point of view: users with different user models get different texts as a content of the same page.

5.2. ADAPTIVE NAVIGATION SUPPORT

The idea of adaptive navigation support techniques is to help users to find their paths in hyperspace by adapting the way of presenting links to goals, knowledge, and other characteristics of an individual user. Though this area of research is very new, a number of interesting techniques have been already suggested and implemented. These techniques can be classified in five groups according to the way they use to adapt presentation of links. We distinguish five technologies for adapting link presentation which are different from a "what can be adapted" point of view: direct guidance, sorting, hiding, annotation, and map adaptation (Figure 4). To compare these technologies we first need to understand how and in which context the links are usually presented. Here we mean links in the user's sense (i.e., visible and "clickable" representation of the related pages to which the user can navigate). We distinguish four kinds of link presentation which are different from the point what can be altered and adapted:

Local non-contextual links. This type includes all kinds of links on regular hypermedia pages which are independent from the content of the page. They can appear as a set of buttons, a list, or a pop-up menu. These links are easy to manipulate – they can be sorted, hidden, or annotated.

Contextual links or "real hypertext" links. This type comprises "hotwords" in texts, "hot spots" in pictures, and other kinds of links which are embedded in the context of the page content and cannot be removed from it. These links can be annotated but can not be sorted or completely hidden.

Links from index and content pages. An index or a content page can be considered as a special kind of page which contains only links. These links are usually presented in a fixed order (content order for content pages and alphabetic order for index pages). As a rule, links from index and content pages are non-contextual, unless such a page is implemented in a form of a picture.

Links on local maps and links on global hyperspace maps. Maps usually graphically represent a hyperspace or a local area of hyperspace as a network of nodes connected by arrows. Using maps, the user can directly navigate to all nodes visible on the map just by clicking on a representation of the desired node. From a navigation point of view, these clickable representations of nodes are exactly what we mean above by links, while the arrows serving as a representation of links are not used for direct navigation.

Now we can compare existing technologies of link adaptation. *Direct guidance* is the most simple technology of adaptive navigation support. Direct guidance can be applied in any system which can decide what is the next "best" node for the user to visit according user's goal and other parameters represented in the user model. To provide direct guidance, the system can outline visually the link to the "best" node as it is done in Web Watcher (Armstrong et al., 1995), or present an additional dynamic link (usually called "next") which is connected to the "best" node as in ISIS-Tutor (Brusilovsky & Pesin, 1994), SHIVA (Zeiliger, 1993), HyperTutor (Pérez et al., 1995a), and Land Use Tutor (Kushniruk & Wang, 1994). The former way is more clear, while the latter is more flexible, because it can be used to recommend the node which is not connected directly to the current one (and not represented on the current page). Direct guidance is a clear and easy to implement technology, it can be used with all four kinds of link presentation listed above. The problem with direct guidance is that it provides limited support: "follow me or no help". Direct guidance can hardly be the primary form of navigation support because it provides no support for the users who would not like to follow the system's suggestion. Direct guidance is useful but it has to be used together with a "more supportive" technology.

The idea of *adaptive ordering* technology is to sort all the links of a particular page according to the user model and to some user-valuable criteria: the more close to the top, the more relevant the link is. Adaptive ordering has a limited applicability: it can be used with non-contextual links, but it can hardly be used for indexes and content pages and can never be used with contextual links and maps. Another problem with adaptive ordering is that this technology makes the order of links non-stable: it may change each time the user enters the page. At the same time, some recent research shows that the stable order of options in menus is important for novices (Debevc et al., 1994; Kaptelinin, 1993). However, this technology seems to be useful for information retrieval (IR) applications (Armstrong et al., 1995; Kaplan et al., 1993; Mathé & Chen, 1996). Experimental research (Kaplan et al., 1993) showed that adaptive ordering can significantly reduce navigation time in IR applications where each page can have many non-contextual links. A similar area where adaptive ordering can be used is on-line documentation systems (Hohl et al., 1996). There are also some suggestions on using adaptive ordering in educational hypermedia (Tomek et al., 1993).

Hiding is currently the most often used technology for adaptive navigation support. The idea of navigation support by hiding is to restrict the navigation space by hiding links to "not relevant" pages. The page can be considered as not relevant for several reasons: for example, if it is not related to the user's current goal (Boy, 1991; Brusilovsky & Pesin, 1994; Grunst, 1993; Höök et al., 1996; Vassileva, 1996) or if it presents materials which the user is not prepared yet to understand (Brusilovsky & Pesin, 1994; Clibbon, 1995; Gonschorek & Herzog, 1995; Pérez et al., 1995a). From the surface view, hiding looks like the most obvious and the most easy to implement technology. It protects users from the complexity of the unrestricted hyperspace and reduces their cognitive overload. Hiding has a wide applicability: it can be used with all kinds of non-contextual, index, and map links by real hiding buttons or menu items (Brusilovsky & Pesin, 1994), and with contextual links by transferring clickable "hot words" to normal text (Gonschorek & Herzog, 1995; Pérez et al., 1995a). Hiding is also more transparent to the user and looks more "stable" for them than adaptive ordering (links are usually added incrementally, but not removed or reordered).

The idea of *adaptive annotation* technology is to augment the links with some form of comments which can tell the user more about the current state of the nodes behind the annotated links. These annotations can be provided in textual form or in the form of visual cues using, for example, different icons (de La Passardiere & Dufresne, 1992; Schwarz et al., 1996), colors (Brusilovsky & Pesin, 1994; Brusilovsky & Zyryanov, 1993), or font sizes (Hohl et al., 1996). A good review of various visual cues which can be used in hypermedia systems can be found in (Arens & Hammwöhner, 1995). Link annotation is known as an effective technology of navigation support in hypermedia (Zhao et al., 1993). The typical kind of annotation considered in traditional hypermedia is static (user independent) annotation. Adaptive navigation support can be provided by dynamic user model-driven annotation. Adaptive annotation in its simplest history-based form (outlining the links to previously visited nodes) has been applied in some hypermedia systems including several World-Wide Web browsers. Even this simplest form of adaptive annotation which can distinguish only two states of links (links to visited/not visited nodes) appears to be quite useful. Current adaptive hypermedia systems (Brusilovsky & Pesin, 1994; Schwarz et al., 1996) can distinguish and annotate differently up to six states on the basis of the user model (see Section 6.4).

Annotation seems to be a very relevant form of adaptive navigation support. Annotation can be naturally used with all four possible forms of links. This technique supports stable order of links and avoids problems with incorrect mental maps. Annotation is generally a more powerful technology than hiding: hiding can distinguish only two states for the nodes – relevant and non-relevant – while annotation, as mentioned above, up to six states, in particular, several levels of relevancy as it implemented in Hypadapter (Hohl et al., 1996). Annotations do not restrict cognitive overload as much as hiding does, but the hiding technology can be quite well simulated by the annotation technology using a kind of "dimming" instead of hiding for "not relevant" links. Dimming can decrease cognitive overload in some extent (the user can learn to ignore dimmed links), but dimmed links are still visible (and traversable, if required) which protects the user from forming wrong mental maps.

Map adaptation technology comprises various ways of adapting the form of global and local hypermedia maps presented to the user. Such technologies as direct guidance, hiding, and annotation also can be used to adapt hypermedia maps, but all these technologies do not change the form or the structure of maps. Human-computer interaction research offers a number of techniques to adapt the structure and the form of various kinds of networks, including hypermedia maps (Furnas, 1986; Mukherjea & Foley, 1995; Mukherjea et al., 1995; Rivlin et al., 1994). However, most of these ideas have not been applied yet in adaptive hypermedia systems. The only known exeption (see Section 6.4) is the HYPERCASE system (Micarelli & Sciarrone, 1996) which is partly based on the ideas of (Rivlin et al., 1994).

Direct guidance, sorting, hiding, annotating, and map adaptation are the primary technologies for adaptive navigation support. As we will see in the following sections, most existing adaptation techniques use exactly one of these ways to provide adaptive navigation support. However, these technologies are not contradictory and can be used in combinations. For example, ISIS-Tutor (Brusilovsky & Pesin, 1994) uses direct guidance, hiding, and annotation and Hypadapter (Hohl et al., 1996) uses sorting, hiding, and annotation. In particular, the direct guidance technology can be naturally used in combination with any of the three other technologies.

6. How Adaptive Hypermedia Can Help

In this section we consider methods by which adaptive hypermedia systems can help to solve some hypermedia problems and describe the most interesting techniques applied by existing AH systems to implement these methods. Since content adaptation techniques and adaptive navigation support techniques are intended to solve different problems we consider them separately.

6.1. HOW CONTENT ADAPTATION CAN HELP: METHODS

At present, content adaptation is used in three classic hypermedia application areas: on-line information systems – Hypadapter (Hohl et al., 1996), MetaDoc (Boyle & Encarnacion, 1994), KN-AHS (Kobsa et al., 1994), and PUSH (Höök et al., 1996), on-line help systems – Lisp-Critic (Fischer et al., 1990), EPIAIM (de Rosis et al., 1993), WING-MIT (Kim, 1995), and ORIMUHS (Encarnação, 1995b), and educational hypermedia – Anatom-Tutor (Beaumont, 1994), ITEM/IP (Brusilovsky, 1992b), C-book (Kay & Kummerfeld, 1994b), and SYPROS (Gonschorek & Herzog, 1995) (Table II).

The goal of the most popular method of content adaptation (we call it *additional explanations*) is to hide from the user some parts of information about a particular concept which are not relevant to the user's level of knowledge about this concept. For example, low level details can be hidden from users with a poor level of knowledge of this concept because they cannot understand these details. On the contrary, additional explanations usually required by novices to understand the concept can be hidden from users with a good level of knowledge of the concept because they do not need these explanations anymore. In more general terms, in

Table II. Adaptive presentation: methods, techniques, and systems.

	Conditional text	Stretchtext	Fragment variants	Page variants	Frame-based technique
Additional, prerequisite, and comparative explanations	C-Book ITEM/IP Lisp-Critic	MetaDoc KN-AHS PUSH			EPIAIM PUSH
Explanation variants	C-Book		Anatom-Tutor Lisp-Critic WING-MIT	Anatom-Tutor C-Book EPIAIM ORIMUHS SYPROS	Hypadapter
Sorting					EPIAIM Hypadapter

addition to the basic presentation, some category of users can get some additional information which is specially prepared for this category of users and will not be shown to users of other categories. This method is used in MetaDoc (Boyle & Encarnacion, 1994), KN-AHS (Kobsa et al., 1994), ITEM/IP (Brusilovsky, 1992b), EPIAIM (de Rosis et al., 1993), and Anatom-Tutor (Beaumont, 1994). A goal-based variant of this method is to hide from the user some parts of information about a particular concept which are not relevant to the current user's goal (Höök et al., 1996).

Two other methods *prerequisite explanations* and *comparative explanations* change the information presented about a concept depending on the user knowledge level of related concepts. The first method is based on prerequisite links between concepts. The idea is the following: before presenting an explanation of a concept the system inserts explanations of all its prerequisite concepts which are not sufficiently known to the user. This method is used in Lisp-Critic (Fischer et al., 1990) and C-book (Kay & Kummerfeld, 1994b). The second method is based on similarity links between concepts. If a concept similar to the concept being presented is known, the user gets a comparative explanation which stress similarities and differences between the current concept and the related one. Such comparative explanations are particularly effective in the domain of programming languages. Interestingly, all systems which apply this method (ITEM/IP, Lisp-Critic, and C-book) belong to this domain.

Another method (we call it *explanation variants*) assumes that showing or hiding some portion of the content is not always sufficient for the adaptation because different users may need essentially different information. With this method, the system stores several variants for some parts of the page content and the user gets the variant which corresponds to his or her user model. This method is used in Anatom-Tutor (Beaumont, 1994), Lisp-Critic (Fischer et al., 1990), Hypadapter

(Hohl et al., 1996), ORIMUHS (Encarnação, 1995b), SYPROS (Gonschorek & Herzog, 1995), and WING-MIT (Kim, 1995).

An interesting method which can take into account both the user's background and knowledge level is *sorting* the fragments of information about the concept where the information which is most relevant to user's background and knowledge is placed toward the front. This method is implemented in Hypadapter (Hohl et al., 1996) and EPIAIM (de Rosis et al., 1993).

6.2. HOW CONTENT ADAPTATION CAN HELP: TECHNIQUES

A simple, but effective technique for content adaptation is the *conditional text* technique which is used in ITEM/IP (Brusilovsky, 1992b), Lisp-Critic (Fischer et al., 1990), and C-book (Kay & Kummerfeld, 1994b). With this technique, all possible information about a concept is divided into several chunks of texts. Each chunk is associated with a condition on the level of user knowledge represented in the user model. When presenting the information about the concept, the system presents only the chunks where the condition is true. This technique is a low-level technique – it requires some "programming" work from the author to set all the required conditions – but it is also very flexible. By choosing appropriate conditions on the knowledge level of the current concept and related concepts represented in the user model, the author can implement all the methods of adaptation listed above excluding sorting. A simple example is hiding chunks with irrelevant explanations if the user's knowledge level of the current concept is good enough, or turning on a chunk with comparative explanations if the corresponding related concept is already known.

A more high level technique which can also turn off and on different parts of the content according to the user knowledge level is suggested in the MetaDoc (Boyle & Encarnacion, 1994) and developed further in KN-AHS (Kobsa et al., 1994). This technique is based on *stretchtext* which is a special kind of hypertext. In a regular hypertext, a result of activation of a hot word is moving to another page with related text. In stretchtext this related text can simply replace the activated hotword (or a phrase with this hotword) extending the text of the current page. If required, this extended or "uncollapsed" text may be collapsed back to a hotword. Each node in MetaDoc is a stretchtext page which may contain many "uncollapsable" hotwords. The idea of adaptive stretchtext presentation in MetaDoc is to present a requested page with all stretchtext extensions non-relevant to the user being collapsed and all extensions relevant to the user being uncollapsed. To achieve this result an author can declare some uncollapsable textual information contained in a node as an additional explanation of a particular concept, or as a low level detail of a particular concept. Optionally, the user of MetaDoc with a high degree of knowledge of a concept will always get additional explanations of this concept hidden (collapsed) and all low level details uncollapsed. On the contrary, the user with poor knowledge of a concept will always get additional explanations of this concept visible and all low level details collapsed. The user with medium level knowledge will see both kinds of information. An important feature of the adaptive stretchtext technique is that it lets both the user and the system adapt the content of a particular page and that it can take into account both the knowledge and the preferences of the user. After optional presentation of the stretchtext page, it can be further adapted by the user who can uncollapse and collapse appropriate explanations and details according to his or her preferences. The system updates the user model according to the preferences demonstrated by the user to ensure that the user will always see a preferred combination of collapsed and uncollapsed parts. For example, if the user has collapsed additional explanations of a particular concept, the system will always show additional explanations of this concept collapsed until the user changes the preferences.

The *explanation variants* method can be implemented by *fragment variants* and *page variants* techniques. *Page variants* is the most simple adaptive presentation technique. With this technique, a system keeps two or more variants of the same page with different presentations of the same content. As a rule, each variant is prepared for one of possible user stereotypes. When presenting a page, a system selects the page variant according to the user stereotype. This technique is used in Anatom-Tutor (Beaumont, 1994) with background stereotypes, in ORIMUHS (Encarnação, 1995b) and WING-MIT (Kim, 1995) with knowledge stereotypes, and in C-book (Kay & Kummerfeld, 1994b) with stereotypes reflecting user proficiency with the language of presentation (English). A similar technique is used in EPIAIM (de Rosis et al., 1993) and C-book to adapt example presentation to the user's background. These systems store several examples illustrating particular concept and offers the user the example which is most suitable to the user's previous experience and interests.

Fragment variants is a more fine-grained implementation of *explanation variants* method. An good example here is Anatom-Tutor (Beaumont, 1994). In Anatom-Tutor, a page is not equal to a concept as in some other systems and it can include explanations of several concepts. The system stores several variants of explanations for each concept and the user gets the page which includes variants corresponding to his or her knowledge about the concepts presented in the page. This idea is supported by the work of Paris (Paris, 1988) who shows that users with different knowledge of a particular concept need structurally different explanations about the concept. An interesting feature of Anatom-Tutor is a combination of page variants and fragment variants methods to support adaptation to both the user's background and the user's knowledge. The current page variant for an accessed node is selected according to the user's background. This page can be further adapted: for each concept mentioned in the page, the system selects the explanation which is most suitable to the user's knowledge level.

The most powerful of the all content adaptation techniques is the *frame-based technique* implemented in Hypadapter (Hohl et al., 1996), and EPIAIM (de Rosis et al., 1993). With this technique all the information about a particular concept is represented in form of a frame. Slots of a frame can contain several explanation variants of the concept, links to other frames, examples, etc. Special presentation rules are used to decide which slots should be presented to a particular user and in which order. More exactly, in EPIAIM these rules are used to select one of the existing presentation schemes (each scheme is an ordered subset of slots) and the scheme is used to present the concept. In Hypadapter, the rules are used to calculate the "presentation priority" for each slot and then a subset of slots with high priority is presented in order of decreasing priority. In their conditional parts, these rules can refer not only to the user knowledge level of a concept being presented, but also to any feature represented in the user model. In particular, both systems which use this technique take into account the background of the user. In Hypadapter and EPIAIM, the frame-based technique is used to implement all methods mentioned above except prerequisite and comparative explanation. However, the latter two methods also can be implemented with the frame-based technique by setting appropriate conditions on the knowledge level of related concepts.

The very recent technique developed in the PUSH project (Höök et al., 1996) can be considered as a combination of stretchtext and frame-based adaptation. A hypermedia page in this on-line information system provides a complete description of a particular object structured as a ordered sequence of typed information entities. Each type of objects in PUSH has its own assortments of information entity types which are used to describe an object of this type. It is very close to the frame-based model where information entities play roles of slots describing various aspects of an object. A specific feature of PUSH, however, is that each information entity is a reasonably big portion of hypertext. The complete description of an object is usually very big and takes several pages of information. To protect users from the information overflow and to help them to find a required piece of information, the system use hiding: it presents only those types of information entities about the current object which are relevant to the current goal of the user (the goal can be set by the user or deduced by the system). At the same time, to keep the adaptation transparent, the system maintains the stable presentation order of the information entities and never hides non-relevant entities completely: the titles of hidden non-relevant entities are always shown. If the user is not satisfied with the system's decision to show or to hide a particular entity, he can collapse or uncollapse the content of the information entity by clicking on an icon near its title. The resulting interface looks quite similar to MetaDoc stretchtext interface: non-relevant pieces of material are not presented to the user, showing only a keyword (in MetaDoc) or the title (in PUSH), but the user can override the adaptation by opening and closing any desired piece of information.

6.3. HOW ADAPTIVE NAVIGATION SUPPORT CAN HELP: METHODS

Adaptive navigation support techniques are used to achieve several adaptation goals: to provide global guidance, to provide local guidance, to support local

Table III. Adaptive navigation support: goals, technologies, and systems.

	Direct guidance	Sorting	Hiding	Annotation	Map adaptation
Global guidance	WebWatcher ITEM/IP ISIS-Tutor SHIVA	Adaptive HyperMan CID HYPERFLEX			
Local guidance	Land Use Tutor HyperTutor	Adaptive HyperMan ELM-PE Hypadapter HYPERFLEX	Hypadapter PUSH	ISIS-Tutor ELM-ART	HYPERCASE
Local orientation support (knowledge)		Hypadapter ELM-PE	[Clibbon] HyperTutor Hypadapter ISIS-Tutor	ELM-ART ISIS-Tutor ITEM/PG Manuel Excel	
Local orientation support (goal)			Hynecosum HyPLAN ISIS-Tutor PUSH SYPROS	ELM-ART ISIS-Tutor	HYPERCASE
Global orientation support			[Clibbon] Hynecosum HyperTutor ISIS-Tutor SYPROS	ITEM/PG ISIS-Tutor ELM-ART Manuel Excel	HYPERCASE

orientation, to support global orientation, and to help with managing personalized views in information spaces (Table III). Generally, these goals are different, but at the same time each pair of neighboring goals in this list has something in common. So, it is rather a continuum of goals where the borders between neighbors are not clear cut, and some methods and techniques work for more than one goal (Figure 3).

6.3.1. Global guidance

Global guidance can be provided in hypermedia systems where users have some "global" information goal (i.e., need information which is contained in one or several nodes somewhere in the hyperspace) and browsing is the way to find the required information. The goal of global guidance methods is to help the user to find the shortest way to the information goal with minimal floundering. Global guidance is the primary goal of adaptive navigation support in IR hypermedia and also an important goal in on-line help and on-line information systems with reasonably big hyperspaces. The user's information goal which is usually clearly (Kaplan et al., 1993) or partly (Armstrong et al., 1995; Mathé & Chen, 1996) provided by the user is the primary user feature for adaptive guidance. The most direct method of providing global guidance is to suggest to the user at each step of browsing which of the links from the given node to follow (i.e., to apply the direct guidance technology). This method is used in WebWatcher (Armstrong et al., 1995). A more supportive method is to apply adaptive sorting technology and to sort all the links from the given node according to their relevance to the global goal (the most relevant – first). Here, users still have the possibility of proceeding along the first most relevant link, but also have some more information (relevance of the other links) to make a free choice. This method is used in Adaptive HyperMan (Mathé & Chen, 1996), and HYPERFLEX (Kaplan et al., 1993).

A special case for global guidance is educational hypermedia. In an educational hypermedia system a student usually has a global goal, but it is the learning goal – the knowledge which the user has to learn. The learning goal is different from an information goal, it is not a small piece, but a big subset of the hyperspace (sometimes the total hyperspace). Another specific feature of educational hypermedia is that to provide global guidance a system has to know not only the global learning goal itself, but also the current state of user knowledge of the subject being taught. What is similar with IR hypermedia is the choice of adaptation technologies: it can be either direct guidance or adaptive sorting. A most popular method of providing global guidance in educational hypermedia is direct guidance with the dynamic button "next". There are a number of different elaborated techniques which implement this method. Usually, these techniques are hypermedia-adjusted implementations of curriculum sequencing techniques from the domain of intelligent tutoring systems (ITS). Curriculum sequencing techniques (Brusilovsky, 1992a) can build for a user the shortest individual sequence of learning units (presentations, examples, problems) to achieve the learning goal. The button "next" in educational hypermedia activates a similar sequencing mechanism which selects the node with most relevant educational material according to the current user knowledge, learning goal, and system tutoring strategy (Brusilovsky & Pesin, 1994; Brusilovsky, 1992b; Zeiliger, 1993).

As for the use of adaptive sorting for global guidance in educational hypermedia, at least one method based on sorting links according to the global learning goal was suggested (Tomek et al., 1993), but there are no techniques which implement it. Direct guidance seems to be a very relevant technology for global guidance in educational hypermedia. Users of educational hypermedia are usually novices who have problems with making their own choice and rely heavily on the suggestion of the system. For the novices, the button "next" is the most often used navigation tool (Reed et al., 1995). On the contrary, sorting seems to have a limited applicability in educational hypermedia. First, it can be used only with non-contextual links which are not very popular in educational hypermedia. Second, even for non-contextual links it is not as relevant as in IR hypermedia (where users are mostly professionals) because novices prefer to have a stable order of items (i.e., links) in menus (Debevc et al., 1994; Kaptelinin, 1993).

6.3.2. *Local guidance*

The goal of local guidance methods is to help the user to make one navigation step by suggesting the most relevant links to follow from the current node. This goal is somewhat similar, but more "modest" than the goal of global guidance. Local guidance methods do not expect a global goal to provide a guidance. They make a suggestion according to the preferences, knowledge, and background of the user – whatever is more important for the given application area. For example, a relevant method of local guidance for IR hypermedia and on-line information systems is sorting links according to user preferences (Adaptive HyperMan, HYPERFLEX) and background (Adaptive HyperMan). Methods used in educational hypermedia are: sorting links according to the user's knowledge (Brusilovsky & Weber, 1996) and direct guidance according to the user knowledge (Kushniruk & Wang, 1994; Pérez et al., 1995a). The latter method is usually applied to select the most relevant problem from the set of problems available from the current point. If a system shares the features of both on-line information systems and educational hypermedia like Hypadapter (Hohl et al., 1996), a local guidance technique can take into account all the features mentioned above: preferences, knowledge, and background.

6.3.3. *Local orientation support*

The goal of local orientation support methods is to help the user in local orientation (i.e., to help them in understanding what is around and what is his or her relative position in the hyperspace). Existing AH systems implement local orientation support by two different ways: providing additional information about the nodes available from the current node (i.e., use of annotation technology) and limiting the number of navigation opportunities to decrease the cognitive overload and let the users concentrate themselves on analyzing the most relevant links (i.e., use of hiding technology).

Methods based on hiding technology have the same idea: to hide from the user all the links (either from index or from a local node) which are not relevant to him or her at the given moment, or in other words, to show only relevant links. Methods differ with respect to the principles used to decide which links are relevant and which are not. This decision can be made according to the user's knowledge, goals, experience, and preferences. The most simple method in this category is to show only the links relevant to the user's preferences (Waterworth, 1996), but existing implementation of this method is not really adaptive. The most universal method is to show only the links which are relevant to the user's current goal. This method was used in the on-line help system HyPLAN (Grunst, 1993), the institutional hypermedia system Hynecosum (Vassileva, 1996), and in the on-line information systems CID (Boy, 1991) and PUSH (Höök et al., 1996). Another method which is based on the user's experience in the given hyperspace is to show more links for users who have more experience in the hyperspace, as is done in HyperTutor (Pérez et al., 1995a) and Hynecosum (Vassileva, 1996). Novices in these systems will see quite a small number of links. Along the growth of users' experience they will be able to see gradually more links from the same place.

Two methods based on the hiding technology are specific for educational hypermedia. A very popular method in this application area is to hide the links to the nodes which are not yet ready to be learned (usually it means that these nodes have unlearned prerequisite nodes). This method is used in several systems: ISIS-Tutor (Brusilovsky & Pesin, 1994), HyperTutor (Pérez et al., 1995a), (Clibbon, 1995), and Hypadapter (Hohl et al., 1996). Another method specific for educational hypermedia is to hide the links to the nodes which belong to the educational goals of subsequent lessons and do not belong to the current educational goal, as is done in ISIS-Tutor and SYPROS (Gonschorek & Herzog, 1995).

The idea of methods based on annotation technology is to inform the user about the current "state" of the nodes behind visible links. At present, four basic methods have been suggested for this. First, annotation can be used to show several gradations of link relevancy. For example Hypadapter uses three different font sizes to annotate links as very relevant, relevant, and less relevant. Second, annotation can reflect several levels of user knowledge of the nodes behind the annotated links. At present the techniques implementing this method distinguish three levels of user knowledge of the node: not-known, in-work and well-learned (Brusilovsky & Pesin, 1994; Brusilovsky & Zyryanov, 1993; de La Passardiere & Dufresne, 1992; Schwarz et al., 1996). Two other methods use annotation in situations where hiding is usually used. The first one is outlining the links related to the current goal (Brusilovsky & Pesin, 1994). The second one is providing special annotation for links to not ready to be learned nodes (ITEM/PG and ISIS-Tutor use a kind of dimming and ELM-ART uses "red" traffic light icon). The latter examples show that in many cases methods based on the hiding technology also can be implemented with the annotation technology either by outlining the relevant links or by dimming not relevant links. However, annotation can hardly be used in the cases where the number of visible links is very big (and where hiding is still applicable).

As we see, local orientation support methods do not guide the user directly, but provide help in understanding what are the proximal links and in making well-grounded navigation choices. From another perspective, global and local guidance methods based on sorting technology can support local orientation to some extent, but not as effectively as special orientation support methods described above because the position of a link in a sorted list gives the user very little additional information about this link.

6.3.4. *Global orientation support*

The goal of global orientation support methods is to help the user to understand the structure of the overall hyperspace and his or her absolute position in it. In non-adaptive hypermedia, this goal is usually achieved by providing visual landmarks and global maps which can directly help the user in global orientation and by providing guided tours to help the user gradually learn the hyperspace (Linard & Zeiliger, 1995). Adaptive hypermedia can provide more support for the user along the same lines by applying hiding and annotation technologies. In fact, all those hiding and annotation methods considered above which are systematic – i.e., when the decision about hiding and annotating a link depends only on the state of the node behind the link and does not depends not from the user's position in the hyperspace – support also user global orientation.

Annotations function as landmark: since a node keeps the same annotation when the user looks at it from different positions in the hyperspace, the user can more easily recognize the nodes he or she met before and understand the current position. Especially useful here is the method which provides different annotations depending on the user knowledge level (Brusilovsky & Pesin, 1994; Brusilovsky & Zyryanov, 1993; de La Passardiere & Dufresne, 1992; Schwarz et al., 1996). Hiding reduces the size of the visible hyperspace and can simplify both orientation and learning. In such application areas as educational or institutional hypermedia where the hyperspace is not especially big, hiding can effectively support gradual learning of the hyperspace. The useful hiding methods for this purpose are those which gradually show the user incrementally larger parts of the hyperspace. The examples from educational hypermedia are the methods of hiding not-ready-to-be-learned nodes as in ISIS-Tutor (Brusilovsky & Pesin, 1994), HyperTutor (Pérez et al., 1995a), (Clibbon, 1995), and Hypadapter (Hohl et al., 1996) and nodes which are the educational goals of subsequent lessons as in ISIS-Tutor and SYPROS (Gonschorek & Herzog, 1995). An example of a more universal method is the method which shows gradually more links with the growth of the user experience in the given hyperspace, as is done in HyperTutor and Hynecosum (Vassileva, 1996).

A promising direction of adaptive global orientation support is *adaptation of local and global maps* (Zyryanov, 1996), but this direction is really underinvestigated. Generally, all systematic hiding and annotation methods can be applied to adapt hyperspace maps, but no existing AH systems really do that. Another possibility is applying the map adaptation technology (i.e., the adaptive construction of local and global maps where the very structure of the map can depend on the user characteristics). The only existing work in this area is the HYPERCASE system (Micarelli & Sciarrone, 1996) which suggests a technique to generate global and local maps according to the current user goal.

6.3.5. *Managing personalized views*

Managing personalized views is a new goal for adaptive hypermedia systems. Personalized views is a way to organize an electronic workplace for the users who need a access to a reasonably small part of a hyperspace for their everyday work. The usual way to protect these users from the complexity of the overall hyperspace is to let them organize personalized goal-oriented views. Each view is just a list of links to all hyperdocuments which are relevant to a particular working goal. Traditionally, it is the duty of the users to create and to manage their personalized views (adaptability). Classic hypermedia systems and modern WWW browsers suggest bookmarks and hotlists as a way to make personal views. More advanced systems suggest some more high-level adaptability mechanisms based on metaphors (Waterworth, 1996) and user models (Vassileva, 1996).

Adaptive solutions, i.e., system supported management of personalized views, are required in WWW-like dynamic information spaces where items can appear, disappear, or evolve. By now we can mention only BASAR (Thomas & Fischer, 1996) as an example of a system which provides adaptive management of personalized views. BASAR uses intelligent agents to collect and maintain an actual set of links relevant to one of the user's goals. The agents can search regularly for new relevant items and identify expired or changed items. Currently we can hardly formulate any methods (as generalization of existing techniques) for managing personalized views, but it can be done very soon because several research groups are start working on BASAR-like systems for WWW.

6.4. HOW ADAPTIVE NAVIGATION SUPPORT CAN HELP: TECHNIQUES

One of the most often referenced techniques for adaptive sorting of links was implemented in HYPERFLEX (Kaplan et al., 1993) which can be considered as an on-line information system or IR hypermedia system. HYPERFLEX provides the user with global and local guidance by displaying an ordered list of nodes related to the current node. The links are ordered according to their relevance to the current node (most relevant – first). If the user selects the current search goal from the list of existing goals, sorting also takes into account the relevance of the displayed links to the selected goal. New goals can be also created by users themselves. The main component of the user model in HYPERFLEX is a matrix of relevance which stores relevance values between each pair of documents and from each goal to each document. This matrix reflects mainly user preferences on the link order: in HYPERFLEX the user can move the links to tell the system directly his or her preferences regarding the relative order of links (i.e., which are the relevant links and in which order he or she would like to see them when a particular document is the current document or when a particular goal is the current goal). These preferences are processed by the system to update the user model. Therefore the preferences shown in one context can influence adaptation in another context.

A powerful and universal technique for ordering the links according their relevance is implemented in Adaptive HyperMan (Mathé & Chen, 1996). The system takes into account many factors or *inputs*: user background (profile), user search goal (set of keywords), current node of interest, etc., and returns as an output an ordered set of documents relevant to the provided input. If the search goal is set, the system can provide global guidance, otherwise it can provide local guidance. To calculate the relevancy for the documents the system uses a personal relevance network which stores in this special form individual preferences of the users. To provide feedback, the user judges the set of nodes selected by the system as relevant or not relevant to the input from his or her personal point of view. This feedback is used by the system to update the individual relevance network so it gradually learns user preferences.

A flexible original (and actually the first known) technique for local guidance and local orientation support is implemented in Hypadapter (Hohl et al., 1996). A node in Hypadapter is represented as a frame which usually has several "relation" slots storing different kinds of links to related nodes. Hypadapter uses a set of rules to calculate the relevance of links for each relational slot from the current node. Each applicable rule can increment or decrement the relevance value of the link depending on specific features of the link and the node behind it. Then the system uses a combination of sorting, hiding, and annotation to show relevance to the user: first, the links are sorted according to the relevance, second, the system uses three different font sizes to annotate very relevant, relevant, and less relevant links, third, the system hides irrelevant links. For example, the links to concepts not ready to be learned can be hidden in this way.

Another example of a rule-based adaptive navigation support technique is the rule-based hiding technique implemented in the educational hypermedia systems HyperTutor (Pérez et al., 1995a) and SYPROS (Gonschorek & Herzog, 1995). Both systems use special sets of pedagogical rules to decide which concepts and nodes should be visible at a given moment and which should not. These rules take into account the type of the concept, the types of its links to other concepts, and the current state of the user's knowledge as reflected in the user model. If a node is not to be visible, then all contextual links to this node will be changed from hot words to normal text. The rule-based hiding technique is very flexible. By manipulating with hiding rules it is possible to implement several local and global orientation support methods based on hiding, such as hiding not ready to be learned nodes, or hiding nodes which belong to the subsequent lessons. In SYPROS hiding is used to implement the *explanation variants* method of content adaptation. The hyperspace contains several nodes devoted to the same concepts which are oriented toward users with different levels of knowledge. Hiding rules always keep visible only those nodes which suit to the user's current level of knowledge.

A very different hiding technique is suggested in Hynecosum (Vassileva, 1996). This system supports hierarchies of tasks for users of different categories. Each hyperspace node in the system is indexed by the elementary (terminal) tasks which require access to this node. Thus, for each terminal task the system can compile the associated list of nodes relevant to this task. By definition, a list of relevant nodes for higher level tasks includes all the nodes relevant at least to one of its subtasks. Using this knowledge Hynecosum can provide local orientation support by hiding. Working with Hynecosum the user always informs the system which task he or she is currently performing by selecting one of the tasks from a personal hierarchy. Knowing the user's task, the system can hide from the user all nodes which are not relevant to the current task. This makes the set of visible nodes manageable. When the selected task is a high level task in the hierarchy, the number of visible nodes can still be too big. To provide additional support for novices, Hynecosum will not show links to document nodes until the user sets the current task more exactly by selecting a lower level task in the hierarchy. The more experienced the user is, the higher the level is when the user gets access to document nodes. Thus, the technique implemented in Hynecosum supports both goal-based and experience-based methods of hiding.

The techniques implemented in ISIS-Tutor (Brusilovsky & Pesin, 1994), ITEM/ PG (Brusilovsky & Zyryanov, 1993), and ELM-ART (Schwarz et al., 1996) support several methods of local and global orientation support based on annotation and hiding. The backbone of the hyperspace in these systems is formed by a conceptual network which represents the pedagogical structure of the subject being taught. Each concept in the conceptual network is represented by a node of the hyperspace. Concept nodes in the network are connected by different kinds of relationships such as "is-a", "part-of", and "prerequisite". Another kind of node in the hyperspace is a learning unit (such as a textbook section, a problem, or an example). Each learning unit is connected to all concept nodes which are required to work with this unit. The overlay student model separately represents the level of the student's knowledge of each of the concepts. Using this student model and prerequisite links, the systems can distinguish four educational states for each node represented by a hypermedia page: not-ready-to-be-learned (i.e., has unlearned prerequisites), ready-to-be-learned, in-work (learning started), and learned (student has solved the required number of problems for the concept). The idea is that concepts with different educational states have different meanings for the student and making educational states visible would help the student in hyperspace navigation. To make educational states visible, links to the concepts with different educational states are annotated differently using different colors (ITEM/PG and ISIS-Tutor) and different icons (ELM-ART). As an option, the links to not-ready-to-be-learned pages in ISIS-Tutor can be hidden.

The same framework was used in ISIS-Tutor and ELM-ART to implement one additional adaptation method based on the learning goal. The teacher can set for each student a sequence of learning goals (here a goal is a set of concept nodes of the network which have to be learned). Each goal serves as a chapter in a book: Concepts belonging to the same goal are expected to be learned together and then mastered by solving a number of problems before a student moves to the next goal. Two technologies are used for adaptation to the learning goal: first, to attract the student's attention the system outlines links to the concepts belonging to the current goal (ISIS-Tutor, ELM-ART), second, to decrease the student's cognitive load it hides concepts which belong to the next learning goals (ISIS-Tutor).

The technique used in HYPERCASE (Micarelli & Sciarrone, 1996) is the only known example of map adaptation. This technique supports local and global orientation by adapting the form of local and global maps to the didactic or information goal of the users. Similar to HYPERFLEX, HYPERCASE represents and uses knowledge about possible goals for goal adaptation, but the type of goal knowledge is very different from HYPERFLEX. HYPERCASE uses a case-based approach and a neural network technology to store in the database of cases several typical navigation paths for each of the didactic goals. Using this knowledge, the system can find the most similar standard path (and thus the most probable didactic goal) for the navigation path of a real student supplied as an input to the case-based mechanism. When the student requests help, HYPERCASE can show where he or she is located in the hyperspace by drawing a wide-area or local area hierarchical map using the technique suggested in (Rivlin et al., 1994). As the root of the hierarchy the system uses the "central node" of the hyperspace (which is computed by a special method) for the wide-area map and the closest node of a deduced standard path for the local-area map. This technique is suitable for educational hypermedia and on-line information systems.

7. User Modeling in Adaptive Hypermedia

All previous sections were devoted to the issues related to adaptation techniques in adaptive hypermedia (i.e., techniques which use the student model to provide some kind of adaptation to the user). This is, however, only the second part of the overall adaptation process (Figure 1). In this chapter we will consider some issues related with the first part of this process – the user modeling. We will not discuss here all issues of user modeling in adaptive hypermedia because most of them are not really specific to adaptive hypermedia (unlike the issues related with adaptation) and have been discussed in a number of other papers on adaptive systems – see (Kobsa, 1993; Kok, 1991) for a comprehensive review. What seems to be quite specific for user modeling in adaptive hypermedia is the sharing of the duties between the user and the system in the process of user modeling. The discussion in this section is centered around the problems of collaborative user modeling in AH systems.

A recent review of adaptive user interfaces (Dieterich et al., 1993) provides a very fine-grained taxonomy to describe sharing duties between the system and the user in the process of adaptation. We will base our discussion on a different model which is more suitable for our domain. We outline three stages in the adaptation process (Figure 1): collecting data about the user, processing the data to build or update the user model, and applying the user model to provide the adaptation. In our case, the last stage of this process is always performed by the system because we define as adaptive hypermedia systems exactly the systems which can provide automatic adaptation on the basis of the user model. In the case of "classic" or fully adaptive systems, the system also performs both of the previous stages of the overall process: while the user is simply working in an application system, the adaptation component watches what the user is doing, collects the data describing user's activity, processes these data to build the user model, and then provides an adaptation. Unfortunately, such an ideal situation is very rarely met in adaptive hypermedia systems. Almost all of them rely on external sources of information about the user. The main source of information for many of the systems is the information provided by the users themselves in several forms.

7.1. PROBLEMS WITH AUTOMATIC USER MODELING IN HYPERMEDIA SYSTEMS

There are some general problems related to automatic user modeling in adaptive systems. We name only two of them. First, automatic user modeling is not completely reliable. As it was pointed out in (de Rosis et al., 1993), systems which perform both user modeling and adaptation without user influence are twice unreliable - they can make an error when deducing the student model and they can make an error when providing adaptation (even if the model itself is correct). Second, some components of the user model, such as background and preferences of the user, cannot be deduced at all and have to be provided directly by the user. At the same time, research on adaptive dialogue systems demonstrates a number of effective technologies of automatic user modeling. In particular, two widely used standard technologies which have been shown to be effective for different applications involve (1) tracking the user's actions to understand which commands and concepts are known to the user and which are not, and (2) using the plan knowledge base to deduce the goal of the user.

The situation with automatic user modeling in adaptive hypermedia seems to be specific. Unlike in other kinds of application systems, watching what the user is doing in hypermedia provides insufficient information for user modeling. This fact was emphasized in several works on adaptive hypermedia (Beaumont, 1994; Boyle & Encarnacion, 1994; Vassileva, 1996). Most known techniques for automatic user modeling can hardly be applied in this area. The only information about the user's actions which the system can record is the user's path through the hyperspace and the time spent on each node. The user's path itself and patterns of user navigation are an interesting source of information, but it is very hard to update the user model using only this information. There are only two adaptive hypermedia systems which offer some techniques for this. Hynecosum can deduce the user level of experience based on the patterns of user navigation and HYPERCASE (Micarelli & Sciarrone, 1996) can deduce the user's didactic goal from the user's path. Some cumulative information about user navigation, such as the time spent on a particular node or the number of visits to it is easier to use. For example, HYPERFLEX uses the time spent on a node to measure how relevant the node is to the current goal, and ISIS-

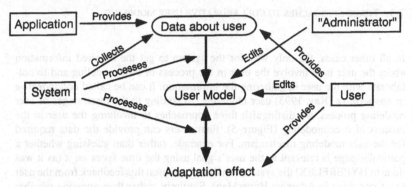

Figure 5. Collaborative user modeling in adaptive hypermedia.

Tutor uses the number of visits to predict the user knowledge level of the visited concept nodes. However, the fact that the user has visited a page several times or spent reasonable time on it does not even guarantee that the user attentively read its content. This kind of information is not reliable and cannot be used as the only source for building the user model. In fact, both HYPERFLEX and ISIS-Tutor use this information along with additional sources to update the user model.

7.2. ADDITIONAL SOURCES OF INFORMATION FOR AUTOMATIC USER MODELING

If automatic user modeling in adaptive hypermedia is hard and unreliable what are the ways for these systems to learn the information about the user? The answer depends on the application area. Two kinds of adaptive hypermedia systems – on-line help systems and educational hypermedia in intelligent tutoring systems – are more lucky to have an additional source of information to update the user model (Figure 5). On-line help systems are designed to serve as a part of a complex interactive system. Regular methods of user modeling can be applied in these systems to recognize the goal and the level of user experience. A good example is provided by HyPLAN (Grunst, 1993) which can infer the goal of the user working in a spreadsheet application and offer an adaptive help index which shows only the links relevant to this goal. Educational hypermedia in intelligent tutoring systems can use the information about the user (i.e., the student) from the student model which is an important part of any ITS. The student model in ITS is updated mainly by analyzing the student's answers to the offered tests, questions, or problems. This information about the student is usually more reliable than information inferred by watching the student navigation. It is not surprising that most existing adaptive educational hypermedia systems (Anatom-Tutor, ELM-ART, ELM-PE, HyperTutor, ISIS-Tutor, ITEM/PG, Land Use Tutor, SHIVA, SYPROS) are designed in ITS context.

7.3. THREE APPROACHES TO COLLABORATIVE USER MODELING

In all other cases, the only way for the system to get the required information about the user is to involve the user in the process of user modeling and to collaborate with the user in gathering the information. It can be called *collaborative* or *cooperative* (Kay, 1995) user modeling. According to the three stages of user modeling process, we distinguish three approaches to involving the user in the process of user modeling (Figure 5). First, users can provide the data required for the user modeling mechanism. For example, rather than guessing whether a particular page is relevant to the user's goal using the time spent on it (as it was done in HYPERFLEX) the system can directly request this feedback from the user (as it was done in Adaptive HyperMan). Similarly, rather than guessing whether the user understands a particular page, the system can get feedback from the user. Such a feedback is a more reliable source of information and not very difficuilt for the user to provide. Data received from the user can be further processed by the system to update the user model.

Second, users can make the desired adaptation themselves, directly showing the system what they would like to see on the screen in the given context. HYPERFLEX (Kaplan et al., 1993), MetaDoc (Boyle & Encarnacion, 1994), KN-AHS (Kobsa et al., 1994), and PUSH (Höök et al., 1996) demonstrate how this can be done in adaptive hypermedia for both link and content adaptation. HYPERFLEX adapts the list of links to related nodes by sorting the links according to their relevance to the current node and current user goal. The users can drag the links in the list to change their order thus telling the system which order of links they expect to see for the current goal and node. HYPERFLEX takes this information into account updating the main part of the user model – the relevance matrix. MetaDoc, KN-AHS, and PUSH adapt the context of a stretchtext page before presenting it to the user by showing or hiding some pieces of stretchtext according to the user's knowledge. Users can further adapt the content of the page by collapsing or uncollapsing pieces of stretchtext thus showing the system which information they actually want (or do not want) to see on the given page. These changes let MetaDoc and KN-AHS update the user knowledge level in the user model and help PUSH to infer the user's goal.

To proceed according to this second approach the system has to provide users with special interface features to make the adaptation (such as the possibility of dragging the links or collapsing/uncollapsing the text), i.e., the system should be user-adaptable. At the same time, the system has to be able to update the user model according to the preferences demonstrated by the user-driven adaptation. As a result, the preferences demonstrated by the user in one context can be used to adapt the interface in other contexts. The latter feature distinguish systems like HYPERFLEX and MetaDoc from simple user-adaptable systems which just store the set of user preferences "as is" and which cannot apply it in different contexts.

Third, the information in the user model can be updated directly by the information received from the users. In adaptive hypermedia systems Adaptive HyperMan (Mathé & Chen, 1996), Hypadapter (Hohl et al., 1996), Anatom-Tutor (Beaumont, 1994), EPIAIM (de Rosis et al., 1993), and C-Book (Kay & Kummerfeld, 1994b) as well as in many other kinds of adaptive systems, this method is used to set various features related to user background (profession, relevant experience, prospects, etc.) which can be provided only by the users themselves. More specific to adaptive hypermedia systems (Armstrong et al., 1995; Höök et al., 1996; Kaplan et al., 1993; Mathé & Chen, 1996; Thomas & Fischer, 1996; Vassileva, 1996) is the possibility for users to set their current goals (which are hard for the system to infer). The final step here is to make the user model viewable and changeable (Cook & Kay, 1994; Kay, 1995) – i.e., to provide a special interface for the users to inspect the content of the user model and to update it. With such an interface, the users can inspect all aspects of their models (Hohl et al., 1996) and make quite complicated changes, for example, changing the personal task hierarchy and visibility of nodes (Vassileva, 1996). In some cases, end users are not skilled enough to change a non-trivial part of the user model reliably while this part is very important for the correct functioning of the adaptation. In these cases the system can provide an interface for a skilled responsible person (administrator) to set the model correctly (Figure 5). For example, setting user classes and hierarchies in Hynecosum is expected to be done by an administrator. In educational hypermedia systems, the role of such an administrator is usually played by the teacher. In ISIS-Tutor it is the role of the teacher to set individual sequences of learning goals (an important part of the student model) for each student.

What is similar for the three analyzed approaches is the idea of involving the user in the process of user modeling to get additional information from the user and – as a result – to make user modeling more simple and more reliable. What is different with these approaches is the applicability. Providing feedback is the most simple method for users. It requires very small changes in the interface and can be used with any category of users. This method can provide some reliable data for inferring student preferences or knowledge. From another perspective, the amount of information provided with the feedback method is limited. Providing feedback is a side activity for users and should not disturb them from their main work. Feedback which requires more than two mouse clicks can be considered obtrusive. However, even one-click feedback combined with a powerful user modeling technique can give good results as demonstrated by Adaptive HyperMan (Mathé & Chen, 1996).

Receiving information for the user model directly from the student is the most simple method for the system. It requires a rather complicated interface but does not require complicated inference methods. It is definitely the most relevant method of getting the information which can be provided easily – such as goal or background aspects. Updating some more complicated data as an overlay knowledge model or a goal hierarchy requires considerable time and experience level. Understanding the relationships between updated information in the user model and changed behavior also implies reasonable experience. This method is suitable for an experienced user who uses the system in everyday work or for an administrator.

The method based on user-driven adaptation is in the middle between the above extremes. To provide adaptation requires more time for the user than to provide feedback, but it is still not very distracting and can be done by a not very skilled user (because the user has to provide just a desired effect, not the changes in the user model). Data provided by the user still have to be processed to update the student model, but the amount of information provided is greater and the processing methods cannot be as complicated. This way is also the most transparent one for users because the relation between their actions and the received adaptation is straitforward. Finally, it naturally joins adaptivity and adaptability (Fischer, 1993; Höök et al., 1996) and opens the way to apply such a promising method as adaptively supported adaptability (Oppermann, 1994a; Oppermann, 1994b). We think that this approach is the most relevant one for the continuum of users excluding beginners on one side (for them feedback is more easy) and experienced professionals on the other side (they can get more control by updating the user model).

8. Concluding Remarks

Adaptive hypermedia is a new but very quickly developing area of research. More than 20 truly adaptive hypermedia systems have been developed and described within the last three years. By now, most existing AH systems are applied in the traditional hypertext and hypermedia areas, such as on-line information systems, on-line help systems, and educational hypermedia. Some recent work demonstrates that AH techniques can be applied in a number of other application areas: IR hypermedia, institutional hypermedia, and personalized information spaces. In each of these application areas AH techniques can help to solve several groups of problems related to navigation in large hyperspaces and differences between hypermedia users.

Though adaptive hypermedia is a new area where most existing AH systems are original and very different from each other, it is already possible to identify a set of effective AH methods which have been implemented in several systems. These methods can be used as a set of building tools for creating future AH systems. In real AH systems, these methods have been implemented by different techniques which use different knowledge representations and different adaptation algorithms. Many of these techniques are well-described in the literature and can be re-used by the designers of AH systems.

The main characteristic of all methods and techniques of adaptive hypermedia is the applied technology of adaptation. We have identified seven adaptation technologies which are different from a "what can be adapted" point of view: adaptive text presentation, direct guidance, adaptive sorting, hiding, and annotation of links, adaptive multimedia presentation, and map adaptation. The first five of these technologies are well-investigated and used by many AH methods and techniques. The last two technologies are currently under-investigated and need further research. More work has to be done in applying current techniques of adaptive multimedia presentation to real-world hyperspaces and in making known techniques for generation of hypermedia maps adaptive.

One of the special features of AH systems is the important role of users in the user modeling process. Most existing AH systems cannot rely on "classic" automatic user modeling and must use external sources of information about the user. Many of the systems extend traditional "look and browse" hypermedia interface with special features that let users provide more information about their goals, knowledge, and preferences. A promising approach here is to let the user adapt presented hypermedia pages and take the user's changes into account to update the user model.

This paper is an attempt at conducting a comprehensive review of existing AH systems. The review classifies existing AH techniques and methods according to several introduced dimensions and systematically presents the most interesting AH methods and techniques for both the adaptation and user modeling parts of the overall adaptation loop. At the end, we want to mention three important issues related with the topic of the paper which have been left outside the scope of the review. These issues are currently underinvestigated. For each of them we can name 2–4 papers which are useful as a background for further research but cannot be used for providing a comprehensive review. We consider the three issues listed below as the important directions of research in AH area.

The first issue is the efficiency of AH methods and techniques. Unfortunately, the situation with experimental testing of AH systems is not as advanced as the situation with development of these systems. As we have shown, a good number of interesting techniques were suggested and implemented in AH systems. The problem is that very few of them have been evaluated by a properly designed experiment. By now, we can name only three systems which have been tested by a comprehensive experiment with the number of subjects large enough to get statistically significant data: MetaDoc (Boyle & Encarnacion, 1994), HYPERFLEX (Kaplan et al., 1993), and ISIS-Tutor (Brusilovsky & Pesin, 1995). The lack of experimental studies is a weak point of AH research and more work has to be done in this direction.

The second issue which is related to the previous one is the usability of adaptation. This issue is important for any adaptive computer system. Adaptivity is not a silver bullet. Adding adaptivity does not always makes a system better, moreover, it can make system much less usable if the users will not be able to understand what is going on in an adaptive system and lose the control over the system. What are the conditions and features of "usable" adaptation? Currently, very few papers contribute directly to this issue. We should specially mention the paper (Vassileva, 1996) which introduces the idea of "stepwise" adaptation and the papers (Höök et al., 1996; Kay, 1995) which discuss the problems of "transparent" adaptation.

The third issue to mention is the relations between AH research and the World Wide Web. WWW, a hyperspace spread over the Internet, has potentially unlimited number of nodes and variety of users. WWW is currently a promising direction for application of AH techniques. Moreover, we think that WWW will be the most important factor stimulating AH research in the next several years. In fact, several AH systems reviewed in this paper are completely or partly implemented on WWW (Armstrong et al., 1995; Höök et al., 1996; Schwarz et al., 1996; Thomas & Fischer, 1996). These works are very different and can hardly be used to provide some generalizations, for example, which adaptation techniques are most suitable for WWW. However, they already show some useful and re-usable ways of implementing AH methods and techniques on WWW.

Acknowledgments

I would like to thank Julita Vassileva, Gerhard Weber, Kristina Höök, Richard Keller and John Eklund for providing comments on the earlier version of this paper. Special thanks to Alfred Kobsa for his permanent support in preparing this review. I would like to thank also the reviewers of this paper for their useful and constructive comments. Part of this work was supported by an Alexander von Humboldt-Stiftung Fellowship to the author.

Appendix 1: List of Adaptive Hypermedia Systems

"REAL" AHS

Adaptive HyperMan (Mathé & Chen, 1994, Mathé & Chen, 1996),
Anatom-Tutor (Beaumont, 1994),
Basar (Thomas, 1995; Thomas & Fischer, 1996),
C-Book (Kay & Kummerfeld, 1994a; Kay & Kummerfeld, 1994b),
CID (Boy, 1991),
[Clibbon] (Clibbon, 1995),
DHS (Shibata & Katsumoto, 1993; Katsumoto et al., 1994; Katsumoto et al., 1996),
ELM-ART (Brusilovsky, Schwarz & Weber, 1996; Schwarz, Brusilovsky & Weber, 1996),
ELM-PE (Brusilovsky & Weber, 1996),
EPIAIM (de Rosis et al., 1993; de Rosis et al., 1994),
Hynecosum (Vassileva, 1994, Vassileva, 1996),
Hypadapter (Böcker et al., 1990; Hohl et al., 1996),
HYPERCASE (Micarelli & Sciarrone, 1996),
HYPERFLEX (Kaplan et al., 1993),
HyperTutor (Pérez et al., 1995a; 1995b),
HyPLAN (Fox, Grunst & Quast, 1993; Grunst, 1993),
ISIS-Tutor (Brusilovsky & Pesin, 1994; Brusilovsky & Pesin, 1995),
ITEM/PG (Brusilovsky, Pesin & Zyryanov, 1993; Brusilovsky & Zyryanov, 1993),
KN-AHS (Kobsa et al., 1994),
Land Use Tutor (Kushniruk & Wang, 1994),

Lisp-Critic (Fischer et al., 1990),
Manuel Excel (de La Passardiere & Dufresne, 1992)
MetaDoc (Boyle & Encarnacion, 1994),
ORIMUHS (Encarnação, 1995a; Encarnação, 1995b),
PUSH (Höök et al., 1996),
SYPROS (Gonschorek & Herzog, 1995)
SHIVA (Zeiliger, 1993),
WebWatcher (Armstrong et al., 1995),
WING-MIT (Kim, 1995).

SOME SYSTEMS CLOSE TO AHS

ITEM/IP (Brusilovsky et al., 1993; Brusilovsky, 1992b),
Information Islands (Waterworth, 1996),
PPP (André & Rist, 1996),
[Yetim] (Yetim, 1993).

References

Agosti, M., M. Melucci, and F. Crestani: 1995, 'Automatic Authoring and Construction of Hypermedia for Information Retrieval'. *Multimedia Systems* 3(1), 15–24.
André, E. and T. Rist: 1996, 'Towards a New Generation of Hypermedia Systems: Extending Automated Presentation Design for Hypermedia'. Report, DFKI GmbH, Saarbrücken.
Arens, S. and R. Hammwöhner: 1995, 'Ein graphischer Browser für das Konstanzer Hypertext-System'. In: R. Kuhlen and M. Ritterberg (eds.): *Hypertext – Information Retrieval – Multimedia.* Universitätsverlag Konstanz, Konstanz, pp. 175–189.
Armstrong, R., D. Freitag, T. Joachims, and T. Mitchell: 1995, 'WebWatcher: A Learning Apprentice for the World Wide Web'. *AAAI Spring Symposium on Information Gathering from Distributed, Heterogeneous Environments*, Stanford, CA, http://www.isi.edu/sims/knoblock/sss95/mitchell.ps.
Beaumont, I.: 1994, 'User Modeling in the Interactive Anatomy Tutoring System ANATOM-TUTOR'. *User Modeling and User-Adapted Interaction* 4(1), 21–45 (reprinted in this volume, pp. 91–115).
Benyon, D. R. and D. M. Murray: 1993, 'Applying User Modeling to Human-Computer Interaction Design'. *AI Review* 6, 43–69.
Böcker, H.-D., H. Hohl, and T. Schwab: 1990, 'ϒπAdaptερ – Individualizing Hypertext'. In: D. Diaper (ed.): *INTERACT'90*. North-Holland, Amsterdam, pp. 931–936.
Boy, G. A.: 1991, 'On-Line User Model Acquisition in Hypertext Documentation'. *IJCAI'91 Workshop 'Agent Modeling for Intelligent Interaction'*, Sydney, Australia, pp. 34–42.
Boyle, C. and A. O. Encarnacion: 1994, 'MetaDoc: An Adaptive Hypertext Reading System'. *User Modeling and User-Adapted Interaction* 4(1), 1–19 (reprinted in this volume, pp. 71-89).
Brusilovsky, P. L.: 1992a, 'A Framework for Intelligent Knowledge Sequencing and Task Sequencing'. In: C. Frasson, G. Gauthier and G. I. McCalla (eds.): *Intelligent Tutoring Systems*. Springer-Verlag, Berlin, pp. 499–506.
Brusilovsky, P. L.: 1992b, 'Intelligent Tutor, Environment and Manual for Introductory Programming'. *Educational and Training Technology International* 29(1), 26–34.
Brusilovsky, P. and L. Pesin: 1994, 'ISIS-Tutor: An Adaptive Hypertext Learning Environment'. *JCKBSE'94, Japanese-CIS Symposium on Knowledge-Based Software Engineering*, Pereslavl-Zalesski, Russia, pp. 83–87.
Brusilovsky, P. and L. Pesin: 1995, 'Visual Annotation of Links in Adaptive Hypermedia'. *CHI'95 Conference Companion*, Denver, pp. 222–223.

Brusilovsky, P., L. Pesin, and M. Zyryanov: 1993, 'Towards an Adaptive Hypermedia Component for an Intelligent Learning Environment'. In: L. J. Bass, J. Gornostaev and C. Unger (eds.): *Human-Computer Interaction*. Lecture Notes in Computer Science, Vol. 753, Springer-Verlag, Berlin, pp. 348–358.

Brusilovsky, P., E. Schwarz, and G. Weber: 1996, 'ELM-ART: An Intelligent Tutoring System on World Wide Web'. *Third International Conference on Intelligent Tutoring Systems, ITS–96*, Montreal.

Brusilovsky, P. and G. Weber: 1996, 'Collaborative Example Selection in an Intelligent Example-Based Programming Environment'. *International Conference on Learning Sciences, ICLS–96*, Evanston, USA.

Brusilovsky, P. and M. Zyryanov: 1993, 'Intelligent Tutor, Environment and Manual for Physical Geography'. *Seventh International PEG Conference*, Edinburgh, pp. 63–73.

Clibbon, K.: 1995, 'Conceptually Adapted Hypertext for Learning'. *CHI'95 Conference Companion*, Denver, pp. 224–225.

Cook, R. and J. Kay: 1994, 'The Justified User Model: A Viewable, Explained User Model'. *Fourth International Conference on User Modeling*, Hyannis, MA, pp. 145–150.

de La Passardiere, B. and A. Dufresne: 1992, 'Adaptive Navigational Tools for Educational Hypermedia'. In: I. Tomek (ed.): *Computer Assisted Learning*. Springer-Verlag, Berlin, pp. 555–567.

de Rosis, F., N. De Carolis, and S. Pizzutilo: 1993, 'User Tailored Hypermedia Explanations'. *INTERCHI'93 Adjunct Proceedings*, Amsterdam, pp. 169–170.

de Rosis, F., N. De Carolis, and S. Pizzutilo: 1994, 'User Tailored Hypermedia Explanations'. *Workshop on Adaptive Hypertext and Hypermedia at the Fourth International Conference on User Modeling*, Hyannis, MA, http://www.cs.bgsu.edu/hypertext/adaptive/deRosis.html.

Debevc, M., S. Rajko, and D. Donlagic: 1994, 'Adaptive Bar Implementation and Ergonomics'. *Informatica: Journal of Computing and Informatics* 18, 357–366.

Dieterich, H., U. Malinowski, T. Kühme, and M. Schneider-Hufschmidt: 1993, 'State of the Art in Adaptive User Interfaces'. In: M. Schneider-Hufschmidt, T. Kühme and U. Malinowski (eds.): *Adaptive User Interfaces: Principles and Practice*. North-Holland, Amsterdam, pp. 13–48.

Encarnação, L. M.: 1995a, 'Adaptive Help for Interactive Graphics Systems: An Application-Independent Approach'. *Workshop Adaptivität und Benutzermodellierung in interaktiven Softwaresystemen (ABIS 95)*, München.

Encarnação, L. M.: 1995b, 'Adaptivity in Graphical User Interfaces: An Experimental Framework'. *Computers & Graphics* 19(6), 873–884.

Fischer, G.: 1993, 'Shared Knowledge in Cooperative Problem-Solving Systems – Integrating Adaptive and Adaptable Components'. In: M. Schneider-Hufschmidt, T. Kühme and U. Malinowski (eds.): *Adaptive User Interfaces: Principles and Practice*. North-Holland, Amsterdam, pp. 49–68.

Fischer, G., T. Mastaglio, B. Reeves, and J. Rieman: 1990, 'Minimalist Explanations in Knowledge-Based Systems'. *23th Annual Hawaii International Conference on System Sciences*, Kailua-Kona, HI, pp. 309–317.

Fox, T., G. Grunst, and K.-J. Quast: 1993, 'HyPlan – A Context-Sensitive Hypermedia Help System'. Report No. 743: Arbeitspapiere der GMD, GMD, Germany.

Furnas, G. W.: 1986, 'Generalized Fisheye Views'. *CHI'86*, pp. 16–23.

Gonschorek, M. and C. Herzog: 1995, 'Using Hypertext for an Adaptive Helpsystem in an Intelligent Tutoring System'. *AI-ED'95, 7th World Conference on Artificial Intelligence in Education*, Washington, DC, pp. 274–281.

Greer, J. and G. McCalla (eds.): 1993, *Student Modeling: The Key to Individualized Knowledge-Based Instruction*. NATO ASI Series F, Vol. 125, Springer-Verlag, Berlin.

Grunst, G.: 1993, 'Adaptive Hypermedia for Support Systems'. In: M. Schneider-Hufschmidt, T. Kühme and U. Malinowski (eds.): *Adaptive User Interfaces: Principles and Practice*. North-Holland, Amsterdam, pp. 269–283.

Hammond, N.: 1989, 'Hypermedia and Learning: Who Guides Whom?'. In: H. Maurer (ed.): *Computer Assisted Learning*. Lecture Notes in Computer Science, Vol. 360, Springer-Verlag, Berlin, pp. 167–181.

Helmes, L., M. Razum, and A. Barth: 1995, 'Concept of a Hypertext Interface for the Information Retrieval in Complex Factual Databases'. In: R. Kuhlen and M. Ritterberg (eds.): *Hypertext – Information Retrieval – Multimedia*. Universitätsverlag Konstanz, Konstanz, pp. 175–189.

Hohl, H., H.-D. Böcker, and R. Gunzenhäuser: 1996, 'Hypadapter: An Adaptive Hypertext System for Exploratory Learning and Programming'. *User Modeling and User-Adapted Interaction* 6(2-3), 131–156 (reprinted in this volume, pp. 117–142).

Höök, K., J. Karlgren, A. Wærn, N. Dahlbäck, C. G. Jansson, K. Karlgren, and B. Lemaire: 1996, 'A Glass Box Approach to Adaptive Hypermedia'. *User Modeling and User-Adapted Interaction* 6(2-3), 157–184 (reprinted in this volume, pp. 143–170).

Kaplan, C., J. Fenwick, and J. Chen: 1993, 'Adaptive Hypertext Navigation Based on User Goals and Context'. *User Modeling and User-Adapted Interaction* 3(3), 193–220 (reprinted in this volume, pp. 45–69).

Kaptelinin, V.: 1993, 'Item Recognition in Menu Selection: The Effect of Practice'. *INTERCHI'93 Adjunct Proceedings*, Amsterdam, pp. 183–184.

Katsumoto, M., M. Fukuda, N. Irie, and Y. Shibata: 1994, 'Dynamic Hypermedia System Based on Perceptional Link Method for Distributed Design Image Database'. *9th International Conference on Information Networking (ICOIN–9)*, pp. 49–54.

Katsumoto, M., M. Fukuda, and Y. Shibata: 1996, 'The Kansei Link Method for Multimedia Database'. *10th International Conference on Information Networking (ICOIN–10)*, pp. 382–389.

Kay, J.: 1995, 'The UM Toolkit for Cooperative User Models'. *User Modeling and User-Adapted Interaction* 4(3), 149–196.

Kay, J. and R. Kummerfeld: 1994a, 'Adaptive Hypertext for Individualised Instruction'. *Workshop on Adaptive Hypertext and Hypermedia at the Fourth International Conference on User Modeling*, Hyannis, MA, http://www.cs.bgsu.edu/hypertext/adaptive/Kay.html.

Kay, J. and R. J. Kummerfeld: 1994b, 'An Individualised Course for the C Programming Language'. *Second International WWW Conference "Mosaic and the Web"*, Chicago, IL, http://www.ncsa.uiuc.edu/SDG/IT94/Proceedings/Educ/kummerfeld/kummerfeld.html.

Kim, D.-W.: 1995, 'WING-MIT: Das auf einer multimedialen und intelligenten Benutzerschnittstelle basierende tutorielle Hilfesystem für das Werkstoffinformationssystem WING-M2'. *Workshop Adaptivität und Benutzermodellierung in interaktiven Softwaresystemen (ABIS 95)*, München.

Kobsa, A.: 1993, 'User Modeling: Recent Work, Prospects and Hazards'. In: M. Schneider-Hufschmidt, T. Kühme, and U. Malinowski (eds.): *Adaptive User Interfaces: Principles and Practice*. North-Holland, Amsterdam, pp. 111–128.

Kobsa, A., D. Müller, and A. Nill: 1994, 'KN-AHS: An Adaptive Hypertext Client of the User Modeling System BGP-MS'. *Fourth International Conference on User Modeling*, Hyannis, MA, pp. 31–36.

Kok, A. J.: 1991, 'A Review and Synthesis of User Modeling in Intelligent Systems'. *The Knowledge Engineering Review* 6(1), 21–47.

Kushniruk, A. and H. Wang: 1994, 'A Hypermedia-Based Educational System with Knowledge-Based Guidance'. *ED-MEDIA'94 – World Conference on Educational Multimedia and Hypermedia*, Vancouver, Canada, pp. 335–340.

Linard, M. and R. Zeiliger: 1995, 'Designing a Navigational Support for Educational Software'. In: B. Blumental, J. Gornostaev, and C. Unger (eds.): *Human-Computer Interaction*. Lecture Notes in Computer Science, Vol. 1015, Springer-Verlag, Berlin, pp. 63–78.

Mathé, N. and J. Chen: 1994, 'A User-Centered Approach to Adaptive Hypertext Based on an Information Relevance Model'. *Fourth International Conference on User Modeling*, Hyannis, MA, pp. 107–114.

Mathé, N. and J. Chen: 1996, 'User-Centered Indexing for Adaptive Information Access'. *User Modeling and User-Adapted Interaction* 6(2-3), 225–261 (reprinted in this volume, pp. 171–207).

Maybury, M. T. (ed.) 1993, *Intelligent Multimedia Interfaces*. AAAI Press/MIT Press, Boston.

Micarelli, A. and F. Sciarrone: 1996, 'A Case-Based Toolbox for Guided Hypermedia Navigation'. *Fifth International Conference on User Modeling, UM–96*, Kailua-Kona, Hawaii, pp. 129–136.

Moore, J. D. and W. R. Swartout: 1989, 'Pointing: A Way toward Explanation Dialogue'. *Eight National Conference on Artificial Intelligence*, pp. 457–464.

Mukherjea, S. and J. D. Foley: 1995, 'Visualizing the World-Wide Web with navigational view builder'. *Third International World-Wide Web Conference. In: Computer Networks and ISDN Systems* 27(6), 1075–1087.

Mukherjea, S., J. D. Foley, and S. Hudson: 1995, 'Visualizing Complex Hypermedia Networks through Multiple Hierarchical Views'. *CHI'95*, Denver, pp. 331–337.

Oppermann, R. (ed.): 1994a, *Adaptive User Support – Ergonomic Design of Manually and Automatically Adaptable Software*. Computers, Cognition, and Work, Vol. 40, Lawrence Erlbaum Associates, Hillsdale, NJ.

Oppermann, R.: 1994b, 'Adaptively Supported Adaptability'. *International Journal on Human-Computer Studies* 40, 455–472.

Paris, C. L.: 1988, 'Tailoring Object Description to a User's Level of Expertise'. *Computational Linguistics* 14(3), 64–78.

Pérez, T., J. Gutiérrez, and P. Lopistéguy: 1995a, 'An Adaptive Hypermedia System'. *AI-ED'95, 7th World Conference on Artificial Intelligence in Education*, Washington, DC, pp. 351–358.

Pérez, T., P. Lopistéguy, J. Gutiérrez, and I. Usandizaga: 1995b, 'HyperTutor: From Hypermedia to Intelligent Adaptive Hypermedia'. *ED-MEDIA'95, World Conference on Educational Multimedia and Hypermedia*, Graz, Austria, pp. 529–534.

Reed, W. M., J. M. Oughton, D. J. Ayersman, S. F. Giessler, and J. R. Ervin: 1995, 'Computer Experience and Learning Style: Linear versus Nonlinear Navigation'. *ED-MEDIA'95 – World Conference on Educational Multimedia and Hypermedia*, Charlottesville, 802 pp.

Rivlin, E., R. Botafogo, and B. Shneidermann: 1994, 'Navigating in Hyperspace: Designing a Structure-Based Toolbox'. *Communications of the ACM* 37(2), 87–96.

Schwarz, E., P. Brusilovsky, and G. Weber: 1996, 'World-Wide Intelligent Textbooks'. *ED-MEDIA'96 – World Conference on Educational Multimedia and Hypermedia*, Boston, MA.

Shibata, Y. and M. Katsumoto: 1993, 'Dynamic Hypertext and Knowledge Agent Systems for Multimedia Information'. *ACM Hypertext'93*, Seattle, WA, pp. 82–93.

Thomas, C. G.: 1995, 'Basar: A Framework for Integrating Agents in the World Wide Web'. *IEEE Computer* 28(5), 84–86.

Thomas, C. G. and G. Fischer: 1996, 'Using Agents to Improve the Usability and Usefulness of the World-Wide Web'. *Fifth International Conference on User Modeling, UM–96*, Kailua-Kona, Hawaii, pp. 5–12.

Tomek, I., H. Maurer, and M. Nassar: 1993, 'Optimal Presentation of Links in Large Hypermedia Systems'. *ED-MEDIA'93, World Conference on Educational Multimedia and Hypermedia*, Orlando, FL, pp. 511–518.

Vassileva, J.: 1994, 'A Practical Architecture for User Modeling in a Hypermedia-Based Information System'. *Fourth International Conference on User Modeling*, Hyannis, MA, pp. 115–120.

Vassileva, J.: 1996, 'A Task-Centered Approach for User Modeling in a Hypermedia Office Documentation System'. *User Modeling and User-Adapted Interaction* 6(2-3), 185–223 (reprinted in this volume, pp. 209–247).

Waterworth, J. A.: 1996, 'A Pattern of Islands: Exploring Public Information Space in a Private Vehicle'. In: P. Brusilovsky, P. Kommers, and N. Streitz (eds.): *Multimedia, Hypermedia and Virtual Reality: Models, Systems, and Applications*. Lecture Notes in Computer Science, Springer-Verlag, Berlin, pp. 266–279.

Yetim, F.: 1993, 'User-Adapted Hypertext Explanation'. In: T. Grechenig and M. Tscheligi (eds.): *Human-Computer Interaction*. Springer-Verlag, Berlin, pp. 348–358.

Zeiliger, R.: 1993, 'Adaptive Testing: Contribution of the SHIVA Model'. In: D. Leclercq and J. Bruno (eds.): *Item Banking: Interactive Testing and Self-Assessment*. NATO ASI Serie F, Vol. 112, Springer-Verlag, Berlin, pp. 54–65.

Zhao, Z., T. O'Shea, and P. Fung: 1993, 'Visualization of Semantic Relations in Hypertext Systems'. *ED-MEDIA'93, World Conference on Educational Multimedia and Hypermedia*, Orlando, FL, pp. 556–564.

Zukerman, I. and R. McConachy: 1993, 'Consulting a User Model to Address a User's Inferences during Content Planning'. *User Modeling and User-Adapted Interaction* 3(2), 155–185.

Zyryanov, M.: 1996, 'Adaptive Local Maps in the Hypermedia Components of Intelligent Learning Environments'. In: P. Brusilovsky, P. Kommers, and N. Streitz (eds.): *Multimedia, Hypermedia and Virtual Reality: Models, Systems, and Applications.* Lecture Notes in Computer Science, Springer-Verlag, Berlin, pp. 306–310.

Author's Vita

Dr. Peter Brusilovsky
Carnegie Mellon University, School of Computer Science, Pittsburgh, PA 15213, U.S.A.

Dr. Peter Brusilovsky received his Ph.D. degree in Computer Science from the Moscow State University in 1987. Until recently he has been a Senior Research Scientist in the International Center for Scientific and Technical Information, Moscow. His research interests lie in the areas of Intelligent Tutoring Systems and Shells, Student and User Modelling, Adaptive Interfaces, and Adaptive Hypermedia.

Adaptive Hypertext Navigation Based On User Goals and Context

CRAIG KAPLAN
The I.Q. Company

JUSTINE FENWICK
Harvard Business School

JAMES CHEN
University of California at San Diego

(Received 26 October 1992; in final form 5 July 1993)

Abstract. Hypertext systems allow flexible access to topics of information, but this flexibility has disadvantages. Users often become lost or overwhelmed by choices. An adaptive hypertext system can overcome these disadvantages by recommending information to users based on their specific information needs and preferences. Simple associative matrices provide an effective way of capturing these user preferences. Because the matrices are easily updated, they support the kind of dynamic learning required in an adaptive system.

HYPERFLEX, a prototype of an adaptive hypertext system that learns, is described. Informal studies with HYPERFLEX clarify the circumstances under which adaptive systems are likely to be useful, and suggest that HYPERFLEX can reduce time spent searching for information by up to 40%. Moreover, these benefits can be obtained with relatively little effort on the part of hypertext authors or users.

The simple models underlying HYPERFLEX's performance may offer a general and useful alternative to more sophisticated modelling techniques. Conditions under which these models, and similar adaptation techniques, might be most useful are discussed.

Key words: adaptive interface applications, hypertext, user models, human–computer interaction, associative matrices, intelligent information retrieval, relevance feedback

1. Introduction

Hypertext systems are becoming an increasingly popular approach to the problem of information retrieval. In a hypertext system, information is usually chunked into discrete, independently meaningful topics. Associated topics are connected via links. Highlighted words or icons embedded in the text typically indicate the presence of links. Users retrieve a new topic by selecting a link.

Boyle and Encarnacion (1994) have explored the possibility of using standard user modelling techniques to adapt the content of hypertext nodes. Our approach differs from this research in two important ways. First, we focus on the information access, retrieval, and navigational aspects of hypertext. Like Boyle and Encarnacion, we are fundamentally concerned with linking users to the information that is most relevant to them, but our approach is to recommend different information

P. Brusilovsky et al. (eds.), Adaptive Hypertext and Hypermedia, 45–69.
© 1998 *Kluwer Academic Publishers.*

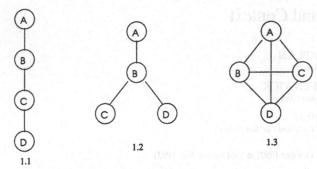

Figure 1. A structural continuum for online systems.

topics, rather than changing the content of the information topics. Secondly, our system relies on, and demonstrates the effectiveness of, a simple, but nonstandard user modelling approach which may have potential for a variety of domains.

Consider first the information access aspects of hypertext. Online systems can be viewed along a structural continuum ranging from sequential text to a maximally interconnected hypertext system. Figure 1 illustrates three points along this continuum.

Figure 1.1 illustrates the structure of a sequential document. Note that sequential structure forces users to transverse intermediate states that they may not be interested in. For example if a user wants to access topic D from topic B, intermediate topic C must first be transversed.

Hypertext differs from online sequential documents in that it can provide more direct and flexible access to information. For example, in Figure 1.2, a user could go directly from topic B to topic D.

Figure 1.3 illustrates a maximally flexible hypertext document. Because every topic is linked to every other topic, many potential paths through the topics exist. Direct access to any topic from any other topic is possible without ever having to navigate through intermediate topics.

Flexible and direct access is an important benefit of hypertext because it is virtually impossible to construct a sequential document that is optimally ordered for all possible users. Hypertext provides the flexibility to skip more directly to what is of interest.

Unfortunately, with added flexibility comes the possibility that users may lose the benefit of the information implicit in a sequential ordering. They may become disoriented or 'lost in hyperspace', and they may have to explore many links before finding the desired information (e.g. see Conklin, 1987; Horton, 1991).

These dangers increase as the numbers of links increase, so most authors of hypertext balance the gains in flexibility and direct access against the dangers of losing a coherent path through the information. The resulting systems typically fall somewhere in the middle of the continuum depicted in Figure 1.

One of the major challenges for hypertext system designers has been to find new ways to exploit the flexibility of hypertext while minimizing the accompanying perils.

One response has been to supplement hypertext systems with keyword-based retrieval functions. The FIND or SEARCH commands common to word processing programs are good examples. If users know the specific terms they are looking for, then keyword-based retrieval systems provide an easy and efficient way to find information. More sophisticated keyword-based retrieval systems such as Latent Semantic Indexing (Dumais, 1988), Thesauruses (Reisner, 1966), and Adaptive Indexing (Furnas, 1985) can improve this method of retrieval.

Another way to supplement hypertext links is to include navigational aids. For example, fisheye views (Furnas, 1986), guides (Salomon et al., 1989), and network browsers (Anderson et al., 1990) help users find their way through hypertext networks. Despite the inclusion of these aids, however, authors still rely on a fixed sequential structure as the primary means of providing guidance to users.

In contrast, an adaptive approach to information access issues might start with a maximally flexible hypertext document and evolve a dynamic structure based on the needs of users. In so doing, the approach maximizes the benefits of hypertext while minimizing its dangers. First, authors may include unlimited numbers of links without fear that the users will become lost. The system recommends links that best suit the user's needs. Secondly, authors are relieved of the impossible task of trying to create documents that are all things to all people. An adaptive hypertext document tailors its organization to its readers as it learns their information preferences and goals. Finally, the presence of many links ensures that users can access topics directly, without having to navigate through intermediate topics. If other types of access are desired, any of the search and navigation techniques mentioned above could complement a system with adaptive capabilities.

2. Simple, General, User Models

At the heart of most intelligent and/or adaptive systems are models of the user and task domain. For example, Kobsa and Wahlster (1989) include intelligent help systems, intelligent CAI systems, multiple-agent planning systems, computer games, text generation/understanding systems, intelligent database query evaluation systems, expert systems, and natural language dialog systems among the research areas that rely heavily on user modelling techniques. Within these areas, one can find a diversity of approaches towards knowledge representation, ranging from simple propositional representations, to scripts, to stereotypes, to statistically-based schemes. While powerful, many of these representational approaches are also quite complex. By comparison, our approach towards modelling is relatively simple, and general.

From an applications viewpoint, a simple approach is important because extensive knowledge engineering requirements and the complexity of most intelligent systems have proven to be major obstacles to the practical application of AI and adaptive technology. If a simple, and general, approach to these problems can be found, even if it is only partially successful, it will facilitate the evolution and adoption of more powerful modelling schemes.

The simplicity of our approach stems from two observations. The first is that hypertext is itself a semantic network. Thus it is possible to leverage the semantics that already exist in a hypertext network, without creating a separate domain model. The second observation is that the complexity of a user model tends to be proportional to the complexity of the interaction between the system and the user. A carefully constrained method of interaction between the user and system allows a minimal user model to be maximally effective. This observation has been one of the factors underlying success in some intelligent tutoring systems (e.g. see McKendree, 1990).

Presenting advice in the form of an ordered list of recommended topics, transforms the complex problem of advice-giving into the much simpler problem of rank ordering a list. An adaptive hypertext system does not need to explicitly represent the semantic content of these list items – the semantics are in the information topics themselves. The system needs only to represent a user's preference for one item over another in a particular context.

Theoretically, context could include the time and place of the user's interaction with the system, the Dow Jones Industrial average on a particular day, or any number of factors that might be relevant to anticipating the user's information needs. In our prototype, only two kinds of context are taken into consideration: user goals and user preferences for specific topics.

Initially, we were drawn to connectionist networks as the basis for our knowledge representation, for three reasons. First, elements of context can be represented simply as nodes in a network. Second, preferences can be represented easily by weighted links in a network. And third, hypertext itself is a network. In fact, an earlier approach to building our adaptive hypertext system used connectionist networks and learning algorithms (Kaplan and Wolff, 1990). However experimentation with that system made it clear that a simpler scheme using association matrices (semantic nets), would be more effective.

As in semantic network models of human memory, the primary idea is to capture the strength of association between two nodes.

Figure 2 shows an associative matrix that captures the strength of relationships between information topics that might appear in a cookbook. For example, the matrix indicates that the topic, Gravy, is most strongly associated to Potatoes. An intelligent hypertext system could use the information in this matrix to recommend that a potato lover read first about gravy and then perhaps about soups (since the Potatoes – Soups link has the second largest weight).

Topic / Topic	Potatos	Cakes	Gravy	Soups
Potatos	X	1	10	3
Cakes	1	X	3	1
Gravy	10	3	X	5
Soups	5	1	5	X

Figure 2. The topic-to-topic associative matrix.

Goal / Topic	Potatos	Cakes	Gravy	Soups
Cook first course	5	1	2	10
Make dessert	2	10	8	2

Figure 3. The goal-to-topic associative matrix.

Note that the strengths of relationships between topics should be a function of context. In the context of cooking a first course, a potato lover might want to be directed to (potato) soups, rather than gravy.

Context can be incorporated by adding more matrices. The Goal-to-Topic matrix shown in Figure 3 is a matrix that takes the user's goals into account. Based on this matrix, the system would recommend soups to someone with the goal of cooking a first course. If that someone also happened to be a potato lover (i.e. if the Topic title 'Potatoes' was specified to be of interest) then the system should use that information along with the goal information to make its recommendation.

Figure 4 illustrates graphically what happens in the network. With no goal information, the system recommends that a potato lover read about gravy since that topic has the strongest association to Potato (Fig. 4.1). However, in the context of a goal to cook a first course, Soup ends up having a stronger association to Potato then Gravy does. In this case, the system determines the strength of the association by adding the information contained in the Topic-Topic and Goal-Topic matrices. (Details of the algorithm for combining information from multiple matrices are discussed later in this paper.)

Theoretically, as many matrices as desired could be added to the system, reflecting a variety of context elements.

Because user preferences are represented numerically, the information can be subjected to a wide variety of mathematical transformations, including averaging the preferences of groups of users. Determining the rank order for the list of

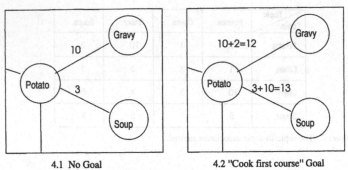

| 4.1 No Goal | 4.2 "Cook first course" Goal |

Figure 4. What happens when a goal is activated.

recommendations proves to be computationally simple as well. Conceptually, one sums the association strengths to a topic from all other active topics. Then one orders the topics according to these resulting sums. In practice, one can often read the rank ordering from the matrix, making the representation extremely computationally efficient. Finally, unlike many connectionist models, the representation is simple enough that it has face validity. That is, one can understand what knowledge has been captured by examining the matrix of numbers together with a list of titles for topics and goals.

3. Learning

While associative matrices allow a hypertext system to make intelligent recommendations, the system must learn if it is to adapt to its users. Specifically, the system must learn to adjust the structure and weights of its network to match the goals and preferences of different users. As in most learning systems, feedback plays a critical role.

In a simple associative matrix, user feedback tells the system how to adjust the association strength between two topics so as to improve the system's performance. This idea of weighting more heavily information that users find useful is sometimes referred to as relevance feedback. The effectiveness of relevance feedback has been demonstrated in several information retrieval systems .

For example, Ide and Salton (1971) reported that relevance feedback can improve retrieval effectiveness by 50% in situations where users are interested in finding all relevant materials, and by 20% in situations where users are interested in finding only some of the material.

3.1. A RELEVANCE-FEEDBACK CONTINUUM

Methods for gathering relevance feedback from users can be viewed on a continuum. Users may have to do more or less work translating their preferences into specific feedback that the system can use.

For example, Belew's (1989) Adaptive Information Retrieval (AIR) system requires users to rate explicitly documents suggested by the system. AIR uses a four-point rating scale for both documents and their related features: keywords and authors. In this system, users must know what they like and explicitly state their preferences using the system's tri-partite model.

In Holynski's (1988) Adaptive Graphics Analyzer system, users do not have to translate their preferences into feedback on individual features. Instead users provide an overall preference rating for an image. However, for the system to determine which features users like, users must rate a series of ten images.

In contrast, Kok and Botman's prototype of an Active Data Base (1988) makes inferences about users' preferences without requiring users to use a rating scale. Users are shown a list of automobiles and asked to choose the cars they like best. From their choices, the system infers the features that were most important to the users. It uses these inferences to show the users more cars with similar attributes. Note that users are asked to behave in much the same way they would if shopping for a car. Specifically, they do not have to rate individual attributes of the cars, and there is no requirement for a specific number of ratings before the system can use the relevance feedback information.

Asking users to provide relevance feedback for particular features can be useful when it is unclear how to infer these features ratings from more general ratings, or when users are willing and able to do the extra work involved in providing detailed relevance feedback.

In some cases users cannot provide detailed relevance feedback. For example, the users may not be aware of all the features that influence their preference for a particular car. Or, users may be aware of these features, but simply don't want to have to specify all of them to a computer system.

3.2. ADAPTIVE AND ADAPTABLE LEARNING

Perhaps the best approach, is to incorporate both ends of the relevance feedback continuum discussed above in an adaptive hypertext system. This leads to two distinct learning mechanisms, which might be called adaptive and adaptable learning capabilities, following a distinction drawn by Totterdell and Rautenbach (1990).

An adaptable system allows users to teach the system explicitly. For example, by moving titles up or down in a list, users might communicate how they think the system ought to rank order a list of recommended topics. The system could then change the weights in its association matrices to match the order specified by the users.

Users might also add new goals or context items to the system. The system could create a new item in its matrix of associations for each new goal specified by the user. Again, users could specify the weights from this goal item to the various topics in the system by moving topic titles in an ordered list.

Finally, the system should be able to create, save, and merge user profiles. Each profile would be a complete set of matrix weights for a particular user or group of users. Each profile would support recommendations based on the preferences stored in that profile. Users could merge the preferences contained in two or more profiles to create new profiles. The new profile could weight the preferences contained in the old profiles equally, or according to a scheme determined by the user. This feature of merging profiles would allow new knowledge to be created dynamically. For example, a new member of a group might want to begin with a default profile that contained an average of the preferences of the existing group members. The new member could then customize this default profile through his or her subsequent interactions with the system.

In addition to these adaptable capabilities, the system could incorporate an adaptive ability. In automatic learning mode, the system could observe what goal the user has specified and what topics are visited during the user's search for information related to the goal. By noting the amount of time the user spends on each topic (normalized by a measure of the information contained in the topic), an Interest Index could be computed. This Interest Index could be used to rank order the topics visisted. Thus, rather than the user specifying how topics ought to be ranked, the system would infer a rank ordering based on observations of the user's behavior. Of course, the user would be free to override the system's inferences by adding, deleting, or changing the order of topics on the list of recommendations.

4. The HYPERFLEX Prototype – Algorithms

So far, the discussion of an adaptive hypertext system has been theoretical. To test the theory that such a system could work, and to gain some idea of its effectiveness, we built a prototype. HYPERFLEX (so named because it is a maximally flexible hypertext system) implements the intelligent and adaptive capabilities described in Section 3.2. The remaining sections of this paper describe the algorithms used by HYPERFLEX, its features and user interface, some preliminary experiments with the system, and our conclusions.

Readers not interested in the algorithmic implementation of the concepts discussed in the previous sections, may want to skip to section 5 for an overview of the system.

The following section describes the implementation of the adaptive functions described earlier, including:

1. how the rank order data structure is maintained and updated in a user's profile of a hypertext document

2. how multiple profiles from different users of the same document can be selectively merged.
3. how HYPERFLEX can incrementally maintain an adaptive system profile for a document that reflects the average rank-order preferences of multiple users over time.
4. the implementation of HYPERFLEX's automatic learning feature.

4.1. MAINTAINING AND UPDATING PROFILES

HYPERFLEX profiles are implemented by associative weight matrices. Each topic is connected to all other topics in the document, as well as to nodes representing specific task goals created by the user. (Note: although theoretically all nodes are connected to all other nodes, in actual practice, only those links with non-zero weights need be explicitly represented in the system.) Associated with each connection is a weight, which corresponds to the strength of the association between two topics or between a goal and a topic. More specifically, the weight associated with the connection from topic A to topic B represents the rank of importance of topic B, among all topics in the current document, given that topic A is the current topic of interest. Similarly, the weight associated with the connection from a goal to a topic is the rank of importance of that topic among all topics, given interest in the specific goal.

Users specify a topic of interest, a goal of interest, or both. Based on this 'current topic' and/or 'current goal' HYPERLFEX makes recommendations by displaying a rank-ordered list of related topics. If only one of the current topic and task goal is specified, HYPERFLEX looks at the rank order matrix for the weights from the current topic or goal to all topics, and displays a sorted list of topic names. If both the current topic and task goal are specified, HYPERFLEX sums the two weight vectors before sorting.

The weight matrix is updated when a user moves a topic in the ordered list. If only one of the current topic and the task goal is specified, HYPERFLEX simply updates the associated weight vector accordingly. That is, the weight associated with the connection from the current topic or task goal to the topic being moved is updated according to the moved topic's position in the ordered list. The weights associated with the connections to the topics that are within the moving range of the moving topic are reduced by one, if the move is upward, or incremented by one if the move is downward.

When a user moves a topic in the ordered list with both the current topic and the current goal specified, the system must decide how much to change the weight from the moved topic to the current goal, and how much to change the weight from the moved topic to the current topic. By default HYPERFLEX changes the two weights equally, although this ratio can be set to any proportion. HYPERFLEX then calculates the change of sum of ranks needed in order for the topic to be moved to the right place in the ordered list, and updates each of the two ranking vectors proportionally. If the topic's current rank in either of the two weight vectors is already at the top or bottom of the list and cannot be adjusted further, the surplus change gets transferred to the other weight vector.

We investigated several variations before deciding on this ordering algorithm. For example, an alternative approach would have been to adjust the rankings in accordance with a weighted history scheme. In this case, a single user's actions would not necessarily change the order of items on the recommendations list. Or the order might change but not as much as the user would like.

We chose to make the system maximally responsive to new input from each user. If a user wants to move an item that used to be last on the list, the user has only to move that item once – not several times while waiting for a history-weighted algorithm to catch up. However, we still wanted the capability to create profiles that reflected the past history of the system's use, and to assign a reasonable weight to that past history. These objectives can be accomplished by merging profiles, or by maintaining an Adaptive System Profile as described below.

4.2. MERGING SELECTED PROFILES

Different profiles for the same hypertext document can be merged to combine different users' knowledge and preferences. Users can select the profiles they would like to combine, and can also specify the relative importance (weights) they would like to assign to each of the profiles. HYPERFLEX takes a weighted average over different profiles for each of the rank vectors in the matrices, where a rank vector contains the list of ranks of all topics given a particular current topic or a particular task goal.

As some hypertext document systems may grow with time, different profiles may contain different numbers of topics. Hence, corresponding rank vectors for the same current topic or task goal in different profiles may have different maximal rank values as well as different vector lengths. To ensure fair comparison between ranks, rank vectors are normalized to the same scale before a weighted average is taken. Also, to accommodate different vector lengths, the weighted average of the ranks of a target topic is only taken across the profiles which contain that topic, and the result is adjusted by the total weights of those profiles. Specifically, the weighted average of the normalized rank is

$$\sum_{p \text{ in } P} R_{ijp} \times W_p / \sum_{p \text{ in } P} W_p$$

where R_{ijp} denotes the normalized rank of topic j given topic i or task goal i in profile p, W_p the weight assigned to profile p, and P the set of profiles that contains both topics i and j.

The system then sorts the computed weighted averages of all target topics (that is, across all js, for each current topic/goal i) and reassigns ordered ranks to vectors in the new combined profile.

4.3. ADAPTIVE SYSTEM PROFILE

HYPERFLEX is also capable of maintaining an incrementally adaptive system default profile for a hypertext document. This profile captures the knowledge and experience of active users by keeping a moving average of user profiles that de-emphasizes older profiles.

The merge algorithm used for the adaptive system profile is similar to that used to merge selective user profiles (described in the last section), but the relative weights given to the current system profile and the profile to be merged into the system profile are predetermined. HYPERFLEX maintains a constant K, which reflects the size of the initial pool of profiles needed to establish a reasonable moving average. The system keeps track of N, the number of updates (the number of times some profile is added to the system) already made to an incrementally adaptive system profile.

Let R denote the normalized rank matrix of the system profile, and $R1$ denote that of the profile to be added. To build the initial system average, that is, when $N < K$, update R by

$$R = (R \times N + R1)/(N + 1).$$

After the initial system profile is established, that is, $N \geq K$, update the normalized rank matrix by

$$R = (R \times (K - 1) + R1)/K.$$

At any point, the matrix is a weighted average of the entire collection of profiles added in the history. Older ones are down-weighted exponentially each time by a factor of $(K - 1)/K$, and the total weights of all profiles always sum to one. Index subscripts for topics and goals are not used in the formula here for simplicity, but the same algorithm used to handle missing topics applies here as well. HYPERFLEX maintains two versions of an adaptive system profile. A real-valued version of the normalized rank matrix is kept for incremental updates to avoid significant round-off errors. The updated matrix is then sorted and converted into a regular rank order matrix after every update and the new system profile is made available to users of HYPERFLEX.

4.4. AUTO-LEARN

When the user turns Auto-learn on, the system records the time that the user views each subsequent topic. Viewing time is divided by an index that quantifies the amount of information presented on a given topic (e.g. number of lines of text). This normalized view time is used to estimate the user's interest level. The longer the view time, the more interested a user is assumed to be.

When Auto-learn is used to associate topics to a new goal, no previous recommendations exist, and HYPERFLEX adds the viewed topics to the recommendations list, ranked in order of their normalized view times. When recommendations exist from prior use of the system, HYPERFLEX must convert the normalized view times to rankings. The generic conversion formula is:

$$R = \text{int}(K/T)$$

where: R = the rank; K = a constant parameter; T = the normalized view time for a topic; int = a function that returns an integer value.

In cases where two normalized view times convert to the same rank, the one with the higher normalized view time is placed higher in the list or recommendations.

There are trade-offs with any learning algorithm. One of the disadvantages of the learning algorithm just described is that there is no way to know for sure whether increased time spent accessing a topic means the user is really interested in the topic. The system has no way of telling whether the user is having a cup of coffee, talking on the phone, or actually reading the text on the screen. Yet it assumes that if text is there, the user is reading it.

At one extreme, one can imagine a system that tracks the user's eye movements, and calculates interest according to what part of the text is being fixated. This would solve the problems, but it is a very intrusive measure, and most users would not put up with it. A less intrusive option would be to simply ask the user to rate his or her satisfaction with each piece of information. As discussed earlier, this is the approach taken by many relevance feedback systems.

We experimented with this approach. For example, in an earlier version of HYPERFLEX users were asked to rate their satisfaction by clicking on a (five-point) Likert scale. This required some extra effort on the part of the user, but it provided more reliable feedback than the automatic learning algorithm described above. Ultimately such design decisions come down to trade-offs between accuracy and the intrusiveness of the system.

We chose the automatic learning method described above, not because these other techniques would not work, but primarily to see how much progress could be made with a simple and completely non-intrusive approach. We addressed the inherent difficulties in such an approach, namely that the system would make incorrect inferences about interest levels, by making the user the final arbitrator. Because they can rearrange items in the recommendation list, users can correct any false inferences made by the system.

5. Features, User-Interface, Usage Scenario, and Scaling Considerations

5.1. FEATURE SUMMARY

HYPERFLEX's capabilities include the following:
- dynamically models users' goals and information preferences using associative matrices (profiles)
- allows users to change profiles directly, or updates profiles automatically via Auto-learn feature
- stores profiles of individuals or groups of users

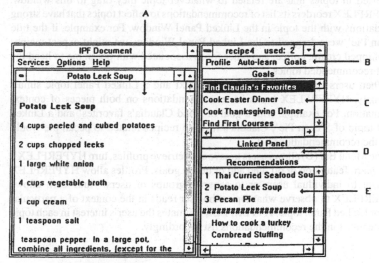

Figure 5. The HYPERFLEX interface.

- can merge two or more existing user profiles to create new profiles
- recommends topics in a rank ordered list based on user profiles
- allows users to link directly to a recommended topic or to any other topic in the document.

5.2. USER INTERFACE

Figure 5 shows the user interface for HYPERFLEX. In this example, the system displays a cookbook document, but any document that can be broken down into discrete topics can be used. The large window (A) displays a recipe. Users can jump to any other recipe in the cookbook by selecting the title of another recipe from the Recommendations Window (E). The topics in this window listed above the fence (#####) are ranked using context specified by the user.

For example, users provide a GOAL Context by selecting any of the GOALS (listed in Window C). The system reorders the recommendations window in accordance with the specified goal. With an active goal of 'Find Claudia's Favorites' (Figure 5-C) the system suggests that the user look at Thai Curried Seafood Soup as the top ranked topic (Figure 5-E). Potato Leek Soup and Pecan Pie might also be of interest. New goals can be added or deleted from the system by the user.

The Linked Panel Window (Figure 5-D) provides another way users can specify context. The Linked Panel Window allows users to tell the system that they are interested in topics that are related to whatever topic they drag to this window. HYPERFLEX reorders its list of recommendations to reflect topics that have strong associations with the topic in the Linked Panel Window. For example, if the title 'Pecan Pie' were dragged to the Linked Panel Window, we might expect recipes for whipped cream, coffee, and other foods associated with pecan pie to head the list of recommended topics.

When users specify both a GOAL Context and a Linked Panel topic simultaneously, HYPERFLEX bases its recommendations on both pieces of context information. For example with a goal of 'Find Claudia's favorites' and a Linked Panel topic of 'Pecan Pie', Claudia's favorite recipes related to pecan pie would head the recommendations list.

The Menu Bar (B) allows users to save and retrieve profiles, turn HYPERFLEX's Auto-learn feature on or off, and add or delete goals. Profiles allow HYPERFLEX to adapt to individual users or to separate groups of users. Auto-learn allows HYPERFLEX to observe what topics the user reads in the context of a particular goal or Linked Panel topic. HYPERFLEX estimates the user's interest in each topic and locates it in the recommendations list accordingly.

5.3. USAGE SCENARIO

The first step in using HYPERFLEX is to create a document. The author of the document decides the grain-size of the topics of information and writes the document in chunks of the appropriate size. Or, if the document already exists, a convenient chunk size (e.g. topic headings) can be determined. When the document is read into the system, it can create links between every topic and every other topic. Thus, in theory, the document could be completely inter-linked, allowing users to get to any topic from any other topic. However, in practice, the initial link weights default to zero and need not be explicitly represented until they change to a non-zero value.

The author now decides which chunks ought to have strong associations with each other, and uses the Linked Panel Window (described above) to create associations between topics. Note that so far the scenario is equivalent to the standard procedure for creating hypertext documents except that HYPERFLEX is many times more efficient at creating links than using a tag language to create links and having to compile the hypertext – the existing process used at IBM. In a timed comparison of the two methods, HYPERFLEX was 9.5 × faster at creating links and 17 × faster to use for modifying links compared with the existing hypertext authoring tool.

The author may also create a starter set of goals judged to be useful to most users of the system. Topics are associated to these goals using GOAL Contexts (described above). Note that it is not necessary for the authors to create associations between every topic, nor is it necessary to think of all possible user goals, and link these to every topic.

In fact, the advantage of an adaptive system from an author's point of view is that some of the work that normally goes into creating an effective hypertext system can be done by those who are most capable – the users. For example, normally a good deal of task analysis and audience analysis is necessary to produce a good static hypertext system. If the authors miss their mark, the user is stuck with what ever links the authors thought were important. However in an adaptive hypertext system, users can correct and augment the associations initially put into the system by the author.

When a user first reads the document, the usefulness of the recommendations depends on the how well the author anticipated his needs. However, the more the user interacts with the document, the more the associations come to reflect the goals and associations of that user. By adopting or merging the profiles of other users, a user is able to gain the benefit of other people's goals and associations. This is a powerful way that users with the same general concerns can leverage each other's knowledge.

For example, if the head chef of a particular restaurant has already created associations and goals that reflect his judgement of good recipe combinations, the other chefs can start with his profile and adjust it to fit their own particular tastes. If the profiles of all the chefs are merged into a master profile for the restaurant, a new chef can use this profile to learn the style of the restaurant.

5.4. SCALING CONSIDERATIONS

Given that the recipe example described in Section 2 was quite simple, an issue remains as to whether HYPERFLEX can 'scale up' to a size that would be useful. Since we have conducted informal studies with a real world technical manual from IBM (see Section 6), the system is already capable of handling documents of practical size. However it is worth exploring the issue of scalability in more depth.

There are two sources of limitation that might affect how well a system like HYPERFLEX could scale up: human limitations and system limitations.

Human limitations include factors such as the willingness and ability of users to create new goals and associations, and the ability to process long lists of recommendations. Fortunately it is not necessary to specify how every topic is linked to every other topic, nor is it necessary to specify every conceivable user goal.

Consider our chef example. Suppose the document used by the chefs contained the information in all the world's cookbooks. It might arrive at the restaurant with some general associations and user goals that were created by the author. The number of these associations and goals is completely variable but the task of creating them might reasonably be compared to the task of creating a index for the work – something that authors (or teams of authors) of encyclopedias do routinely.

Just as encyclopedia authors are not expected to cross-reference every topic with every other topic, so we would not expect the authors of our world-wide cookbook to come up with associations between every topic. In fact most of the link weights between topics would default to zero. However the chefs (users) remain free to change the association strength between any two topics or between any topic and a goal.

The association strengths that change will be those that are most useful to the chefs. The system adapts on demand.

This demand-driven characteristic is one of the features that allows the system to scale up. Unlike many user models whose complexity is a exponential function of the domain size, HYPERFLEX adapts only where users indicate there is a need for adaptation.

Moreover, the list of recommendations for a particular topic, far from being overwhelming, reflects the number of associations that naturally occur in human memory. A chef might think of twenty dishes that go well with a strawberry cream sauce. A master chef might come up with a hundred. But no chef, or team of chefs, is going to come up with ten thousand recipes using strawberry cream sauce. And of the hundred that a master chef might come up with, only handful are going to be the most popular. Thus, the number of topic-to-topic associations mirrors the natural limitations of human memory.

In a sense, asking how HYPERFLEX scales up to handle large documents is like asking how human memory handles the tremendous complexity of the real world. According to most current thinking on human memory, the answer is that while our minds are capable of an astronomical number of associations, we make only those that are important to us or that come into our lives. Similarly, HYPERFLEX can make associations between any of its topics and goals. But rather than try to anticipate these associations in advance, the authors who initially use HYPERFLEX can choose a relatively small 'starter set' of associations. Users can adapt the system to their needs.

System limitations are another source of potential concern. For documents the size of technical manuals, it is feasible to automatically link every topic with every other topic. Links are assigned a default value of zero. However since the number of potential links goes up as the square of the number of nodes, a dynamic linkcreation algorithm, similar to those used by relational database programs, would be better for large documents.

A final consideration for large documents would be to add a hierarchical structure. That is, instead of having one flat network, one could have a hierarchical organization of networks. Within a (small number of) level(s) of the hierarchy, topics could be completely inter-connected in a HYPERFLEX system. However to reach topics several levels away in the hierarchy would require hierarchical navigation to a distinct HYPERFLEX system covering those levels. Although we have not implemented a hybrid adaptive-hierarchical system, our experience with large hierarchical databases suggests that this would be a way to improve performance in a very large system.

Table I. Search results with and without availability of GOAL contexts

	Goal Contexts	No Goal Contexts
Search Time	462 sec.	716 sec.
# Topics Searched	8.8	12.2
Time/topic	53 sec.	59 sec.
% correct	83%	75%

6. Experimental Studies

We conducted two experimental pilot studies on small groups of HYPERFLEX users. The first pilot study explored the potential benefits of HYPERFLEX'S GOAL Contexts. The second explored the benefits of the system's adaptive capabilities.

In Pilot study #1, four subjects were asked questions relating to information in a technical manual for an IBM expert systems product. For example, one question was: 'Describe how to start The Integrated Reasoning Shell and how to define a new rule.'

The subjects used a special version of HYPERFLEX to search for the information needed to answer the question. This special version prohibited users from adding, deleting or modifying GOAL Contexts. Thus we were able to examine the usefulness of GOAL Contexts supplied by the document author – as opposed to those created by the user.

Each user answered ten questions. GOAL Contexts were provided for five of the questions. For example, the GOAL Context for the question described above might have been 'Getting Started'.

We measured the total time it took subjects to answer each question, the total number of topics searched before answering, and the number of correct answers. The mean results are shown in Table I.

Having a GOAL Context available decreased search time (by 35%), reduced the number of pages of information that were searched (by 28%), and increased accuracy (by 8%). While these results should be interpreted with caution due to the small sample size, they are consistent with our expectations. The results suggest that author-created, relevant, GOAL Contexts help users find information.

One of the objectives of Pilot Study #2 was to see if user-created GOAL Contexts would be effective as well. We were also interested in whether users would find the GOAL Contexts or the Linked-Panel features of HYPERFLEX most useful. Finally, we wanted to measure the time required by users to 'train' HYPERFLEX. This measurement would help us determine whether HYPERFLEX would be useful in real-world environments.

Subjects in Pilot Study #2 used one of three versions of HYPERFLEX: GOAL Enabled, Linked-Panel Enabled, or Fully Functional. The GOAL Enabled system,

Table II.   SEARCH task performance using three versions of
HYPERFLEX

System	n	Mean Time	# Topics	Time/Topic
GOAL Enabled	19	387 sec.	8.6	45 sec.
Linked-Panel	16	356 sec.	6.8	52 sec.
Fully Functional	34	345 sec.	9	38 sec.
Overall Average:		359 sec.	8.4	43 sec.

allowed users to create GOAL Contexts and 'train' the system to associate specific
topics with these GOAL Contexts. However, users were not able to use the Linked-
Panel Window (see Section 5.2).

In the Linked-Panel Enabled system, users were able to the Linked-Panel Window, but not GOAL Contexts. In the Fully Functional system, users could use both
GOAL Contexts and the Linked-Panel Window.

Eighteen users participated in Pilot #2. Six subjects used each of the three
versions of HYPERFLEX. All subjects worked with the same document – a 50+
page technical report describing the activities of members of IBM's Publications
organization.

Each user was asked to perform four SEARCH tasks and two TRAIN tasks. A
typical SEARCH task was: 'Find four topics that new personnel should access if
they want to know more about chunking information for hypertext.'

The TRAIN tasks were identical to the SEARCH tasks, except that users were
asked, in addition to finding information, to create/update GOAL Contexts (in
the GOAL enabled version), or to create/update topic-to-topic associations (in
the Linked-Panel Enabled version). Users of the Fully Functional system did no
training.

TRAIN tasks allowed subsequent users to benefit from the experience of those
who went before them. That is, users of the Goal-Enabled system could see and use
the GOAL Contexts and associations created by prior users. Users of the Linked-
Panel Enabled system could use the topic-to-topic associations created by prior
users. Users of the Fully Functional system could use both the GOAL Contexts and
the Linked-Panel associations created by prior users of both of the other systems.

The order of the tasks was counter-balanced to control for possible order effects.
The version of HYPERFLEX that subjects used was determined at random.

Dependent measures were the time to complete each task and the number of
topics searched for each task. Since all subjects completed the tasks successfully, %
correct was not a relevant measure. Table II compares the performance of subjects
using these three versions of HYPERFLEX on SEARCH tasks. Table III presents
similar data for TRAIN tasks.

Table III. TRAIN task performance using three versions of HYPER-
FLEX

System	n	Mean Time	# Topics	Time/Topic
Goal Enabled	20	427 sec.	9.3	45 sec.
Linked-Panel	13	604 sec.	12.5	48 sec.
Overall Average:		497 sec.	10.6	47 sec.

The trends in Tables II and III are in the direction we would expect. Users of the Fully Functional system (who had the option of using either GOAL Contexts or the Linked-Panel Window) had the lowest absolute SEARCH time, as well as the shortest time per topic. GOAL Contexts are somewhat easier to use in our system than the Linked-Panel Window. As a result, the time per topic for the GOAL Enabled system was slightly less than for the Linked-Panel Enabled system.

Perhaps the most interesting results come from comparing the SEARCH times in Table II with the TRAIN times in Table III. Recall that TRAIN time includes the time to search for the information AND to create associations that might be helpful to subsequent users. A comparison of the two tables shows that 'training' the system adds very little additional overhead to the time required to search for information without training. On average, it takes only 4 seconds more per topic to create associations which subsequent users can take advantage of when they use the system.

In the case of the GOAL Enabled system, users are just as fast (per topic) training the system as they are using the system to search for information. The difference in total time spent training versus searching is due solely to the greater number of topics visited by trainers. Users may have felt that they needed to visit more topics to ensure that they selected the best ones to associate with GOAL contexts.

Nevertheless, for the GOAL-Enabled system, the time differential between search alone and search with training is only about 10%. This result is important because it demonstrates not only that users can create GOAL contexts, but that they can do so with very little additional effort.

Given that HYPERFLEX can adapt to user preferences with relatively little additonal 'training effort' on the part of the users, does this adaptation actually help?

Table IV attempts to answer this question by showing how the time and number of topics visited during SEARCH tasks changed as the system adapted to more and more users. Mean data from all three versions of HYPERFLEX are shown, in order to obtain the most stable estimates of the system's performance.

Table IV suggests that adaptation is beneficial. There is a fairly consistent downward trend in the time spent per topic as the system adapts to more users. We

Table IV. SEARCH task performance as a function of prior training

# Trainings	n	Search Time	# Topics	Time/Topic
0	6	448 sec.	8	56 sec.
1	12	342 sec.	6.5	53 sec.
2	12	268 sec.	5.8	46 sec.
3	12	349 sec.	7.2	48 sec.
4	12	395 sec.	10.8	37 sec.
5	12	399 sec.	11.2	36 sec.

feel this reflects the ability of users to access topics more easily using the GOAL Contexts and Linked-Panel mechanisms once these have adapted to users.

Moreover users spend less total time searching for information when they can use the GOAL Contexts and Linked-Panel associations provided by previous users. For example, users are 24% faster at finding information after one prior user has 'trained' the system. After two prior trainings, users were 40% faster.

After two trainings something interesting happens. Although the time per topic continues to decrease (despite a slight bump at 3 trainings) the number of panels visited begins to climb. The result is that the overall search time increases, although never reaching the level of the initial users who had no benefits of prior training.

Our interpretation is that users get faster as the system learns, but they also have more recommendations to sort through. As a result, they consider more information before answering the questions. They spend less time on each page of information, scanning rather than reading, but they take more total information into account in their answers to questions.

Both pilot studies support the hypothesis that providing context-based advice can speed information retrieval. This idea is consistent with the beneficial effects of incorporating context in other interface designs (Totterdell et al., 1990), and with arguments that context ought to play a larger role in human computer interaction. However Pilot #2 suggests there may be a point of diminishing returns after which it no longer becomes useful to add more contexts. At this point, the system (or users) should concentrate on improving the accuracy of the associations to existing contexts.

Viewed more generally, these preliminary results raise some interesting design issues. First, they highlight the need for adaptive learning mechanisms. Both human and AI systems face a learning curve. Devoting more resource to learning during the difficult part of the curve, and less as the returns diminish from additional learning, helps maximize the effectiveness of an adaptive system. The parameters of a learning mechanism may need to adapt (e.g. Weir, 1991) or a completely different learning mechanisms may need to be invoked.

	Same Task	New Task
Same User	YES	YES
New User	YES	NO

Figure 6. Conditions where adaptive interfaces are useful.

In HYPERFLEX, for example, it might be best to concentrate on acquiring new GOAL Contexts and topic-to-topic associations during the early part of learning. But in later stages, rather than allowing users to continue to add contexts and new associations ad infinitum, perhaps HYPERFLEX should concentrate of getting feedback to help fine-tune the weights of order the associations that already exist.

Similarly, other adaptive systems may begin adaptation with one learning algorithm, and then switch to other adaptation strategies as the environment changes.

If a system is to make intelligent choices about when to adapt its learning method, it will require some model of when different types of learning are beneficial. Even more fundamental is the question of whether to invoke a learning mechanism at all. There may be times when the best thing a system can do is to wait for explicit instruction from a user. While this paper is not the place to go into such considerations in detail, Figure 6 summarizes some general thoughts on this point.

Learning is not possible unless there is some regularity that the system can discern. If neither the user nor the task remains constant from experience to experience, then an adaptive system cannot learn. This condition is represented by the lower right quadrant of Figure 6.

The lower left and upper right quadrants represent benefits that might accrue from transfer of knowledge about the task or about the user respectively. The upper left quadrant represents a situation in which an adaptive system can use knowledge of both the user and the task to adapt. An adaptive system might do well to determine the quadrant it is operating in before selecting a learning mechanism. In that way, it can tailor its learning to its environment.

7. Conclusions

Adaptive hypertext systems offer one way to help users cope with the explosion of online information. Such systems can provide flexible and direct access to information without some of the disadvantages typically associated with hypertext. The HYPERFLEX prototype demonstrates that it is possible to build an adaptive hypertext system that addresses information access issues using simple modelling techniques. HYPERFLEX's features include:

- Direct access to any topic from any other topic in the system.

- Recommendations based on user GOAL Contexts and/or topics of interest to the user.
- The ability to add GOAL Contexts dynamically.
- User profiles that capture unique interests (associations and goals).
- The ability to merge profiles to create new group profiles.
- The ability to observe, and learn from, user actions.
- The ability to adjust recommendations based on explicit feedback from users.
- Intelligent and adaptive capabilities based on very simple user models.

The results of two preliminary studies suggest that HYPERFLEX's advice can cut search time for information up to 40%, without imposing significant additional demands on either the author or user of the hypertext system. The studies also suggest some guidelines for the design of adaptive (learning) systems.

Perhaps most significant, however, are the simple models that underlie HYPER-FLEX's advice-giving and learning capabilities. HYPERFLEX represents its expertise in simple associative matrices. Each number in a matrix reflects the strength of an association between two information topics, or between a goal and an information topic. These simple models work, because the nature of the interaction with the user is quite constrained. HYPERFLEX is only expected to give the user a rank ordered listing of what information to jump to next. A simple numerical representation is all that is needed to provide this level of advice. Yet this advice is still quite effective in constraining search among a number of information topics.

It could be equally effective in other situations – suggesting exercises to a student in a tutoring situation, for example. In this case the nodes in the network could be tutoring exercises and learning goals. The link weights would capture association strengths between specific exercises, and specific learning goals. These link strengths could be modified based on subjective student ratings of how effective they felt the exercises were at meeting the goals, or based on objective criteria linked to student performance. The network scheme would allow the creation of individual student profiles and would allow these profiles to be merged. That is, the tutor could adapt to a group of students by merging the profiles that reflected optimal assignment of remedial exercises for individual members in the group. This average adaptation might not be optimal for a new student joining the group, but it would be computationally simple, and is likely to be better than no adaptation at all.

In general, simple models have tremendous advantages when it comes to learning. Not only is it easy to update knowledge represented as a matrix of numbers, but it is also easy to merge such knowledge using simple mathematical operations (e.g. averaging the preferences of a set of users). Individual user profiles are easy to create, and could be shared over a networked system, facilitating transfer of information. With a learning system, each user becomes a source of expertise for the system.

With the ability to pool these many sources of expertise, it becomes possible to create a reservoir of experience and knowledge that is very difficult and time consuming to acquire via traditional knowledge engineering approaches. Thus adaptive systems can be viewed as one way to address the knowledge engineering bottleneck that currently hinders many of the efforts to create economically viable expert systems.

From an applications perspective, the twin forces of increasing demand for better information access and decreasing cost of computing power and memory are driving us towards more intelligent systems. Systems that learn and adapt are the next evolutionary response to these pressures. Many of these systems will require complex algorithms and sophisticated user models, but HYPERFLEX demonstrates that a simple direct approach can also be effective.

Acknowledgements

The authors wish to thank Ralph Clark, Mitch Forcier, Debbie Mayhew and Greg Wolff for their support. The authors also wish to acknowledge Alfred Kobsa and two anonymous reviewers for their helpful comments. This work was partially supported by the Programming Systems Division of the IBM Corporation. Please address all correspondence to: Dr. Craig Kaplan, The I.Q. Company, P.O. Box 554 Santa Cruz, CA 95061-0554 U.S.A. Email: 73424.2052@COMPUSERVE.COM

References

Anderson, J. R.: 1988, 'The Expert Module'. In: M.C. Polson and J.J. Richardson (eds.), *Foundations of Intelligent Tutoring Systems*. New Jersey: Erlbaum.

Anderson, M. P., M. Darnell, and R. Simons: 1990, 'Network Navigator: A Graphical User Interface for Browsing Networks'. IBM STL Human Factors Center Technical Report #83, San Jose, CA: IBM.

Belew, R. K.: 1989, 'Adaptive Information Retrieval: Using Connectionist Representations to Retrieve and Learn About Documents'. Proceedings of SIGIR, Cambridge, MA., pp. 11–20.

Benyon, D. and D. Murray: (1988). 'Experience with Adaptive Interfaces', *The Computer Journal* **31**, 465–473.

Carroll, J. and J. McKendree: 1986, 'Interface Design Issues for Advice Giving Expert Systems'. IBM Research Report, RC 11984 (#53988). Yorktown Heights, NY: IBM Research Division.

Carlson, D., and S. Ram: 1990, 'HyperIntelligence: The Next Frontier', *Communications of the ACM* **33**, 311–321.

Chin, J. P.: 1989, 'A Dynamic User Adaptable Menu System: Linking It All Together', *Proceedings of the Human Factors Society*, 33rd Annual Meeting, pp. 413–417.

Cole, B. C.: 1990, 'Hypertext Tackles the Information Glut', *Electronics* **63**, 66–68.

Conklin, J.: 1987, 'Hypertext: An Introduction and Survey', *IEEE Computer* **20**, 17–41.

Croft, B. W.: 1984, 'The Role of Context and Adaption in User Interfaces', *International Journal of Man-Machine Studies* **21**, 283–292.

Dumais, S. T.: 1988, 'Textual Information Retrieval'. In: M. Helander (ed.): *Handbook of Human-Computer Interaction*. North-Holland: Elsevier Science Publishers, pp. 673–700.

Dumais, S. T., G. W. Furnas, T. K. Landauer, S. Deerwester, and R. Harshman: 1988, 'Using Latent Semantic Analysis to Improve Access to Textual Information'. *CHI'88 Conference Proceedings*, New York: ACM, pp. 281–285.

Boyle, C. and A. O. Encarnacion: 1994, 'MetaDoc: An Adaptive Hypertext Reading System'. *User Modeling and User-Adapted Interaction* **4**(1), 1–19 (reprinted in this volume, pp. 71–89).

Furnas, G. W.: 1985, 'Experience With an Adaptive Indexing Scheme'. *CHI'85 Conference Proceedings*, New York: ACM, pp. 131–135.

Furnas, G. W.: 1986, 'Generalized Fisheye Views'. *CHI'86 Conference Proceedings*, New York: ACM, pp. 16–23.

Greenberg, S. and I. H. Witten: 11985, 'Adaptive Personalized Interfaces – a Question of Viability', *Behavior and Information Technology* 4 (1), 31–45.

Grice, R. A., L. S. Ridgeway, and E. J. See: 1991, 'Hypertext: Controlling the Leaps and Bounds', *Technical Communications*, First Quarter 48–56.

Holynski, M.: 1988, 'User-Adaptive Computer Graphics', *International Journal of Man–Machine Studies* 29, 539–548.

Horton, W.: 1991, 'Is Hypertext the Best Way to Document Your Product? An Assay for Designers', *Technical Communications*, First Quarter, 20–35.

Ide, E. and G. Salton: 1971, 'Interactive Search Strategies'. In: G. Salton (ed.): *The Smart Retrieval System – Experiments in Automatic Document Processing*. New Jersey: Prentice Hall.

Innocent, P. R.: 1982, 'Towards Self-Adaptive Interface Systems', *International Journal of Man–Machine Studies* 16, 287–299.

Kaplan, C. A. and G. Wolff: 1990, 'Adaptive Hypertext', *Proceedings of the Intelligent Systems Technical Symposium*, Endicott, NY: IBM.

Kass, R. and T. Finin: 1989, 'The Role of User Models in Cooperative Interactive Systems', *International Journal of Intelligent Systems* 4, 81–112.

Kobsa, A. and W. Wahlster (eds.): 1989, *User Models in Dialog Systems*. Heidelberg: Springer-Verlag.

Kok, A. J.: 1991, 'A Review and Synthesis of User Modelling in Intelligent Systems', *The Knowledge Engineering Review* 6(1), 21–47.

Kok, A. J. and A. M. Botman: 1988, 'Retrieval Based on User Behavior'. *Proceedings of the 11th International Conference on Research and Development in Information Retrieval*, Grenoble, pp. 343–358.

McKendree, J.: 1990, 'Effective Feedback Content for Tutoring Complex Skills', *Human Computer Interaction* 5, 381–413.

Nelson, M. J.: 1991, 'The Design of a Hypertext Interface for Information Retrieval', *The Canadian Journal of Information Science* 16 (2), 1–12.

Norcio, A. F. and J. Stanley: 1989, 'Adaptive Human–Computer Interfaces: A Literature Survey and Perspective, *IEEE Transactions on Systems, Man, & Cybernetics* 19, 399–408.

Reisner, P.: 1966, 'Evaluation of a Growing Thesaurus', IBM Research Report RC-1662, Yorktown Heights, NY: IBM Research Center.

Rich, E.: 1983, 'Users as Individuals: Individualizing User Models', *International Journal of Man–Machine Studies* 18, 199–214.

Salomon, G, T. Oren, and K. Kreitman: 1989, 'Using Guides to Explore Multimedia Databases', *Proceedings of the 22nd Annual Hawaii International Conference on System Science*. IEEE Computer Society Press, Vol. 4, pp. 3–11.

Totterdell, P. and P. Rautenbach: 1990, 'Adaptation as a Problem of Design', In: D. Browne, P. Totterdell, and M. Norman (Eds.): *Adaptive User Interfaces*. London: Harcourt Brace Jovanovich.

Totterdell, P., A. Rautenbach, A. Wilkinson, and S. O. Anderson: 1990, 'Adaptive Interface Techniques', In: D. Browne, P. Totterdell, and M. Norman (eds.): *Adaptive User Interface*. London: Harcourt Brace Jovanovich.

Weir, M. K.: 1991, 'A Method for Self-Determination of Adaptive Learning Rates in Back Propagation', *Neural Networks* 4, 371–379.

Authors' Vitae

Craig A. Kaplan
The I.Q. Company, P.O. Box 554, Santa Cruz, CA 95061-0554 U.S.A.

Dr. Kaplan received his B.A. in Computer Science and Psychology from the University of California at Santa Cruz, and his Ph.D. and M.S. degrees in Cognitive Psychology from Carnegie Mellon University. While at IBM, he founded the

Adaptive Technology Project and authored several patents and technical papers in the area of user-interface design. More recently, Dr. Kaplan co-founded The I.Q. Company, an information technology consulting firm. He is also co-author of the book, *Secrets of Software Quality: 40 Innovations from IBM* (McGraw-Hill 1994). Research interests include applications of artificial intelligence to user interface design, adaptive systems, creative problem solving, software quality and software innovation.

James R. Chen
Department of Computer Science and Engineering, University of California, San Diego, Mail Stop 0114, La Jolla, CA 92093-0114, USA.

James Chen received his Ph.D. in Computer Science from U.C. San Diego. He received his M.S. degree in Industrial Engineering from the University of Wisconsin, Madison, in 1981. His recent research projects span the areas of modular neural networks, object-based knowledge systems, adaptive information retrieval and user interfaces.

Justine R. Fenwick
Graduate School of Business Administration Harvard University Boston, MA 02163 U.S.A.

Justine Fenwick is a human factors engineer. She received her B.A. in Psychology from University of California, Santa Barbara, in 1989 and is currently enrolled in the doctoral program at Harvard Business School. Her contributions to this paper stem from research she conducted for IBM in 1991. Her interests continue in the areas of adaptive information retrieval and object-oriented user models.

Metadoc: An Adaptive Hypertext Reading System

CRAIG BOYLE
Information Engineering, P.O. Box 180021, Austin, Texas 78718, USA;
e-mail: boyle@cactus.org

and

ANTONIO O. ENCARNACION
Department of Computer Science, Texas A&M University, College Station, Texas 77843, USA

(Received: 21 February 1992; in revised form: 31 January 1994; accepted: 2 February 1994)

Abstract. Presentation of textual information is undergoing rapid transition. Millennia of experience writing linear documents is gradually being discarded in favor of non-linear hypertext writing. In this paper, we investigate how hypertext – in its current node-and-link form – can be augmented by an adaptive, user-model-driven tool. Currently the reader of a document has to adapt to that document – if the detail level is wrong the reader either skims the document or has to consult additional sources of information for clarification. The MetaDoc system not only has hypertext capabilities but also has knowledge about the documents it represents. This knowledge enables the document to modify its level of presentation to suit the user. MetaDoc builds and dynamically maintains a user model for each reader. The model tailors the presentation of the document to the reader. The three-dimensionality of MetaDoc allows the text presented to be changed either by the user model or through explicit user action. MetaDoc is more a documentation reading system rather than a hypertext navigation or reading tool. MetaDoc is a fully developed and debugged system that has been applied to technical documentation.

Key words: Hypertext, adaptation, user expertise, stretchtext, evaluation, online documentation

1. Introduction

1.1. HYPERTEXT AND ADAPTIVE HYPERTEXT

Hypertext (Nielsen, 1990) provides a means of flexibly organizing and presenting information. The writer of a document need not be rigid in his/her organization of text, since chunks of information can be linked. The reader manipulates the order of text presentation through link selection. In this sense, hypertext is an advance over the essentially linear nature of paper text or simple online documentation. However, hypertext is not an *active participant* in the reading process since the reader is required to adapt and select without assistance from the computer.

This work augments the notion of non-linear hypertext documentation. The addition of a user-modeling component through a system called MetaDoc (so called because it has knowledge about documents) allows the computer to actively participate in the reading process.

Conventional hypertext offers flexibility at the network level: traversal of links allows different nodes to be selected and a 'view' of the entire document to be presented. Another dimension of adaptivity is flexiblity at the node level. Manip-

71

P. Brusilovsky et al. (eds.), Adaptive Hypertext and Hypermedia, 71–89.
© 1998 *Kluwer Academic Publishers.*

ulation of the text inside a single node allows a greater degree of control over the information presented and hence a more readable document. Stretchtext (sometimes called replacement text) permits such node level flexibility (Nelson, 1971). MetaDoc uses stretchtext to implement its user modeling capability. Because of MetaDoc's heavy use of stretchtext, we refer to it as a three-dimensional writing style.

A user-modeling component augments a hypertext document by automatically adapting a document at the node level. A user model (Kobsa and Wahlster, 1989) contains a representation of the reader's knowledge. The model alters the amount of information presented by automatically stretching or contracting the text in a node – this is the essence of MetaDoc. The advantage of such an 'automatic stretchtext' system is that the reader no longer needs to adapt to a document. Instead, the document adapts to the reader and hence the computer actively participates in the reading process. Such active computer mediation (Reinking and Schreiner, 1985) should aid in the reading process.

An adaptive document allows different user-ability levels to be accommodated by a single document. It also allows for a reader to have an uneven scope of knowledge. To some extent, conventional hypertext allows the *user* to adapt to a document by browsing at the network level. *MetaDoc* adapts to the user through automatic node-level operations.

1.2. GOALS OF THIS RESEARCH

Our first goal is to build a hypertext document that automatically adapts to the ability level of the reader. Thus, only one document would be needed for all classes of potential readers. Each reader should feel that the document is personalized to his/her ability level. Ideally, no reader would feel the need to skip text (because the document is too trivial) or seek another document (because of complexity). Our domain is technical documentation, chosen because of the wide range of readers and its regular structure.

Our second goal is to evaluate the resulting work to discover whether such an adaptive document improves the productivity and the satisfaction of both domain-novices and domain-experts.

2. Related Work

In this section, we review previous work concerning stretchtext in several guises and briefly consider user modeling work upon which adaptive system behavior is based.

Ted Nelson, the hypertext pioneer, coined the term stretchtext in his article 'Computopia and Cybercrud' (Nelson, 1971). In this form of hypertext, 'the reader can control the amount of detail to suit himself, as he pulls on a throttle or some other control, additional words end phrases appear on the screen, and the rest move apart to make way; as he pushes the throttle in the other direction, words and phrases disappear, and the rest of the text slides back together.' Stretchtext allows the depth of information presented in a node to be varied. But there is more to it than just varying the number of words or the expansion and compression of a node. To minimize disorientation and maximize user satisfaction smooth transition between levels of stretch is essential.

VisiDoc, developed by Ken Bice in 1987 for on-line help on the TI Explorer Series, used the stretchtext metaphor (Schnase *et al.*, 1988; Texas Instruments, 1988). 'Stretching' text in whole paragraphs or sections (not words or phrases) gives the effect that a whole node had been replaced. Outline processors have similar limited stretchtext features. Since this stretchtext is very chunky, it resembles general hypertext with 'goto' links. In a hypermedia usability study, users found that stretchtext (or replacement buttons) is easy to understand and can improve the usability/readability of the document (Nielsen and Lyngbaek, 1989). These systems used stretchtext instead of 'goto' links.

Guide (Brown, 1987) is another commercial hypertext system that provides stretchtext, referred to here as replacement-buttons. According to Brown, documents with replacement-buttons can be presented in a form suitable to a wide range of readers. Since the text is replaced in-line, all material is seen in context.

The dynamic table of contents used in Superbook (Egan, 1989), DynaText (Dynatext, 1990) and the IBM Operating System/2 on-line documentation (IBMb) display varying amounts of detail chapter and section headings. This is a very limited form of stretchtext.

User modeling is used by an application to explicitly store information about its users to improve interaction. The information stored is used to adapt computer behavior to the user, making the application easier to use and enlarging the population of potential users.

3. MetaDoc

MetaDoc, as indicated in Figure 1, has conventional hypertext capabilities: users can traverse links between nodes, backtrack, follow the network linearly, and search for text. Links can be stretchtext operations concerning detail or expansion, glossary accesses and conventional 'jumps' (reference links).

MetaDoc's adaptive reading capability operates through the use of an Interactive Agent, allowing knowledge about the reader of the document to be stored and used to vary the level of detail in the document presented. If the user explicitly modifies the level of detail presented, then the user model is informed and may decide to vary presentation of future information. Thus, by noting previous user actions, it automatically calculates the best view of the document for the user. MetaDoc's Intelligent Agent stores information about the reader in the form of a user model. Figure 2 shows an overview of the MetaDoc system.

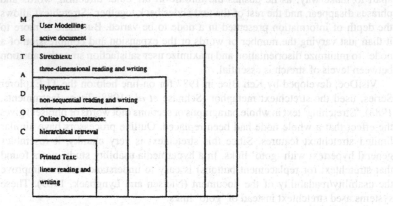

M
E
T
A
D
O
C

User Modelling:
active document

Stretchtext:
three-dimensional reading and writing

Hypertext:
non-sequential reading and writing

Online Documentation:
hierarchical retrieval

Printed Text:
linear reading and
writing

Fig. 1. MetaDoc's relation to other documentation forms

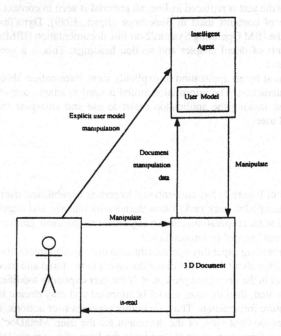

Intelligent
Agent

User Model

Explicit user model
manipulation

Document
manipulation
data

Manipulate

Manipulate

3 D Document

is-read

Fig. 2. An adaptive 3D document

MetaDoc matches the information presented to the information needs of the reader. The presentation styles preferred and amount of information required differ among readers. MetaDoc provides both automatic and manual control of the amount of information presented. Manual control is important as the user may wish to override the presentation decisions of MetaDoc.

MetaDoc is coded in ANSI-C under Microsoft Windows 3.0 on an IBM PS/2 model 80 with a VGA display. No existing hypertext environment was used. It is fully operational and is currently being used to present the contents of two chapters (with seventy paper pages) of the technical manual 'Managing the AIX operating system' for the IBM RT-PC (IBM, 1989). This manual was chosen because of the wide range of readership levels it is expected to address, ranging from inexperienced standalone system users to multi-user system managers. This ability range is typical of what MetaDoc can accommodate. MetaDoc can be applied to other documents without difficulty or recoding.

The linear version of this manual was rewritten in MetaDoc. The rewriting process involved breaking the text into nodes, determining inter-link nodes and intra-node stretchtext structure. The concepts explained in the manual needed to be understood and hierarchically classified by concept to facilitate user-modeling. Creation of this hierarchy could be done by a technical author with little background knowledge of MetaDoc.*

4. User Level and Levels of Information

The presentation styles preferred and the amount of information required are not the same for different readers. Thus, an objective of MetaDoc is to match the information needs and the information presented to the reader. To meet this objective, the readers and their information needs must be classified.

4.1. USERS AND STEREOTYPES

MetaDoc classifies readers with respect to their knowledge of Unix/AIX and general computer concepts into four possible categories, namely novices, beginners, intermediates or experts. This classification is based on UC, a classic user-modeling system for Unix users developed by Chin (Chin, 1986). We assume that readers' knowledge of Unix/AIX concepts and of general computer concepts has the most direct bearing on the comprehension of the prototype manual.

4.2. CONCEPT LEVELS

Concepts in the manual are classified using the same scale as readers' knowledge. A concept is either a Unix/AIX concept, or a general computer concept. A concept

---

* Our discussions with technical authors show that they have a strong structural and semantic understanding of the documents they write. Consequently, hierarchy creation could be learned. However, inter-document hierarchies would be harder to create (because of multiple authors).

that is used both in Unix and in other operating systems is considered a general
computer concept.

4.3. PRESENTING THE CORRECT LEVEL OF INFORMATION

To present the correct level of information to the reader, MetaDoc varies the amount
of explanation or detail information. MetaDoc uses internal information based on
stereotypes about the difficulty of a concept and the reader's knowledge level.

A reader belonging to a classification whose level is lower than the difficulty
of a given concept is assumed to be unfamiliar with this concept. Consequently,
MetaDoc explains it by stretching text. Likewise, an expert reader does not need an
explanation (since he would not find it informative), but would rather want more
detailed information. MetaDoc would therefore display more detailed information
for the expert.

5. The Metadoc Document

5.1. THE AUGMENTED DOCUMENT

MetaDoc allows the reader to view different versions of a single node (with different amounts of information). The reader can manually move from one plane
to another as well as have the system automatically calculate the best level suited
for him/her. The text can be manipulated for more (or less) explanation or detail.
More explanation includes definitions of key vocabulary, simpler and less technical
versions, more examples, and supplemental background information. More detail
includes lower-level concepts in the concepts hierarchy. The appendix shows two
versions of the same node, one for the expert and one for the novice. In the second
version, explanations are added to all technical concepts.

MetaDoc allows the reader to select which parts of the node to adjust, instead of
adjusting the whole node. The reader can control the level of explanation or detailed
information by clicking on stretchtext buttons. This allows selective stretching.
To facilitate the comparison of readers' information needs with the information
presented, concepts are associated with stretchtext buttons.

5.2. WRITING STRETCHTEXT

Ted Nelson (Nelson, 1971) mentioned that his 'slight experience trying to write
stretchtext suggests that it is no harder to write, and perhaps easier, than ordinary
prose', although he admitted that there is no firm evidence to back his claim.

Our experience showed that writing stretchtext, although not much more difficult, is all the more time consuming than writing ordinary prose. We rewrote
an electronic copy of the manual in hypertext and rewrote the result in a three-
dimensional form.

The principles that we followed in writing stretchtext are:

1. It is essential that the document read smoothly between the different levels of stretch. Additional text should conform nicely to the existing text when more stretch information is requested, and also if less is requested. Seamless stretchtext is important in order to maintain the user's view of the document as being personalized.

2. Text cues must be retained between different levels of 'stretch' to minimize reader confusion. Loss of familiar 'landmarks' between levels of 'stretch' forces the reader to backtrack and re-read the node. A 'chunky' stretchtext has the same effect on the reader.

3. There should be common node identifiers for both novice and expert readers, to facilitate discussion by providing a common reference. Having sufficient commonalities between the different 'stretch' versions facilitates node identification among different readers.

4. The stretchtext should be ordered. For example, the reader can move from the most detailed version to the least detailed by directing the 'throttle' in one direction or vice-versa.

Currently MetaDoc documents are written using a text editor. A custom markup language similar to that of the Interleaf (Interleaf, 1990) desktop publishing program is used for formatting and link information. We plan to allow MetaDoc documents to be authored in Interleaf.

6. Stretchtext: Three-Dimensionality in MetaDoc

Three-dimensionality in the form of stretchtext has different forms. In this section, we will consider the different dimensions of stretchtext, the types of stretchtext and the methods of stretchtext presentation.

6.1. DIMENSIONS OF STRETCHTEXT

The information presented in a node can be varied in multiple ways. A simplistic approach would be to vary the number of words in a node, but there is little correspondence between the amount of words and the amount of information. The readability of the text (similar to the Flesch reading levels) and the presentation style (technical reference type versus procedural style) are other factors that can be varied.

In MetaDoc, we chose to vary the information presented in terms of either explanation or amount of detail. Better explanations for a concept are provided in MetaDoc by presenting a definition of key vocabulary; presenting a simpler, less technical version; and presenting supplemental background information, which is a prerequisite for understanding. More detail provides lower-level information in the hierarchy of concepts.

6.2. TYPES OF STRETCHTEXT

There are four possible types of stretchtext, based on the placement of the new text relative to the original:

- prefix – the additional text appears at the beginning of the original text.
- embedded – the additional text becomes embedded inside the old text.
- appended – the additional text is appended at the end.
- replacement – the new text completely replaces the original text.

We favor the embedded and appended stretchtext because they are less confusing to the reader. These two types of stretchtext preserve the position of text cues between 'stretch' operations.

6.3. PRESENTING STRETCHTEXT

The degree of stretch is selected through mouse operations on expansion and detail buttons. It is important to give the user an idea of a button's operation (i.e., stretch, glossary or jump). This becomes more important in a system that employs user modeling to minimize the noise going to the user modeling component. We decided to use a context-sensitive mouse cursor, similar to KMS (Akscyn *et al.*, 1987), to make the button types evident to the reader.

The granularity of stretchtext is an important issue. MetaDoc can handle any granularity of stretchtext from fine (word level) to coarse (paragraph or section level). We favor fine granularity of stretchtext because it is less confusing to the reader and shows smoothness between the different levels of stretch.

Theoretically, the number of stretchtext levels is unlimited, although this is not practical. In MetaDoc we allow recursive stretchtext buttons; an embedded stretchtext button may 'contain' an append button, which 'contains' embed and append buttons, etc. A stretchtext button may 'contain' a jump link.

7. The Adaptive Document

MetaDoc is an active participant in the reading process. MetaDoc keeps track of the level of user knowledge and dynamically adjusts the amount of information to the user level.

The default rules used to determine the depth of information presented to the user are:

- Explanation of concepts associated with higher levels are automatically provided for lower level users.
- Explanation of concepts associated with lower levels are unnecessary for higher level users and are suppressed.
- Higher level details not necessary for understanding a certain concept are suppressed for lower level users.
- Details of equal or lower level concepts are automatically displayed for higher level users.

8. Architecture of MetaDoc

8.1. OVERVIEW

The main components of MetaDoc are the 3D Document and the Intelligent Agent. The 3D Document component has the most interaction with the user. It determines the final form of the node presented to the user and receives commands from the user. The Intelligent Agent component dynamically keeps track of the user knowledge level. The Domain Concepts component bridges the gap between the Intelligent Agent component and the 3D Document component. Figure 3 shows the architecture of MetaDoc in detail.

8.2. 3D DOCUMENT COMPONENT

The 3D Document component provides the interface to the user. It is composed of the Document Presentation Manager and the Base Document.

At any time, the Document Presentation Manager presents a portion of the Base Document (node) and determines its form for display to the user. The user, after reading the node, issues one of the document manipulation commands, and thereby 'jumps' to a regular or glossary node, or to a stretchtext operation. For stretchtext operations and 'jumps' to the glossary, the Document Presentation Manager notifies the Intelligent Agent component to update the User Model. 'Jump' to a regular node is not transmitted to the Intelligent Agent since a regular node includes both explanation and detail information.

The Base Document includes regular nodes and glossary nodes containing the definition of key items. Whenever the user performs document manipulation, the Base Document is updated to reflect the status of the manipulation. Domain concepts are associated with buttons. The Domain Concepts Component keeps track of user manipulation of concepts. The Intelligent Agent component of MetaDoc functions as an assistant to the user in determining the correct level of information provided. The Document Presentation Manager refers to the Intelligent Agent component only when it cannot determine any previous user action on a particular piece of text. The user's actions are more important than the agent's, and cannot be overridden. For example, if the user clicked on a button for more detail, detail information associated with the button will always be shown until the user performs another action on the button. Other buttons associated with the same concept will exhibit the same behavior, provided that they have not been manipulated by the user. In determining the level of information presented, the Document Presentation Manager checks the following in order: button status, concept status, and the Intelligent Agent component.

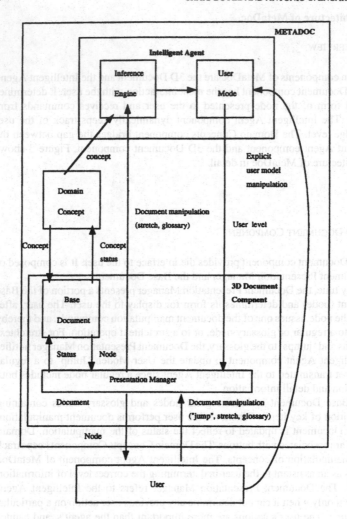

Fig. 3. Functional description of MetaDoc

8.3. INTELLIGENT AGENT COMPONENT

The Intelligent Agent component plays the central role in automatically matching the presented information depth to the user level. It unobtrusively keeps track of the user actions during the session to determine the correct user level.

The Intelligent Agent component uses a user model, consisting of both long-term and short-term elements, to represent the user level. The long-term model, which keeps track of the knowledge state of the user between sessions, is based upon an initial enrollment and the short-term model. The short-term model maintains the immediate user actions within a session.

8.4. EXPLICIT MODELING

Compared to a natural language dialog (a common domain for user-modeling systems), the simple and efficient hypertext interface allows a low bandwidth of information for user modeling. To overcome this limitation, explicit user modeling is used. Users are requested to indicate their experience with computers before their first session. However, to skip the enrollment, users can choose the default user model.

Based on the enrollment, a model of the user is constructed. Two expertise levels, which correspond to the user's presumed knowledge of AIX/Unix and general computer concepts, are maintained for each user. In this effect, dual stereotypes are maintained for each user.

Similarly, AIX/Unix and general computer concepts in the MetaDoc document were classified into different levels. Concept levels and 'concept islands' were artificially created to organize the actual AIX/Unix and general computer concepts. Stereotypically, the actual concepts were grouped into 'concept islands' which form concept levels. Thus, AIX/Unix and general computer concepts are singly stereotyped. Special types of concepts and concept-islands are triggers (similar to Rich (Rich, 1983)) and required (Finin, 1988).

Lack of familiarity with a 'required' concept island forces a reclassification to a lower level, while knowledge of a 'trigger' concept island belonging to a higher level initiates a promotion after a certain threshold is exceeded. The same mechanism holds true at the concept level; ignorance of a 'trigger' concept indicates ignorance of the whole concept island. Concepts and concepts islands may be 'triggers' and 'required' for zero or more concept islands or levels, respectively.

The user is given the option of explicitly changing the user model within the session by specifying which concepts should be explained and which should be shown with more detail. The ability to explicitly change the user model allows users to feel in control of the session (Korfhage, 1985).

8.5. IMPLICIT MODELING

Unobtrusive, implicit user modeling is used throughout the session to refine the user model. A request for more explanation about a concept indicates lack of familiarity with the concept. Requests for more detail imply an understanding of the concept. The stretchtext command for less explanation implies an understanding of a concept; a stretchtext command for less detail implies unfamiliarity with the concept.

Aside from stretchtext operation, 'jumps' to the glossary for definition purposes has the same effect as performing a stretchtext operation for more explanation. 'Jumps' to ordinary nodes do not have an effect on the user model, since these nodes contain both explanation and detail information.

On account of the narrow bandwidth of information for user modeling in this domain, a certain threshold must be set to balance the effect of noise against correct information. Therefore, requesting once for more explanation is not yet considered to be a lack of familiarity with a concept; however, a second request pertaining to the same concept would be.

9. Evaluation of MetaDoc

9.1. HYPOTHESES

Guthrie (Guthrie and Kirsch, 1987) showed that there are two principle reading tasks comprehension and location of specific information. MetaDoc was evaluated with respect to both of these issues.

The experiment primarily compared user performance between hypertext and MetaDoc. Tests on stretchtext were also conducted, since quantitative experiments on stretchtext are not available. The primary experimental hypothesis predicted that MetaDoc users would have better reading performance than stretchtext and hypertext users; i.e., MetaDoc users would have more correct answers.

Additionally, it was predicted that adaptive documents were more efficient to use. That is, MetaDoc users would spend less time, visit less number of nodes and perform fewer operations in answering the reading comprehension questions.

If, as Reinking (Reinking and Schreiner, 1985) suggested, textual manipulations – especially computer-mediated – increase reading comprehension, then subjects using MetaDoc should perform better than stretchtext and hypertext users in reading comprehension tasks. In other words, three-dimensional documents facilitate reading comprehension. Otherwise, there would be no significant difference in the performance of subjects if adaptive documents had no effect.

The secondary experimental hypothesis predicted that MetaDoc users would perform better than stretchtext and hypertext users in search and navigation tasks.

9.2. DESIGN

The design was 2×3 factorial, between-subjects. The independent variables were the readers' expertise level and the system or medium used in presenting information.

The systems compared were the hypertext-only version, the stretchtext version and MetaDoc. MetaDoc was used as the base system. The hypertext-only version used the same system as MetaDoc, but the user modeling and stretchtext features were disabled. The hypertext document was taken from the original manual and re-written in hypertext by fully expanding the detail and explanation elements of each node. The stretchtext version was also based on MetaDoc and utilized the same document, but the user modeling was disabled. Users were still allowed to ask for more or less detail and move between nodes as with regular hypertext.

The dependent variables were the time (in seconds) spent in finding the correct answer, the number of correct answers, the number of nodes visited, and the number of operations (or user commands) used. The time spent in finding the correct answer also included the time spent answering the question. The answers given by the subjects were either right or wrong. The number of nodes visited includes revisits to the same nodes, backtracking and visits to the glossary nodes. This includes the number of stretchtext commands, search commands, and nodes visited. Stretchtext commands were composed of expand and compress text operations and UNDOs of previous stretchtext commands. The number of search operations included new search and continuance of the same search.

9.3. SUBJECTS

The subjects in this experiment were students from the Department of Computer Science. The experts in this experiment belong to the technical support group for the departmental computers. No incentives were offered except for the opportunity to learn more about Unix and AIX.

9.4. APPARATUS AND MATERIALS

The experiments were carried out on an IBM PS/2 model-80 type 8580-311 computer, equipped with ten megabytes of main memory, a 14-inch IBM PS/2 color display type 8514 and an IBM mouse. MetaDoc requires a VGA monitor, a two-button mouse and Windows 3.00 running in 386-enhanced mode.

Materials used were three booklets containing the experimental questions.

9.5. PROCEDURE

Subjects were randomly assigned to one of the three systems. The distribution was balanced between all combinations of system and expertise level. Subjects were introduced to MetaDoc, then trained on their system to an objective compefence standard, using a test document and verbal instruction. After the subject had browsed through the actual document for two minutes, the booklet of experimental questions was given to the subject. Five search and navigation questions preceded the eight reading comprehension questions. The subject was allowed three minutes to find the answer in the search and navigation questions and then five minutes for the reading comprehension question. For each question, the subject was allowed three tries in finding the correct answer. For the search and navigation questions, the

Table I. Summary of Results

	Hypertext		Stretchtext		MetaDoc	
	Expert	Novice	Expert	Novice	Expert	Novice
Reading comp. time	1780	1930	1250	1780	810	1420
Mean search time	755	725	645	530	555	575
Read. comp. correct	5	3	6.5	7	7	7
Search correct	3.5	2.5	3.5	3	3.5	3.5

Note: Times are in seconds; maximum number of correct answer is 8.

subject simply pointed out the location of the answer. The subject orally provided the answer in a few phrases or sentences for the reading comprehension questions. If the answer was vague, the subject was required to explain. The correct answer was provided if the subject failed after three attempts.

9.6. RESULTS

Two-way between-subjects Analysis of Variance (ANOVA) was the primary statistical test used. Table I summarizes the results.

9.6.1. *Time*

The main effects of both the system used and the expertise level on reading comprehension time were very significant at the 1 percent level (see line 1 in Table I). Applying Tukey's Studentized Range test to the data indicated that hypertext and stretchtext users had significantly higher mean times than MetaDoc users; however, no significant difference was found between stretchtext and hypertext users. The mean times of the novice and expert subjects also differed at the 1 percent level of significance. Interaction effects were not significant.

For search and navigation questions (see line 2 in Table I), the main effects of the system used were very significant at the 1 percent level; i.e., the mean times of the hypertext, stretchtext and MetaDoc users were different at the 1 percent level of significance. Tukey's Studentized Range test indicated that hypertext users had significantly higher mean search times than the stretchtext and MetaDoc users, although no significant difference was found between stretchtext and MetaDoc users. No significant main effect was found at the expertise level. An interaction effect between system and expertise was not significant.

9.6.2. *Number of correct answers*

For reading comprehension (see line 3 in Table I), the main effects of the system used on the number of correct answers (hits) was very significant at the 1 percent level. Tukey's Studentized Range test indicated that hypertext users correctly answered significantly fewer reading comprehension questions than the stretchtext and MetaDoc users, although no significant difference was found between stretchtext and MetaDoc users. MetaDoc users answered more questions correctly than stretchtext users. No significant main effect was found at the expertise level. An interaction effect between the system and expertise was not significant.

For search and navigation questions (see line 4 in Table I), the main effects of both the system used and the expertise level were not statistically significant. MetaDoc users answered more questions correctly than the users of both systems, and stretchtext version users had more correct answers than the hypertext version users. Expert users answered more questions correctly than novice users.

9.6.3. *Number of nodes*

In both search and reading comprehension questions, there was no significant difference in the number of nodes visited which can be attributed to the system used or to the expertise level.

9.6.4. *Number of operations*

In both search and reading comprehension questions, there were no significant differences in the number of operations which can be attributed to the system used or to the expertise level.

9.7. COMPARISON OF METADOC AND THE STRETCHTEXT VERSION

To test whether MetaDoc users – who answered more questions – had to perform more stretchtext operations than the stretchtext users, the number of stretchtext operations performed by users in both systems was compared. Stretchtext operations included both text expansion and compression operations.

The main effects of the system used on the number of stretchtext operations was significant at the 5 percent level for the reading comprehension questions. The difference between the means in the number of stretchtext operations performed by novice and expert users was not significant. Expert users performed more stretchtext operations.

For search and navigation questions, the main effects of both system and expertise were not significant. MetaDoc users performed slightly fewer stretchtext operations than the stretchtext version users. Expert users performed more stretchtext operations than novices.

9.8. DISCUSSION OF RESULTS

The results of this experiment, in terms of the four dependent measures to indicate reader performance, are consistent with the primary and secondary hypotheses.

The results from the reading comprehension tasks are consistent with the primary hypothesis: users of adaptive documents spent less time answering the reading comprehension questions than stretchtext and hypertext users and also had significantly more correct answers. An appropriate explanation for this finding could be found in what Reinking (Reinking and Schreiner, 1985) suggested in the first place – that computer-mediated text manipulations enhance reading comprehension.

The timing results from the search and navigation questions are consistent with the secondary hypothesis – users of adaptive documents spent less time (although not statistically significant) in answering search and navigation questions. Interestingly, novices were consistently *faster* than experts in search and navigation, perhaps indicating a fixation on keyword searching. This contrasts with the superior performance of experts in reading comprehension.

Both primary and secondary hypotheses are not confirmed by the results of the number of nodes visited. Hypertext subjects used the string-search function more often than MetaDoc and stretchtext subjects. Through the string-search function, hypertext users visited a large number of nodes but spent more time reading the nodes than MetaDoc and stretchtext users. MetaDoc subjects used a browsing strategy most often to find information within the document. Although browsing requires an understanding of the contents of the document, MetaDoc users were able to visit a large number of nodes since they spent less time reading the nodes. Perhaps on account of the readability of the MetaDoc document, the MetaDoc subjects preferred browsing to the string-search function.

MetaDoc had greater impact on novice users than experts. Results were more significant in reading comprehension than in search and navigation. This conclusion is consistent with previous reading research, showing reading aids to be more significant to novice than expert readers (Reinking and Schreiner, 1985).

10. MetaDoc in Perspective

Many tools have been devised to aid hypertext users. These tools fall into two categories: those which aid navigation and orientation and those which aid reading. Navigation and orientation tools include graphical browsers as implemented in Intermedia (Yankelovich *et al.*, 1985; Yankelovich *et al.*, 1989) and NoteCards (Halasz *et al.*, 1987), as well as in bookmarks (Bernstein, 1988), hierarchical adaptive indexing (Frisse, 1987; Frisse *et al.*, 1989) and fisheye views (Furnas, 1986).

MetaDoc has no intended relation to any of these navigation and orientation tools. However, we believe that the philosophy behind the adaptive three-dimensional writing style will reduce the possibility of disorientation and navigation problems. By presenting information at the appropriate detail level, users will have less need to browse and consequently are less likely to become lost. Thus, MetaDoc prevents rather than cures one source of 'lost in space' problems.

Reading tools are often trail and path oriented, and typically suggest a path through a hypertext which will lead the user to pertinent information in an ordered sequence. Particular paths may be oriented towards different user-ability levels and may present a number of different options at different nodes. Examples of this approach include Zellwegger's active paths (Zellwegger, 1989).

Some of MetaDoc's personalization capabilities can be simulated through the use of path-based mechanisms. MetaDoc is more sophisticated, however, in that it:

- represents and dynamically alters a model of each user;
- includes a concept-based understanding of the document;
- transparently (to the user) modifies the level of presentation in terms of detail and expansion;
- manipulates text rather than links.

Perhaps the greatest difference is that MetaDoc modifies the entire document to suit the readers ability. It has no explicit notion of guiding the user through the document by forcing a reading order, though. MetaDoc documents could be read either linearly or non-linearly, depending on the readers requirements.

11. Conclusion

MetaDoc is a system rather than a tool. Adaptive documentation is the core of MetaDoc rather than a usability-related tool. MetaDoc seeks to fundamentally improve the way information is presented, rather than to cure known problems.

MetaDoc provides an environment in which the user can read a hypertext document that will adapt to his/her needs. MetaDoc does not take the entire control away from the user. The user can adapt the degree of detail or explanation as needed. MetaDoc can help improve reader performance by enhancing the comprehensibility of the document.

References

Akscyn, R., D. McCracken and E. Yoder: 1987, 'KMS: A Distributed Hypermedia System for Managing Knowledge In Organizations', *Proceedings of Hypertext' 87*. Chapel Hill, North Carolina.

Bernstein, M: 1988, 'The Bookmark and the Compass: Orientation Tools for Hypertext Users', *ACM SIGOIS Bulletin* 9 (4), 34–45.

Brown, P. J.: 1987, 'Turning Ideas into Products: The Guide System', *Proceedings of Hypertext' 87*. Chapel Hill, North Carolina.

Chin, D.: 1986, 'User Modelling in UC: the Unix Consultant', *Proceedings of the CHI-86 Conference*. Boston.

Dynatext Corp: 1990, One Richmond Square. Providence, Rhode Island.

Egan, D., J. R. Remde, T. K. Landauer, C. C. Lochbaum and L. M. Gomez: 1989, 'Behavioral Analysis of a Hypertext Browser', *Proceedings of CHI 89*. Addison Wesley.

Finin, T.: 1988, 'Default Reasoning and Stereotypes', *International Journal of Expert Systems* 1 (2), 131–158.

Frisse, M. E.: 1987, 'Searching for Information on a Hypertext Medical Handbook', *Proceedings of Hypertext' 87*. ACM Press, Baltimore, MD, pp. 57–66.

Frisse, M. F., S. B. Cousins: 1989, 'Query by Browsing: An Alternate Hypertext Information Retrieval Method', *Proceedings of the 13th Annual Symposium on Computer Applications in Medical Care*. IEEE Computer Society Press.

Furnas, G. W.: 1986, 'Generalized Fisheye Views', *Proceedings of the 1986 ACM Conference of Human Factors in Computing Systems*. pp. 16–23.

Guthrie, J. T. and I. S. Kirsch: Distinctions Between Reading Comprehension and Locating Information in Text', *Journal of Educational Psychology* **79**, 220–227.

Halasz, F., T. Moran, and R. Trigg: 1987, 'NoteCards in a nutshell', *Proceedings of the CHI '87 Conference*. Toronto, Canada, pp. 45–52.

IBMa: IBM Advanced Workstations Division, Austin, Texas.

IBMb: IBM Entry Systems Division, Austin, Texas.

Interleaf Inc.: 1990, Waltham, MA.

Kobsa, A. and W. Wahlster: 1989, *User Models in Dialog Systems*. Berlin, Springer-Verlag.

Korfhage, R. R.: 1985, 'Intelligent Information Retrieval: Issues in User Modelling', *Conference paper in Expert Systems in Government Symposium*. IEEE Computer Society Press, Washington, DC.

Nelson, T.: 1971, 'Computopia and Cybercrud', in: Levien (ed.): *Computers in Instruction*. The Rand Corporation.

Nielsen, J.: 1990, *Hypertext and Hypermedia*. Academic Press, NY.

Nielsen, J. and U. Lyngbaek: 1989, 'Two Field Studies of Hypermedia Usability', *Proceedings Hypertext2 Conference*. York, United Kingdom, pp. 29–30.

Reinking, D. and R. Schreiner: 1985, 'The Effects of Computer-mediated Text on Measures of Reading Comprehension and Reading Behavior', *Reading Research Quarterly*, Fall 1985, 536–552.

Rich, E.: 1983, 'Users Are Individuals: Individualizing User Models', *International Journal of Man-Machine Studies* **18**, 199–214.

Schnase, J., J. Leggett, C. Kacmar and C. Boyle: 1988, 'A Comparison of Hypertext Systems', *TAMU Technical Report 88–017*. Dept. of Computer Science, Texas A&M University, College Station, TX.

Texas Instruments (1988), Austin, TX.

Yankelovich, N., N. Meyrowitz and A. van Dam: 1985, 'Reading and Writing the Electronic Book', *IEEE Computer*, Oct. 1985, 15–30.

Yankelovich, N., B. J. Haan, N. Meyrowitz, and S. M. Drucker: 1988, 'Intermedia: The Concept and the Construction of a Seamless Information Environment', *IEEE Computer*, Jan. 1988, 81–96.

Zellweger, P.: 1989, 'Scripted Documents: A Hypermedia Path Mechanism', *Proceedings of Hypertext '89*. Seattle, Washington.

Appendix

```
┌─────────────────────────────────────────────┐
│                   MetaDoc                     │
├─────────────────────────────────────────────┤
│  General System Structure                     │
│                                               │
│  The AIX Operating System has three parts:    │
│                                               │
│  * The AIX Virtual Resource Manager (VRM)     │
│                                               │
│  * The AIX Operating System kernel            │
│                                               │
│  * The shell                                  │
│                                               │
└─────────────────────────────────────────────┘
```

```
┌──────────────────┐
│  User Model:      │
│  Unix/AIX:        │
│    expert         │
│  Gen. Computer:   │
│    expert         │
└──────────────────┘
```

An expert's view of a MetaDoc node.

```
┌─────────────────────────────────────────────┐
│                   MetaDoc                     │
├─────────────────────────────────────────────┤
│  General System Structure                     │
│                                               │
│  The AIX Operating System (a group of         │
│  programs that act as interface between the   │
│  user and computer) has three parts:          │
│                                               │
│  * The AIX Virtual Resource Manager (VRM), a  │
│  set of programs that manages the resources   │
│  of the computer (main storage, disk storage, │
│  display stations, and printers).             │
│                                               │
│  * The AIX Operating System kernel, a set of  │
│  programs that send instructions to the VRM.  │
│  It is a set of programs tha control, using   │
│  the VRM, the system hardware (the physical   │
│  components of the system).                    │
│                                               │
│  * A shell is often called an interface or a  │
│  command interpreter. It is the part of the   │
│  operating system that allows access to the   │
│  kernel.                                       │
│                                               │
└─────────────────────────────────────────────┘
```

```
┌──────────────────┐
│  User Model:      │
│  Unix/AIX:        │
│    novice         │
│  Gen. Computer:   │
│    novice         │
└──────────────────┘
```

A novice's view of the same MetaDoc node

Appendix

An expert's view of a MetaDoc node.

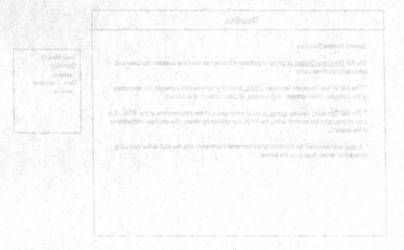

A novice's view of the same MetaDoc node.

User Modelling in the Interactive Anatomy Tutoring System ANATOM-TUTOR

IAN H. BEAUMONT
Fraunhofer Institut für Biomedizinische Technik, Arbeitsgruppe Software Engineering,
Ensheimerstraße 48, 66386 St. Ingbert, Germany;
e-mail: beaumont@ibmt.fhg.de

(Received 11 November 1993; in final form 1 June 1994)

Abstract. This article is a comparative description of the user modelling component of ANATOM-TUTOR, an intelligent anatomy tutoring system for use at university level. We introduce ITSs in general, discussing some of the psychological and pedagogical issues involved in using computers in education, and ANATOM-TUTOR in particular, and locate ANATOM-TUTOR's user modelling component in the field of existing user models. Details of the user model's construction and maintenance, the knowledge representation techniques used in it, and its relation to the domain knowledge base are then discussed. Two applications of ANATOM-TUTOR's user model are described: (1) tailoring hypertext to the level of knowledge of the individual user; and (2) generating explanations and questions in a simulated examination situation, also taking into consideration the individual user's level of knowledge.

Key words: User modelling, CAI, intelligent tutoring systems, hypertext, knowledge representation

1. Introduction

The desire in recent years to make computer applications user friendlier has resulted, among other things, in the development and employment of user models and a consequent "crystallizing out" of techniques for their construction. An overview can be found in Kobsa (1989). The present article describes the use of some of these techniques in the intelligent tutoring system ANATOM-TUTOR (a teaching aid for medical students), which is currently under development at the Fraunhofer Institut in St. Ingbert, Germany, and which makes use of interactive graphics, hypermedia, artificial intelligence knowledge representation and user modelling methods to provide a state-of-the-art automated tutor. ANATOM-TUTOR will only be introduced here in enough detail to provide a setting for the user model.

The article is structured as follows:

In Section 2 we introduce intelligent tutoring systems (ITSs). In Section 3 we describe a space of user models and discuss some modelling techniques. Section 4 is an introduction to ANATOM-TUTOR and we locate this system in the framework provided by the first two sections. The two operating modes, the *question mode* and the *hypermode*, and the use of the user model in them, are discussed in Sections 5 and 6 respectively, and examples are given. In Section 7 we state some conclusions.

Related work is discussed in the course of the text, as are some of the psychological and pedagogical issues arising when using ITSs in education.

P. Brusilovsky et al. (eds.), Adaptive Hypertext and Hypermedia, 91–115.
© 1998 *Kluwer Academic Publishers.*

2. Intelligent Tutoring Systems

An intelligent tutoring system (ITS) is a computer program which teaches in an intelligent way. Although there is no generally accepted definition of intelligence, the taking into account of what the learner already knows is generally accepted as being a characteristic of intelligent teaching (Van Lehn, 1988). In his summary of requirements on ITSs, Kass (1989), lists three forms of knowledge which an ITS should be able to represent: knowledge of the domain, knowledge of how to teach, and the knowledge that the student already has.

2.1. KNOWLEDGE OF THE DOMAIN

The material to be transmitted to the learner is stored in the domain knowledge base (also often referred to as the expert module). Knowledge bases can be categorized according to the way in which knowledge is represented in them. Anderson (1988), lists three basic categories:

- 1) **Black Box Models**. These make use of some way of reasoning about the domain which does not involve actually codifying the domain knowledge. As an example of a black box model Anderson mentions the SPICE electronic circuit simulator (in the tutoring system SOPHIE), which "does not have human knowledge of electronic currents, but can still reason about them by simulating them with its mathematical model . . . Because the SPICE simulator worked by solving a set of equations rather than by humanlike, causal reasoning, it was not possible for SOPHIE to explain its decisions in detail . . . Such a system could provide good advice . . . but it could not explain why".
- 2) **Glass Box Models**. These models are considered by Anderson to be those "prototypically generated in the knowledge-engineering tradition". A glass box model of the electronic circuit domain mentioned above would not use mathematical calculations to predict behaviour in circuits, but would contain some sort of representation of the concepts involved (e.g. atoms electrons, conductors, resistance, etc.). Because the components involved in the domain are explicitly represented they can be used for providing more useful explanations than those possible with black box models.
- 3) **Cognitive Models**. These make use of research in cognitive psychology and attempt to represent and access knowledge in a "humanlike" way. For example, while the above glass box model would have algorithms for juggling with "atoms" and "electrons" etc., a cognitive model of the electronic circuit domain might also know (by way of a structured representation) that both atoms and electrons are elementary particles and be able to deduce, as a human might, further information from this fact. Anderson distinguishes three types of knowledge in his discussion of cognitive models: *procedural* knowledge, i.e. knowledge about how to perform a task; *declarative* knowledge, i.e. knowledge about a set of facts; and *causal* knowledge, for reasoning about

the behaviour of a device, for example in troubleshooting applications. The rule-based modelling approach (i.e. knowledge is formulated as a set of rules which determine what to do in a given situation) is probably the most common when dealing with procedural knowledge, while some sort of hierarchical representation (such as frame systems) with inference procedures built round it is common in dealing with declarative knowledge. (Anderson himself is not convinced that causal knowledge is not a combination of the other two types, op. cit., p. 47.)

2.2. KNOWLEDGE OF HOW TO TEACH

The representation of teaching knowledge is probably one of the most difficult areas to tackle in constructing an ITS. Anderson points out that while "any pedagogy needs to be rigorously founded in a theory of learning" it is currently the case that "no tutoring system actively uses a learning model in its computations" (Anderson, 1988). And usually when constructing teaching modules in ITSs no attempt is made to construct a model of an "expert teacher". Generally, human teachers have a far greater repertoire of teaching techniques, are dealing with a far greater bandwidth of information and are acting in a much more complex situation than their electronic counterparts. Rather, since only small, well definable fragments of an actual human teaching situation are being reproduced, the teaching component is a set of procedures stating how to use the resources available to the machine should the given "fragment" occur. It is often not a single physical unit (as the expert module might be), but distributed over various parts of the program.

Halff (1988) classifies tutoring components into two types, *expository*, i.e. those teaching "factual knowledge and inferential skills", and procedure, i.e. those teaching "kills and procedures that have applications outside of the tutorial situation", and distinguishes between the *curriculum*, i.e. the material to be taught together with an order in which it is to be presented, and the *instruction*, i.e. the act of presenting the material to the student.

2.2.1. *Curriculum Design*

One of the most widely used techniques in designing lessons for computer instruction is that of *task analysis*. Task analysis was proposed by the educational psychologist R. Gagne (1977) as a general procedure for designing effective lessons, and is a top down procedure well suited to the needs of computer instruction. It is basically the process of repeatedly dividing (teaching-) tasks into simpler components called subtasks. Once a set of subtasks has been obtained, *instructional objectives*, i.e. specific statements which identify "the information, skill, or attitude to be learned, and sometimes the means of measuring whether the information is learned" (Rothstein, 1990), can be written for these subtasks. When the instructional objectives of the subtasks have been attained, the composite task which resulted in the generation of the subtasks can be tackled. Although task analysis has been widely used, Lesgold (1988) criticizes the attitude, adopted by many who use the method in constructing tutor systems, of viewing the whole as the sum of its parts and presenting just a collection of individual lessons. He emphasises the need for providing the "glue" with which to "tie together the pieces of knowledge from prerequisite lessons".

After task analysis, there remains the problem of sequencing the material, after which (by Halff's definition) we have a basic curriculum. Here we can be dealing with internal considerations such as the structure and coherence of the material, or external considerations such as coordinating the material with parallel courses or attempting to stimulate student interest by presenting the material in the order of its historical development, etc.

2.2.2. *Instruction*

The purpose of an ITS is to transfer domain knowledge to the student*. The goal state has been reached when the student has (i.e. can demonstrate) an adequate knowledge of the material. Instruction in the ITS sense is a function of the curriculum, the user model, and the procedures in the teaching module. It can be divided into two main tasks:

1) presenting the material, i.e. deciding which parts to shuffle about (to suit the users' current knowledge) or leave out (because the user has, or probably has, the necessary skill or information), and providing the necessary "glue".

2) determining whether the user has attained the desired objectives and recording his** detail knowledge (feedback for the user model).

It also deals with how to respond to user questions and, in strongly procedural applications, how and when to intervene.

For an ITS to instruct in an individual way it obviously has to have very detailed knowledge of what the user knows, and the best way to obtain this information is to ask the user, i.e. to test him in some way. Lesgold mentions two ways of tackling instruction, the *frame* approach and the *pretest/post-test* approach. In the frame approach the material is chopped up into "very microscopic units". After each unit the user takes a test, the result of which determines which frame he should go to next. (This approach, a development of behaviourist educational theories, was also popular in the 60's and 70's for books - the test determined which page the reader should turn to next - but later seemed to go out of fashion.) In the pretest/post-test

---

* This is not to suggest that the knowledge which the user then has is an identical copy of the domain expert's knowledge. The process can be compared with describing a graph by giving the user finitely many points on it. Extrapolating on these points the user could easily come up with a graph which has little to do with that intended by the expert. Depending on the granularity of the material in the ITS a certain amount of deviation can be expected between the learner's model of the domain and that of the expert. This deviation, of course, is invisible to the ITS. At this point it is the job of the human teacher to take over the guidance of the student.

** For want of a better alternative we have decided to use masculine pronouns throughout.

approach the material is organized into larger chunks. Before the lesson the user takes a test, which, if passed, allows the user to skip the lesson. Failure means that he has to take the lesson and then sit a post-test at the end of it. Lesgold notes that there is a degree of inefficiency here in that students spend most of their time taking tests, which is "not very effective instruction". There is also the question of what to do if a student fails a post-test and has to redo the lesson. He basically has to go through the same lesson again "with more examples and more practice" (which may be feasible in procedural domains, but will be difficult in declarative domains). However, it is still basically the same old lesson with the same shortcomings as before. Should he take the same post-test again second time round? Should he be required to redo the same lesson if he fails a second time?

Another approach, building on Gagne's task analysis approach to designing curriculae, would consist in questioning the user at the start of the session and again after the material for each instructional objective has been covered. The above questions also apply here on the subject of what to do with students who fail the post-tests*.

2.3. THE USERS'S KNOWLEDGE

This will be considered more fully later.

3. User Models

Before going into the details of ANATOM-TUTOR's user modelling component, we make a few remarks on user models in general and sketch the "space" of existing models. In Section 4 we attempt to locate our model in this space. For convenience we use the observations made by Finin (1989).

Finin identifies a space of user models by considering them from four angles: who is being modelled, what is being modelled, how is the model to be acquired and maintained and why is the model needed.

1) Who is being modelled: Finin considers two aspects here, the degree of specialization and the temporal extent of the user model.

The degree of specialization refers to whether individual users or classes of users are being modelled. Temporal extent refers to how long the acquired information about the user is to be stored, i.e. is the model rebuilt after every login or is a long term model maintained. Once created, user models can obviously be stored indefinitely (together with changes in knowledge between subsequent sessions should this be deemed useful for progress checking). However, how long models retain their validity is a complex question whose answer depends on various psychological considerations including individual memory ability of the user, time between

---

* This is obviously a point in which present ITS's clearly show limitations and a point at which ITSs could be spliced into a more comprehensive teaching system - users who fail the post-test are prime candidates for some personal contact from the teacher.

lessons, memory deterioration, memory interference due to previous knowledge or misconceptions, etc, and also on the amount and complexity of the material being taught.

2) What is being modelled: (i.e. which aspects of the user are being modelled.) Four types of possible contents of a user model are identified and considered: goals and plans, capabilities, attitudes, and knowledge or beliefs.

Goals are often defined as "states of affairs" which the user wishes to achieve, and are mainly used in problem solving or diagnostic applications, or in teaching skills. Attaining "states of affairs" is a "how to" process where rules and bug rules* are preferred modelling techniques. Capabilities are subdivided by Finin into physical and mental capabilities. The former refer to the user's ability to perform some action and the latter to the "ability to understand a recommendation or explanation", etc.

Acceptance of sex, violence, etc., are examples of attitudes.

Modelling knowledge and belief in the wider sense is a complex area which may be considered as properly encompassing knowledge representation (in the expert system sense) since not only is domain knowledge being represented, but various agents' beliefs about other agents' knowledge and plans are also being considered.

3) Model acquisition and maintenance: Two types of acquisition of knowledge about the user are distinguished, explicit and implicit. Explicit information is that entered by the user as a direct answer to a request for information while implicit information is that gleaned by the system from the user's interaction with the system, possibly using previously entered explicit information. GRUNDY, for example, uses stereotypes to infer further implicit knowledge from information already in the model. Model maintenance, i.e. "incorporating new knowledge about an individual user into an existing model", also treats the problem of what to do when default information in the model is found to be incorrect. This will be considered in more detail below.

4) Why is the model there: Finin lists four uses to which a user model can be put: (1) understanding the user's information-seeking behaviour, (2) providing help and advice, (3) getting input from the user, and (4) providing output to the user.

3.1. MODELLING TECHNIQUES

User modelling is often undertaken by distinguishing a set of concepts in the domain knowledge, imposing a structure or order on these, and utilising the user's familiarity with them to formulate explanations and descriptions. In Chin's KNOME, for example, the concepts are Unix commands and terms from basic computer science such as "file", while in the EPI-UMOD system of de Rosis et al. (1992) concepts

---

* Bug rules are used for representing common misconceptions in procedural knowledge. If the user model contains an entry which can only be explained by a bug rule, then the user probably has the misconception represented by that bug rule.

were taken from epidemiology dictionaries or glossaries of basic texts on medical statistics.

Boyle and Encarnacion's Unix tutor, MetaDoc (Boyle & Encarnacion, 1991), provides a good example of a structure on a set of concepts (influenced by the earlier work of Chin (1986)). The users are first grouped into four categories: novice, beginner, intermediate and experts, and the concepts are then associated with these categories. The actual allocation of concepts to categories is done by observing the commands used by members of these groups. Further observations indicate that knowledge of certain concepts tends to indicate knowledge of certain other concepts (concepts which tend to occur together are refered to as *concept islands*). Similarly, a lack of knowledge of certain concepts (often called *required* or *necessary*, see below on stereotypes) indicates lack of knowledge of others. This allows a default activation and deactivation of concepts. In exactly the same way that concepts go to form islands, these islands can be organised into concept levels. Knowledge of a trigger concept island can cause the user to be promoted to a higher user class.

Stereotypes are another widely employed user modelling technique and are based on the work of Rich in the late 70's (Rich, 1979, 1989). The idea behind stereotypes is that people often assume rather a lot of information about others on observing one or two key items. This allows fast orientation but is not always accurate and can even have undesirable side effects (such as racial prejudices). Rich (1989) states that a stereotype is a "knowledge structure" with body and triggers, and possibly standing in some relation to other stereotypes. If the items* in the trigger are observed in the user model, then the items in the body are added to model. According to Finin (1989, p. 418) "a stereotype is a collection of facts and rules that are applicable for any person who is seen as belonging to that stereotype", i.e. a stereotype is both a collection of facts and rules and a way of categorizing users. He goes on to say that "facts and rules can be either definite or default, allowing for an individual to vary from the stereotypic norm". In effect Finin identifies classes of users with the definite facts and rules in the stereotype. An extension of the basic stereotype paradigm is obtained using the "necessary" and "sufficient" conditions which Shifroni & Shanon (1992, p. 354) describe as being "attached to" their stereotypes - the user's knowledge of the sufficient conditions activates the stereotype, causing the user to be put into the stereotype, while lack of knowledge of the necessary conditions causes him to be removed again (*stereotype deactivation*). Stereotypes and concept structuring as mentioned above are closely related, and concept structuring often forms a basis for stereotyping.

Instead of a fact simply being present in the model if known by the user and absent otherwise, it can have an attached numerical value indicating the certainty with which it is known. Stereotypes or rules which cause an entry to be made in the user model then also cause the (stereotype- or rule-dependent) certainty factor

---

* By "item" we mean facts of the domain, attributes observed in the user, goals and plans, etc.

to be entered with it. Several considerations have to be taken into account in this situation:

Multiple support: A user model entry which is supported by a set of stereotypes should have a higher certainty factor than the same entry would have if it were supported by a proper subset of that set.

Propagation of change: Since the conclusion of a rule or stereotype can be used as a premise in another rule or stereotype, a change in the certainty factor of one entry can cause the need for a whole chain of dependent deductions to be recalculated. Rich (1989) points out that this can result in "substantial effort ... being expended on the propagation of insubstantial changes", and suggests the introduction of a threshold value below which propagation will not occur.

Adaptation: If a prediction is later found to be correct then the certainty factor of the stereotype which caused it should be increased, and similarly, incorrectness should result in a decrease in the certainty factor.

3.2. REALISM IN USER MODELS

Both the possibility and desirability of building user models has been the subject of some debate in the CAI world. Katz and Lesgold (Katz, 1991) mention the two diametrically opposite groups, the "model builders", who consider detailed user modelling essential in individualized CAI, and the "model breakers", who question both the feasibility of constructing adequate user models and the benefits of using them. Sandberg (1987), criticizes that more and more complex user models do not necessarily produce corresponding gains in teaching efficiency. How complex can user models get and how complex need they be?

As an example of a complex user modelling system we mention the Doppelganger (DG) User Modeling System being developed at the MIT Media Laboratory, and described by J. Orwant in (Orwant, 1991). DG is an ambitious undertaking in which as much information about the user as possible is to be gathered - physical location tracking systems, eye tracking systems, model-building cameras are among the sensors mentioned by Orwant. The questionability of this information being processed in a useful way is obvious - natural language is difficult enough to understand without trying to understand body language. But even if we have some way of processing all of this information, what of value are we likely to learn about the user from it. Amongst the uses to which such an all-encompassing model can be put, Orwant mentions "recognizing that a user is going home for the day and consequently needs a reminder to buy milk". Katz and Lesgold mention "behavioral dispositions" and "affective factors such as motivation" being represensed in Sherlock II. How these factors are determined is not mentioned, nor is the use to which the information will be put. Boyle and Encarnacion (Boyle, 1991) mention the time between mouse clicks and the number of user errors as further sources of implicit information about the user. How these are to be realistically interpreted and the effect that the information will have on their program is again left unmentioned. (Do longer than average pauses between mouse clicks indicate that the user is having difficulty with the material, or that he is nibbling his way through a packet of biscuits whilst working at the computer?)

Motivational problems are difficult to tackle, even for human teachers (and they are still more suited to the task than computers). How should the system react to a user it classifies as disinterested or dejected? Tell him to go home and rest for a day or two? (the cause of his depression may be an exam the day after tomorrow). Pile on "helpful" details and depress him some more? The advantage of computer aided instruction is not its ability to water down or liven up its instruction to the level of a bored or dejected student, but in its potential for reducing the teacher's routine workload, leaving him more time to devote to individual students' problems, and in its availability at those times when the student has a desire to learn, whatever time that may be.

4. Overview of Anatom-Tutor

ANATOM-TUTOR is, as the name suggests, a system for teaching anatomy. At present we deal with several aspects of brain anatomy, including the visual system, the pupillary light reflex system and the accommodation reflex system, each looked at from both morphological and functional perspectives. An intelligent knowledge base is used for part of the material and is accessible via menus and mouse-sensitive diagrams, while the remainder, material not suitable for representation in the knowledge base formalism, is treated in a hypertext module.

The three forms of knowledge which Kass lists as being necessary in an ITS correspond in ANATOM-TUTOR to the ANATOM knowledge base, the DIDAK-TIK module, and the user modelling component respectively. We look at these components in more detail in the remainder of this section. The user model documents what the user knows and the DIDAKTIK module "takes this into account" in order to better teach the subject matter.

ANATOM-TUTOR has three operating modes. In the *browsing mode*, menus and mouse-sensitive diagrams are employed for accessing the domain knowledge base. The user model is neither consulted nor modified in this mode. The *question mode*, which makes extensive use of the user model, is a simulated examination situation offering individually tailored responses to student misconceptions. In the *hypermode*, which also makes use of the user model, a hypertext based information system which is functionally independent of the domain knowledge base is used for the structured presentation of domain knowledge in a manner suited to the users' level of knowledge. This is built along the lines of existing "stretchtext" systems such as MetaDoc from Boyle and Encarnacion (Boyle, 1991). In the browsing mode, the user learns in a self-directed, explorative manner. In the hypermode, he is *guided* through the material in a personalised way, the important points are emphasized, and the uses of the material illustrated. The question mode can be used

for examination preparation or as a voluntary intermediate test. Both the question
mode and the hypertext mode will be discussed in later sections.

4.1. THE DOMAIN KNOWLEDGE BASE

The knowledge contained in the domain knowledge base pertains to objects participating in the above-mentioned functional systems together with the functions
which these objects carry out, their relations to each other, and the nerve connections between these objects. We have taken the cognitive approach here - a
frame-based representational formalism is used for the knowledge, each object
being located in an object hierarchy and each function in a function hierarchy.
Deductions are be performed using built-in deduction mechanisms.

4.2. THE TEACHING COMPONENT

The teaching component is responsible for instruction in the sense defined in
Section 2, i.e. presenting the material in a manner suitable for, and checking
whether it has been absorbed by, the student.

We distinguish between global and local teaching knowledge. *Global teaching
knowledge* refers to the general structure of a lesson, and is one of the factors which
go into the design of a (hypertext) lesson and into choosing an order in which to
present material. In the terminology of Chapter 2 it is the knowledge which is used
in producing a basic curriculum. This type of knowledge is usually specified by a
teacher of the subject and is basically hard-coded. *Local teaching knowledge* refers
here to what to do when a student gets into difficulties, and local teaching strategies
make direct use of the user model. Possibilities include completion of correct but
incomplete answers, simply telling him that his answer is wrong and providing
the correct answer, pointing out contradictions, helping the student to deduce an
item of knowledge which he should theoretically know but in actual fact does not,
etc. Requirements of local strategies can require that the global strategy be slightly
altered - i.e. questions asked by the user, his specific knowledge (or lack of it), etc.,
can affect the course of the lesson. (See examples at the end of Section 5.) Local
teaching knowledge is that required for actual instruction.

4.3. THE USER MODELLING COMPONENT

Classification of the user: The user fills in a questionaire at the start of a session.
This gives the system information about the user's semester, which lectures he has
heard already, etc., and results in the *global classification* of the user and consequent
activation of stereotypes. (If the user has used the system before, the information
is integrated into the existing model.)

The user modelling formalism: We wish to model the user's knowledge with
respect to the knowledge base and the hypertext module, so the formalism chosen

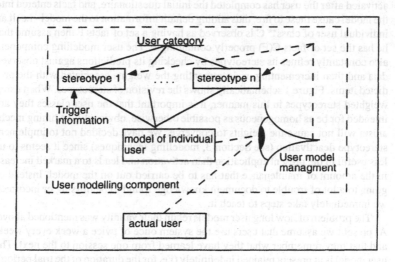

Fig. 1. Stereotype revision in ANATOM-TUTOR.

for the user modelling component must be capable of handling the material in both. For several reasons the knowledge representation formalism employed in the user model is not the frame based formalism used in the knowledge base. Not only does the hypertext module contain material not represented (and not representable) in the knowledge base, but the frame based approach would contain the implicit assumption that the user knows the complete hierarchical structure of the domain objects (which means that in order to document which structural information he knows, we would need an additional representation anyway). Representing knowledge of domain laws and the categorisation of users also make demands which the knowledge base formalism cannot fulfill. We have used the production language Ops5 (Brownston et al., 1985), the hierarchical knowledge implicit in the (hierarchical structure of the) domain knowledge base being recorded in attribute/value fields in the "flat" Ops5 representation, while domain laws are represented in the obvious way as productions.

We now attempt to locate the user modelling component in the space sketched in Section 2 by showing how we have approached some of the topics listed there.

Who is being modelled: The points to be considered here are degree of specialization and temporal extent. Knowledge about classes of users is coded into stereotypes in ANATOM-TUTOR. This class knowledge is then used for extrapolating the actual user's individual knowledge. The appropriate stereotypes* are activated after the user has completed the initial questionaire, and facts entered into the model cause these to fire, thus adding default information to the model - i.e. if an individual user of class** C is observed as having a set of facts F then assume that he has the set of facts C(F) properly containing F. The user modelling component also constantly refines its stereotypes by checking its predictions against observed data and then incrementing or decrementing the weights associated with the predicted items. Figure 1 schematically shows the revision of stereotypes. When using weighted stereotypes in this manner, it is important that the user classes they are intended for be as homogeneous as possible otherwise, obviously, the tuning mechanism will not cause the weights to converge. We have decided not to implement stereotype deactivation (see Section 3, modelling techniques) since it seems to us less useful in the present application than activation and leads to a marked increase in the amount of maintenance that has to be carried out on the model. Instead of going to a lot of trouble to document knowledge found to be missing or incorrect, we immediately take steps to teach it.

The problem of how long user models retain their validity was mentioned above. At present we assume that users use the system once or twice a week every week, and that they remember what they have learned from one session to the next. The user model is at present retained indefinitely (i.e. for the duration of the trial period), and the only changes made to it are those occurring during the course of a session. Detailed studies will be necessary before we can provide "best before" dates on user models or indicate which items are most likely to deteriorate, and such information will probably be based on statistical observations since no current psychological models of memory are powerful enough to accurately predict memory deterioration in a concrete situation.

What is being modelled: Of the types of knowledge mentioned, only the user's knowledge or beliefs play a role in the kind of teaching environment envisioned in ANATOM-TUTOR. We do not differentiate between knowing and believing - correctly entered information is "known" by the user, wrongly entered information is classified under "misconceptions". (It would be possible to label correct entries as known and incorrect entries as beliefs, making belief synonymous with misconception, but this would neither increase the power of the model nor be in accordance with natural language constructions such as "the user correctly believes that . . .".) Multiple agent belief documentation is not needed in ANATOM-TUTOR as there is only one learner at any one time (and it is not necessary for the system to have to figure out what the user thinks the system might be cooking up for him). Since ANATOM-TUTOR is an expository system (see Section 2), the use of goals

---

* Stereotypical information about classes can be thought of as having the form "any member of class C who knows A1 . . . An knows B1 with certainty factor P-B1 and . . . Bm with certainty factor P-Bm". The same basic stereotype may be activated for various classes of user, but obviously the certainty factors for an advanced learner will generally be higher than those for a beginner.

** Classes are not explicitly named, but are defined by the stereotypes which have been activated.

is obviously inappropriate. Plans, defined as sequences of actions leading to the realization of a goal, are thus also not represented. It should be noted, however, that the teaching module can choose subgoals in pursuing a teaching goal - it can decide which item of information to present, and how best to present it. There is, however, no need for the teaching module to occur as an agent in the model. Misconceptions are not stored in the model, but serve rather as prompts for the system to take corrective action. Once such action has been taken and the user has exhibited the appropriate correct knowledge the misconception is removed from the model.

The ANATOM-TUTOR user model first distinguishes certain objects, classes of objects, functions, and classes of functions found in text books on anatomy (Duns, 90; Nieuwenhuys, 1988; Feneis, 1988; Rauber, 1987; Kahle, 1979; Forssmann, 1975). Examples include "parasympathic object", "sulcus", "neuron", "axon" (object classes), "ganglion-ciliare-dext", "thalamus" (objects), "dilation of the pupil", "light reflex" (functions), "sympathic function", "motoric function" (function classes). But not only do we distinguish *concepts* in the domain, we also distinguish certain *relations* between these concepts. Thus we can document that a user not only knows the concepts "nucleus-caudatus" and "corpus-striatum", but also that "nucleus-caudatus is-part-of corpus-striatum". This type of material is also represented in the domain knowledge base.

Being able to represent relations on the domain lays the groundwork for representing *laws* valid in the domain. Thus, distinguishing the relations "belongs-to-class" and "sends-nerve-impulses-to" allows us to formulate the law that "any ganglion which receives nerve impulses from a parasympathic object is itself parasympathic".

We will refer to any item belonging to one of the above three information types as an RI (Representable Item of information). Both domain laws and stereotypes are "production rules" in the sense of Ops5 (Brownston et al., 1985) (in which the modelling component is programmed), but while domain laws represent causal necessities in the domain, stereotypes represent purely statistical dependencies, there being often no anatomical connection between the trigger elements and the body elements. Production rules representing domain laws contain variables while stereotypes (generally) do not.

Model acquisition and maintenance: By its nature, ANATOM-TUTOR obviously requires constant maintenance, and new information is found both implicitly and explicitly. Truth maintenance, however, is not needed, since the assertions in the model are a part of a (logically) consistent body of medical knowledge, and thus also consistent*.

---

* We have not taken into account the problem of different schools of medical thought, with which every medicine student is confronted. This problem reaches back to definitions and results in an inherently inconsistent domain, so we have avoided a major issue in the representation of medical knowledge here.

deth RIs are not just "known" or "unknown" in the ANATOM-TUTOR user model, they also have a certainty factor associated with them. Each stereotype or rule which supports an RI increases the theoretical certainty with which the item is known by the user. An item may qualify as premise for a stereotype if its certainty factor is above a certain (stereotype dependent) threshold. This brings with it the problem of what to do if a default premise is found to be incorrect. As stated above, we adopt the policy of correcting errors on the spot. If a default item is found to be unknown it is not removed and the deductions made using it annulled, but explained to the user (if it was the result of a deduction the premisses and rule with which it should have been deduced are checked and if necessary explained). Since the information is now certainly known by the user, any deductions made using it are justified. As the item was wrongly prognosed as being known, however, the weights associated with it in any stereotypes which supported it are decremented. Rich (1989), mentions the difficulty of starting out with accurate weights in stereotypes and the need for a revision procedure for them, and implemented a similar "tuning" procedure in her system GRUNDY.

The necessary conditions as used by Shifroni and Shanon (Shifroni, 1992) could be adapted for decrementing the certainty factors of items of information instead of removing them. This approach would also involve some sort of tuning procedure, which would then have to be coordinated with that for the sufficient conditions. We decided to trade off the possible gain in model accuracy against the operational simplicity of considering only sufficiency. (Our philosophy of user modelling is in accordance with the views put forward by those authors (e.g. Sandberg (1987), who see user models becoming more and more unwieldy without significant increases in teaching efficiency, and who advocate less complicated user models and repairing anomalies on the spot.)

Why is the model there?: Of the uses mentioned, only the first (i.e. understanding the user's information-seeking behaviour) plays no role in ANATOM-TUTOR. This involves plan recognition strategies and, as mentioned above, plans are not modelled in the system. The fourth use, providing output to the user, is important, especially in hypermode where besides formulating explanations, auxiliary questions, etc., the system tailors text output to the user's level of knowledge. Explanations, auxiliary questions, illustration of the use of domain laws as opportunities for their use arise, etc., are examples of the "glue" which Lesgold mentions as being conspicuously absent in many tutoring systems. "Glue" is not just redisplaying pieces of text or even RIs if the user seems to be lacking these, it is showing the material in action at the user's own level.

The following sections describe ANATOM-TUTOR in the question mode and in hypermode.

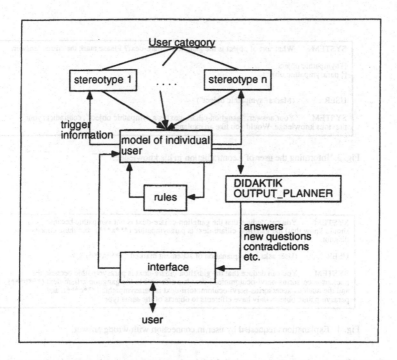

Fig. 2. The role of the user model in the question mode.

5. The User Model in the Question Mode

The questions currently implemented in the question mode are intended for preparing students for the "Physikum", an exam taken by second or third year medical students. Students respond to questions by typing in their answers at the keyboard or clicking objects in active diagrams with the mouse. Both correct and incorrect answers are entered in the user model. The former can cause stereotypes to fire, if causing the addition to the model of items of default information, while the latter are immediately acted upon by the teaching component. Thus the user model retains information which the user has given as a direct answer, information which the average student at the user's knowledge level is expected to know, and information which the user should be able to deduce using his individual knowledge. Any item of information can be supported by several rules and/or stereotypes, each piece of supporting evidence increasing the certainty factor associated with the item.

SYSTEM   What sort of object is the ganglion-ciliare-dext? Please mark the correct answer.

[] sympathic object
[] parasympathic object

USER   (Marks "sympathic object")

SYSTEM   Your answer, "ganglion-ciliare-dext is a sympathic object", contradicts your
previous knowledge. Would you like an explanation?

Fig. 3. Informing the user of a contradiction in his knowledge.

SYSTEM   You can deduce that the ganglion-ciliare-dext is not sympathic because (you
should know that) the ganglion-ciliare-dext is parasympathic (***a***), and these concepts are
disjoint.

USER   (User asks for explanation of statement marked " (***a***) " .)

SYSTEM   You can deduce that the ganglion-ciliare-dext is parasympathic because the
nucleus-accessorius-nervi-oculomotorii-dext has efferents to the ganglion-ciliare-dext (***b***),
and the nucleus-accessorius-nervi-oculomotorii-dext is parasympathic (***c***), and
parasympathic objects only have efferents to objects of the same type.

Fig. 4. Explanations requested by user in connection with wrong answer.

Figure 2 shows how the user model and other components interact in the question mode.

While anatomical knowledge is primarily material learned by rote, there are certain types of user misconception which can be tackled by showing that they stand in contradiction to other knowledge which the user has*. For example sympathic objects and parasympathic objects are disjoint classes. If the user states that the ganglion-ciliare is a sympathic object, but the user model lists that the user should know that it is parasympathic, the system can offer the fact together with all information with which the user should have been able to deduce it**. We do not test every misconception for inconsistency with the model (as a system using a resolution theorem prover, for example, might), but restrict ourselves to these "promising" cases, and although the actual explanation produced is individually found, search spaces remain small.

---

* Or knowledge which he should have according to the user model.
** It may also contradict material which the user should not theoretically know, but which would have been presented a little later in the normal course of the curriculum. This material can be brought forward and integrated into the explanation, resulting in a local fluctuation in the curriculum.

SYSTEM   To which class does an object which has afferents from a parasympathic object belong? Mark the correct answers.

[] sympathic object
[] motoric kernel
[] parasympathic object
[] grey matter

USER   (Marks "parasympathic object")

SYSTEM   Answer correct. You know that any object receiving afferents from a parasympathic object also has to be parasympathic. Do you know a parasympathic object which has efferents to the ganglion-ciliare-dext?

Fig. 5. Checking the user's familiarity with a law of the domain and checking whether he has enough information to apply the law.

On answering a question correctly, the student is told that his answer is correct and the answer is entered in the model. Correct but incomplete answers result in the user being given the full information. If the answer is wrong, the misconception is added to the model and acted upon immediately. Especially at the start of a session, when the model is relatively empty and there is no other information relating to the wrong answer, the user is simply told that his answer is wrong and given the correct answer. The misconception is removed from and the correct information (with certainty factor) added to the user model. Later, however, a misconception may contradict some deduction already in the model. If it contradicts an item supported by a stereotype, the user's knowledge of the supporting items can be checked. If it contradicts an item supported by a domain law, his knowledge of supporting items and of that law can be checked. Figure 5 shows an example of such rule checking. Rules represent laws of the domain, e.g. "any ganglion which receives nerve impulses from a parasympathic object is itself parasympathic".

In Figure 3* the user has entered an answer which contradicts information present in the user model. He is told that his answer is incorrect. The teaching component, i.e. DIDAKTIK module, tells him the correct answer and informs him of the contradiction, asking him whether he would like the contradiction explained. This is one of several possible reactions the teaching component could have made.

Figure 4 shows an example of an explanation. Each statement which occurs in the explanation is indexed (with a letter) so that the user can question any statement he does not understand.

In Figure 5 we consider a situation in which the user is assumed to know that the nucleus-accessorius-nervi-oculomotorii has efferents to the ganglion-ciliare,

---

* We originally intended to include actual colour screen dumps of the system/user interaction, but publishing considerations have forced us to use the following transcriptions. In the original colour screen display objects under discussion in the active diagrams are highlighted in different colours.

and has now been asked what sort of object the ganglion-ciliare is. He answers wrongly. The system responds by checking his knowledge of a law of the domain (not registered in the model as being known), the premisses of which he should, according to the user model, know, and with which he could have deduced the correct answer. His answer shows that he knows the rule, whereupon his knowledge of the premisses is checked. (The answer to this question will result in the weights in the stereotypes supporting the premisses being incremented or decremented.)

6. The User Model in Hypermode

ANATOM-TUTOR uses hypertext* for presenting material. Whereas in a book or in ordinary hypertext the material is simply a piece of prose, ANATOM-TUTOR represents the facts and rules mentioned in the text, and can test the user's knowledge of them. The presence of the user model suggests possibilities for building hypertext windows adapted to the needs of the individual user. Instead of just displaying fixed texts no matter what sort of person is using the system, ANATOM-TUTOR uses information about the user and his domain knowledge to custom-make hypertext displays.

When a user starts a hypermode lesson, a basic text is chosen for him using his global classification (see Section 4). The knowledge contained in the text is then compared to the knowledge contained in the user model, and sufficiently well known items can be deleted from the text, or explanations or detail information can be added. This is a variation on the stretchtext theme.

Figures 6 and 7 graphically illustrate the difference between ordinary Hypertext and ANATOM-TUTOR's Stretchtext.

6.1. PROCESSING THE TEXT FOR USE WITH THE MODEL

The basic text is first divided into units of one or several sentences**. Units of text are not only arranged according to user levels, the system also has a record of which representable items of information (RI's) are contained in the units. This enables the system to include or exclude a unit depending on the certainty factor (as documented in the user model) of the RI's contained in the unit.

As mentioned above, the text units are graded. We have found that medical descriptions are apt to differ in style depending on the level of knowledge of the intended recipients. This is in keeping with the findings of other researchers. C. L. Paris, in her article on the system TAILOR (Paris, 1989), found that texts written

---

   * After experimenting with a commercially available hypertext program we decided to program our own hypertext tool.

   ** When the only distinguished objects are concepts, a simple string search is sufficient for finding their occurrences in a text. Relations are more difficult to handle since they can be formulated in a variety of different ways in natural language. They may even be obviously implied by, although not explicitly mentioned in, a text. This means that determining which relations are contained in a given text cannot be done fully automatically. The same applies for domain laws mentioned in a text.

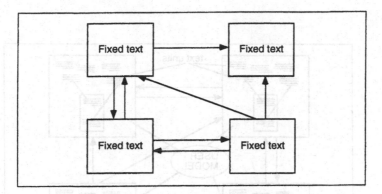

Fig. 6. Ordinary hypertext lessons guide the user while allowing him local freedom to learn exploratively. The concepts in the text units are not represented in a knowledge base.

for users with differing levels of knowledge differed "not only in the amount, but also in the kind of information provided". She distinguished "parts-oriented" and "process-oriented" descriptions*, and proposed a descriptive strategy for each type, (her aim being to generate descriptions in which the sentences were formed according to the descriptive strategy corresponding to the user's knowledge of the concepts involved). Moreover, a beginner will generally need more explanations than an advanced learner and be confused by too many details, whereas an expert will require less explanation of concepts and be more interested in esoteric details (a view also expressed by Boyle and Encarnacion (Boyle, 1991)).

6.2. FEEDBACK

In an information system such as hypertext, the main feedback which the system gets is the request for more information, which is usually done by clicking menu buttons or active fields in the body of the text. Boyle and Encarnacion, (Boyle, 1991), recognise that the mouse click allows only a "narrow bandwidth of information" but make the most of it by enabling the user to remove superfluous information (i.e. information which the user does not understand or which is too basic) from the screen, thus providing another feedback dimension. (We believe that in a realistic situation a user will just gloss over what he cannot use, as he would do when reading a book, and not try to use paragraph deletion as a signaling

* Parts-oriented descriptions focus on the component parts of an object, while process-oriented n descriptions "describe processes associated with the operation of the object". Texts for beginners tend to be process-oriented.

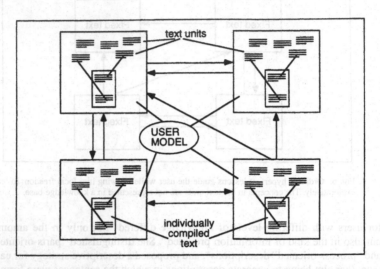

Fig. 7. ANATOM-TUROR's stretchtext is an extension of the hypertext idea in which the user model is consulted to choose a formulation suited to the user's level of knowledge. The concepts (RIs) mentioned in the text are represented in the model, allowing the user's understanding of the material to be checked.

device.) If the user asks for an explanation of an item of information which was assumed known, MetaDoc removes the item from the user model and gives the requested explanation (presumably then re-adding the item to the user model). Paris (1989) avoids the problem, and assumes the existence of an adequate user model somewhere in the background, neglecting the effect that the reading has on the user's knowledge.

Questions in hypermode: While there may be a question of the desirability and user acceptance of putting test questions in an on-line documentation system, ANATOM-TUTOR is a tutoring program and we can use test questions to increase the bandwidth of information available from the user without leaving the teaching paradigm. Adding questions relating to the material is obviously superior to trying to accurately update the model solely from the user's requests for more or less material, and is in keeping with Self's (Self, 1988) advice on bypassing the intractability problem of student modelling - "avoid guessing - get the student to tell you what you need to know". The questions were designed with the task analysis approach to curriculum design in mind and are for confirming that the instructional

> The wall of the eyeball consists of three membranes which differ morphologically and functionally in the front and back parts.
> The exterior membrane (tunica fibrosa bulbi) consists of a transparent, avascular **Hornhaut**, the cornea, and the **Lederhaut**, the sclera. The sclera is very stable and is responsible for the shape of the eye.
> The middle membrane (tunica vasculosa bulbi), on the inside of the sclera, is a vascular membrane consisting of the choroid at the back and the ciliary body and the iris at the front. The ciliary body contains a muscle which controls the curvature of the lens thus regulating its refraction. The iris operates like a shutter, controlling the amount of light entering the eye.
> The interior membrane (tunica interna (sensoria) bulbi) is the interior surface of the eyeball. It is identical with the retina and consists of a light sensitive and a light insensitive part.

Fig. 8. Translation of contents of node presented when user is a beginner with no relevant knowledge.

> The wall of the eyeball consists of three membranes which differ morphologically and functionally in the front and back parts.
> The middle membrane (tunica vasculosa bulbi), on the inside of the sclera, is a vascular memrane consisting of the choroid at the back and the ciliary body and iris at the front. The ciliary body contains a muscle which controls the curvature of the lens thus regulating its refraction. The iris operates like a shutter, controlling the amount of light entering the eye.
> The interior membrane (tunica interna (sensoria) bulbi) is the interior surface of the eyeball. It is identical with the retina and consists of a light sensitive and a light insensitive part.

Fig. 9. Here, the user is a beginner who already has some information on the bulbus oculi (see text).

objectives (see Section 2) in the lessons have been attained. Not only do we get instant reliable feedback on the user's understanding, immediate active recollection is a recognised method of embedding information in the memory. When questions are posed by the system in hypermode, control is temporarily handed over to the question mode thus enabling the system to respond with all available pedagogical strategies, i.e. a wrong user answer can result in comments, additional questions, etc., from the system.

6.3. EXAMPLES

The following figures show how the actual displayed text relating to the concept "bulbus oculi" varies with the type and the assumed knowledge of the user. Figure 8 shows the text displayed for a beginner with no knowledge relating to bulbus oculi. In Figure 9, bulbus oculi is described to a user who knows the various parts of the bulbus oculi by name. Since we have statistically determined that most learners who have delved into the subject deep enough to know these names also know that

> The tunica fibrosa bulbi consists of the transparent, vascular cornea and the whitish sclera.
> Because of its stability the sclera can be thought of as giving the eye it's shape.
> The tunica vasculosa bulbi is a vascular membrane immediately on the inside of the sclera,
> consisting of the choroid at the back and the ciliary body and iris at the front. The corpus ciliare
> contains a muscle which controls the curvature of the lens thus regulating its refraction. The iris
> operates like a shutter, controlling the amount of light entering the eye.
> The tunica interna (sensoria) bulbi is the interior surface of the eyeball. It is identical with the
> retina and consists of the pars caeca and the pars optica.

Fig. 10. Translation of contents of node presented to a more advanced learner with no knowledge relevant to the eyeball (bulbus oculi). The underlined words represent anchors (see text).

the external layer gives the eye its shape, we spare the user with this information. Figure 10 shows the text for an advanced student who is learning this particular subject for the first time.

Texts for more advanced learners contain more "medical latin" than those for beginners. (The difference is more pronounced in German than in English, and whereas doctors would speak of the **retina,** for example, someone not in the medical profession would speak of the **Netzhaut.** Both words would be translated as "retina" in English. We have left the German terms untranslated (bold italics) in second paragraph in Figure 8 to give an idea of the original formulation.)

The fields "retina" and "pars optica" (indicated by underlining in Figure 10) allow the user to request more information on the objects named.

The user can also request all available information on the bulbus oculi.

7. Conclusions

ANATOM-TUTOR is a teaching aid - i.e. it was designed not to replace but to assist teachers by taking over the burden of routine teaching duties such as imparting basic knowledge to students, thus leaving them with more time to attend to problems requiring the abilities which (now and in the foreseeable future) only human teachers possess. The author believes that, while the construction of an electronic tutoring system that is in any way comparable to a human teacher is a long way off, techniques which are available to us now can improve the effectiveness of education, allowing smaller classes, more productive lessons, and more flexible timetables. Moreover, applying new media to education will in itself diversify lessons and help stimulate student interest.

The importance of interpersonal relationships in human psychological development, and in education in particular, has often been stressed, and we believe that, far from computers de-personalizing education, the time gained for the teacher can result in increased contact between the teacher and individual pupils. We have noted in our university test sessions that although the system was designed with single users in mind, students often prefer to work in small groups. Various authors have commented on the phenomenon that computers in class, far from inducing isolation, tend to stimulate student joint activity. Crook (1990), for example, cites LOGO being used with 8- to 11-year-olds over a six week period and states that observers noted "computer activity proved especially potent in facilitating collaborative exchanges". This may also have implications for the construction of future user modelling components in ITSs, since a general tendency in CAI applications, or at least in CAI as applied to certain subjects, to work in groups will limit the types of information we want to gather about "the" user. Monitoring individual capabilities and affective factors will be less applicable, and complex tracking as described above less feasible and desirable than at present. On the other hand stereotype revision, for example, will probably be facilitated since individual extremes will tend to be smoothed out before answers are typed in, which will result in more homogeneous "user" classes and consequently better convergence of weights.

Most work in ITSs seems to have been done in procedure systems (as opposed to expository systems like ANATOM-TUTOR). Interestingly, Spencer (1991) quotes Piaget as stating that teaching machines are better suited to figurative knowledge than to operational knowledge. Generally the knowledge treated in expository systems can be kept within the bounds of the figurative, while much procedural knowledge seems to require a deeper understanding of the domain, and thus belongs more in the realms of the operational. Although it can be argued that procedural knowledge is more challenging and may ultimately lead to greater insights in understanding the mind, we believe that greater benefits can be had for education by taking the expository tack in ITSs and integrating them into existing systems of education, leaving operational aspects largely to human teachers.

The author is not aware of any other work in which a user model has been simultaneously combined with hypertext and an ITS or in which a hypertext system has been equipped to offer custom-tailored explanations and auxiliary questions on encountering user misconceptions, nor (looking at things from a pedagogical point of view) is he aware of a user model having been used with self-directed and guided approaches to instruction simultaneously.

References

Anderson, J. R.: 1988, 'The expert Module'. In: M. C. Polson and J. J. Richardson (eds.): *Foundations of Intelligent Tutoring Systems*. Hillsdale, NJ: Lawrence Erlbaum, pp. 21–53.

Boy, G.: 1991, 'On-line User Model Acquisition in Hypertext Documentation'. In: *Proceedings of the IJCAI Workshop* W4: Agent Modelling for Intelligent Interaction, Sydney, Australia, pp. 34–42.

Boyle, C. and A. Encarnacion: 1991, 'A User Model Based Hypertext Documentation System'. In: *Proceedings of the IJCAI Workshop*, pp. 43–65 (The system is also described in: C. Boyle and A. O. Encarnacion: 1994, 'Meta-Doc: An Adaptive Hypertext Reading System'. *User Modeling and User-Adapted Interaction*, 4(1), 1–19. The latter paper is reprinted in this volume, pp. 71–89).

Brownston, L., et al.: 1985, *Programming Expert Systems in Ops5*. Reading, Massachusetts: Addison-Wesley.

Chin, D.: 1986, 'User Modelling in UC: the Unix Consultant'. In *Proceedings of the CHI-86 Conference, Boston*.

Crook, C.: 1990, 'Computers in the Classroom'. In: O. Boyd-Barret and E. Scanlon (eds): *Computers and Learning*. Addison-Wesley.

de Rosis, F., A. Russo, D. Berry, F. J. N. Molina: 1992, 'Modeling the User Knowledge by Belief Networks'. *User Modeling and User-Adapted Interaction* 2, 367–388.

Duus, P.: 1990, *Neurologisch-topische Diagnostik*. Stuttgart: Thieme Verlag.

Finin, T.: 1989, 'GUMS - A General User Modeling Shell'. In: A. Kobsa and W. Wahlster, *User Models in Dialog Systems*, Springer Verlag, pp. 411–430.

Feneis, H.: 1988, *Anatomisches Bildwoerterbuch*. Stuttgart: Thieme Verlag.

Forssmann, W. G. and Chr. Heym: 1975, *Grundriss der Neuroanatomie*. Springer Verlag.

Gagne, R.: 1977, *The Conditions of Learning*. New York: Holt, Rinehart, and Winston.

Halff, H. M.: 1988, 'Curriculum and Instruction in Automated Tutors'. In: M. C. Polson and J. J. Richardson (eds.): *Foundations of Intelligent Tutoring Systems*. Hillsdale, NJ: Lawrence Erlbaum, pp. 79–108.

Kahle, W., H. Leonhardt and W. Platzer: 1979, *Nervensystem und Sinnesorgane*. Stuttgart: Thieme Verlag.

Katz, S. and A. Lesgold: 1991, 'Modelling The Student in Sherlock II'. In: *Proceedings of the IJCAI Workshop* W4: Agent Modelling for Intelligent Interaction, Sydney, Australia, pp. 93–128.

Kobsa, A. and W. Wahlster: 1989, *User Models in Dialog Systems*, Heidelberg: Springer Verlag.

Lesgold, A.: 1988, 'Toward a Theory of Curriculum for Use in Designing Intelligent Instructional Systems'. In: A. Lesgold and H. Mandl, *Learning Issues for Intelligent Tutoring Systems*. New York: Springer Verlag, pp. 114–137.

Nieuwenhuys, R., J. Voogd, and Chr. van Huijzen: 1988, *The Human Central Nervous System*. Springer Verlag.

Orwant, J.: 1991, 'The Doppelganger User Modeling System'. In: *Proceedings of the IJCAI Workshop* W4: Agent Modelling for Intelligent Interaction, Sydney, Australia, pp. 164–168.

Paris, C.: 1989, 'The Use of Explicit User Models in a Generation System for Tailoring Answers to the User's Level of Expertise'. In: A. Kobsa and W. Wahlster, *User Models in Dialog Systems*, Heidelberg: Springer Verlag, pp. 200–232.

Polson, M. and J. J. Richardson: 1988, *Intelligent Tutoring Systems*. New Jersey: Lawrence Erlbaum Associates.

Leonhardt, H., G. Toendury and K. Zilles (eds.): 1987, *Anatomie des Menschen, Band III*. Stuttgart: Thieme Verlag.

Rich, E.: 1979, 'User Modeling via Stereotypes', *Cognitive Science* 3, 329–354.

Rich, E.: 1989, 'Stereotypes and User Modeling'. In: A. Kobsa and W. Wahlster, *User Models in Dialog Systems*, Heidelberg: Springer Verlag, pp. 35–51.

Rothstein, P.: 1990, *Educational Psychology*. New York: McGraw-Hill.

Sandberg, J.: 1987, *The Third International Conference on Artificial Intelligence and Education*, AICOM.

Self, J.: 1988, 'Bypassing the Intractable Problem of Student Modelling'. In: *Proceedings of the 1st Int. Conf. on Intelligent Tutoring Systems*, Montreal, pp. 18–24.

Shifroni, E. and B. Shanon: 1992, 'Interactive User Modeling'. *User Modeling and User-Adapted Interaction* 2, 331–365.

Spencer, K.: 1991, *The Psychology of Educational Technology and Instructional Media*. Liverpool: United Writers Press.

VanLehn, K.: 1988, 'Student Modelling'. In M. C. Polson and J. J. Richardson (eds.): *Foundations of Intelligent Tutoring Systems*. Hillsdale, NJ: Lawrence Erlbaum, pp. 55–78.

Author's Vita

Beaumont

I. Beaumont received his degree in Mathematics and Computer Science at the University of Kiel, Germany, and is currently a researcher and project coordinator at the Fraunhofer-Institut. Mr. Beaumont's involvement in artificial intelligence includes work in knowledge representation, user modelling, and intelligent tutoring systems. His contribution summarizes the current state of a project in intelligent tutoring being conducted at the Fraunhofer-Institut.

Hypadapter: An Adaptive Hypertext System for Exploratory Learning and Programming

HUBERTUS HOHL[*,1], HEINZ-DIETER BÖCKER[2] and
RUL GUNZENHÄUSER[3]

[1]University of Stuttgart, Department of Computer Science, Breitwiesenstr. 20–22, D-70565
Stuttgart, Germany, E-mail: hohl@informatik.uni-stuttgart.de; [2]GMD IPSI, Dolivostr. 15, D-64293
Darmstadt, Germany, E-mail: boecker@darmstadt.gmd.de; [3]University of Stuttgart, Department of
Computer Science, Breitwiesenstr. 20-22, D-70565 Stuttgart, Germany, E-mail:
rul@informatik.uni-stuttgart.de

(Received 23 January 1995; accepted 14 March 1995)

Abstract. We have developed an adaptive hypertext system designed to individually support exploratory learning and programming activities in the domain of Common Lisp. Endowed with domain-specific knowledge represented in a hyperspace of topics, the system builds up a detailed model of the user's expertise which it utilizes to provide personalized assistance. Unlike other work emerging in the field of adaptive hypertext systems, our approach exploits domain and user modelling techniques to support individuals in different ways. The system not only generates individualized presentations of topic nodes, but also provides adaptive navigational assistance for link-based browsing. By identifying and suggesting useful hyperlinks according to the user's knowledge state and preferences, the system encourages and guides exploration. While browsing through the hyperspace of topics, the system analyses the user's navigational behaviour to infer the user's learning progress and to dynamically adapt presentations of topics and links accordingly.

Key words: adaptive hypertext systems, adaptive navigational support, adaptive presentation techniques, exploratory learning and programming, personal assistants, user modelling, information exploration, information filtering, Common Lisp

1. Introduction

Today, the long-standing, clear-cut distinction between learning and working activities has become blurred in a variety of areas of computer usage. As application areas broaden and application systems increase in size, functionality, and complexity, the classical model of teaching embodied by computer-based instructional systems is no longer sufficient to cope with and, eventually, master these application systems. Instead, learning about the application domain and about software usage increasingly "happens" on the fringe of actual work processes: Users gain new insight while working out solutions, while recovering from breakdown situations, while participating and collaborating in groups, while searching and exploring problem spaces, etc. Thereby, learning and working tasks become tightly interwined;

---

* First author's new address: Siemens AG, ZFE T SN 5, D-81730 München, E-mail: hubertus.hohl@zfe.siemens.de

P. Brusilovsky et al. (eds.), Adaptive Hypertext and Hypermedia, 117–142.
© 1998 *Kluwer Academic Publishers.*

embedded strategies such as *learning by doing*, *learning on demand*, and *learning by discovery* become common practice. To successfully support these incremental learning processes, there is a need for software systems to change character from merely providing tools to also providing intelligent personal assistants that enhance and extend human problem solving capabilities and individually support the much larger and more diverse population that increasingly gains access to computers.

A general framework for integrating learning and working processes in the context of design is described in (Fischer 1995). Designing artifacts is an evolutionary process in which all participants continue to learn new information and insights as the process unfolds. Fischer argues that one of the benefits of integrating learning and working is the potential increase in motivation. Users are willing and motivated to learn when (1) they actively desire and control learning, (2) they are successful in finding and using new information, (3) they can see the immediate benefit of learning something new to their working situation, and (4) their environments are intrinsically motivating and allow them to achieve interesting results with a reasonably small effort.

With the introduction of hypertext, computer-based learning environments have emerged that encourage *exploratory learning* (Jonassen and Mandl 1990). Exploratory learning styles can be characterized by self-initiated, goal-oriented activities to explore a problem domain modelled as a hyperspace of interrelated concepts and topics. Users independently discover information in the hyperspace which is necessary for the immediate solution of their current problem and acquire new domain knowledge by incrementally extending their understanding of known subdomains.

Due to the inherent problems of disorientation and cognitive overload in hypertext, it is usually argued that the freedom of exploration will result in suboptimal learning behaviour (Hammond and Allinson 1989). Hypertext systems face these problems by providing navigational assistance to complement link-based browsing with various real-world navigational metaphors, such as overview maps, footprints, interaction histories, and guided tours for newcomers (Nielsen 1990). However, as a rule, approaches such as these only provide uniform, passive support, not taking the individual's learning and navigational behaviour into account.

With the introduction of adaptive and adaptable system technologies (Schneider-Hufschmidt *et al.* 1993), it seems reasonable to enhance hypertext environments by components that realize the metaphor of a knowledgeable personal assistant. Endowed with domain-specific knowledge about the application and the user, such personal assistants have the potential to support exploratory activities for various levels of knowledge and skills. They can modify their own behaviour, providing customized navigational assistance based on the hypothesized expertise, goals, and needs of the user. They can sense the direction in which the user is working, criticize and correct the user's actual navigational behaviour, suggest useful information not presently known or used, and participate actively in accomplishing tasks. Moreover, by making personal assistants adaptable , they can be adjusted to conform to a user's individual way of learning and doing things.

In this article, we present an adaptive as well as adaptable hypertext system that simultaneously supports exploratory learning and working activities in the domain of programming. The evolution of modern programming environments results in large-scale, high-functionality systems that tend to become unusable because of their size and structural complexity. Advanced interactive object-oriented programming environments, such as VisualWorks (1992) for Smalltalk and CLIM/CLOS for Common Lisp (Steele Jr. 1990), confront programmers with object libraries including thousands of elementary programming units, such as variables, functions, methods, classes, and instances; thousands of chunks of knowledge to be comprehended and, eventually, applied by the programmer.

On the other hand, empirical studies show that programmers effectively use only a small subset of the functionality offered by complex programming systems (Fischer et al. 1985). Also, as has been shown empirically by Fix et al. (1993), programmers with different expertise form different mental representations of program structures. Thus, programmers can be considered truly individuals, seriously differing with respect to programming skills, programming styles, domain knowledge, intentions, and interests (Wender et al. 1995).

Our ultimate objective is to build knowledge-based support systems that act as personal programming assistants when needed. They will have to be flexible enough to adapt to their users' view of the world, generating individualized presentations of information structures and guiding exploratory learning and programming activities. They could also play an active role in knowledge acquisition and transfer by pointing to unknown or unused functionality needed by the programmer to solve the problem at hand.

2. The HYPADAPTER system

The HYPADAPTER system is a first approach to some of the questions posed. HYPADAPTER is an *adaptive* as well as *adaptable* hypertext system designed to individually support exploratory learning and programming activities in the domain of Common Lisp. By using a highly-structured knowledge base of interlinked topics about the Common Lisp domain as a reference point, the system builds up a detailed model of the user's expertise, which it utilizes to provide personalized assistance. The characteristic features of the system can be summarized as follows:

- Individualized presentations of topics and links are tailored to the user's knowledge state and preferences.
- Presentations are dynamically adapted to the user's learning progress which is traced by the system.
- At any time, users have control over the adaptive behaviour of the system. The system is adaptable in that users can modify and overwrite system-inferred

assessments concerning their expertise as well as tailor various presentation-specific aspects to meet their needs.
- While exploring the hyperspace of topics, individual navigational support is provided by the system, allowing users to lay out and maintain their personal paths through the hyperspace.
- Exploratory learning activities are complemented by "learning by examples" and "learning by doing" strategies.

The rest of this article describing HYPADAPTER is organized as follows: First, we show the system in use with screen snapshots illustrating typical user-specific interactions and views of the user interface. We then explain the conceptual background, intrinsics, and behaviour of the system in detail with an architectural model. Finally, we compare our approach to related work in the field of adaptive hypertext systems, discussing current limitations and further prospects for adaptive support in the context of exploratory learning and programming environments.

2.1. HYPADAPTER FROM THE OUTSIDE

Typical users of the HYPADAPTER system are programmers with different programming skills in Common Lisp. To demonstrate the system's adaptability the following dialogue scenarios refer to two of them: *Fred*, a beginner programmer who is just familiar with the basic concepts of Common Lisp, and *Barney*, an experienced Common Lisp expert programmer.

2.1.1. *Acquiring User Characteristics*

In HYPADAPTER, user characteristics concerning programming skills in Common Lisp provide the basis for system-initiated adaptations. The system can infer some of these properties automatically, such as individual knowledge levels of topics, by assigning users to stereotypes and by monitoring users' navigational behaviour with respect to visited topics. To arrive at reasonable initial classifications, users have to self-assess their expertise. These statements are made with the *personal questionnaires* depicted in Figures 1 and 2. Questionnaires not only support self-assessments; they provide a means of controlling and customizing various aspects of the hypertext system based on the user's personal preferences concerning the presentation of learning material. Users should fill in their questionnaire at the beginning of the first session. However, entries can be modified dynamically at any time to express changing needs regarding further adaptations. The system provides reasonable defaults for entries which are left open initially and which can later be overwritten by the user.

2.1.2. *Accessing and Exploring the Hyperspace of Topics*

Programming knowledge about Common Lisp is represented internally as a semantic net of interrelated *topics*, discrete learnable entities referring to particular pro-

Please fill in your personal questionnaire:

☐ *Personal Data*
First Name: Fred
Last Name: Flintstone
Nickname: *your nickname*

Information associated with Computers
General Computer Experience: None **Average** Much
Knowledge about Computers and Operating Systems:

	unknown	unfamiliar	familiar	known
Homecomputer	☐	☐	☐	☒
PC	☐	☐	☒	☐
Vax	☒	☐	☐	☐
Sun	☐	☒	☐	☐
Lisp-Machine	☒	☐	☐	☐
MS/DOS	☐	☐	☒	☐
VMS	☒	☐	☐	☐
UNIX	☐	☒	☐	☐
Genera	☒	☐	☐	☐

Information about CommonLisp Experience
General Lisp Usage: Never **Seldom** Normal Often
Lisp Qualification: Novice Beginner Intermediate Expert **Let it happen**

Tutorial Information
Overall Interest: Curious **If-Needed** Conservative
Desired Detail: Short **Broad** Deep
Preferred Explanation Styles:

	prohibit	dislike	like	require
Show Links	☐	☐	☒	☐
Show Notes	☐	☐	☒	☐
Show Examples	☐	☐	☒	☐

Done   Abort

According to his questionnaire, Fred characterizes himself as an average programmer seldom programming in Lisp. Fred leaves it up to the system to assess his Lisp qualification grade. By default, the system treats any new user as a "novice" initially. Fred regards himself a practical learner, strictly concentrating on topics that are needed immediately to perform the current task. He likes broad explanations of tutorial material covering examples, additional notes, and links to related topics.

Figure 1. Fred's personal questionnaire.

gramming concepts and functions. HYPADAPTER provides a direct manipulation, graphical user interface that mainly supports selection-oriented interaction techniques to access and explore the knowledge base.

By means of *topic browsers*, users navigate through the universe of interconnected topics. Inside a topic browser, topics are arranged and presented in *viewers* – multiple, overlapping windows of arbitrary size on screen. Every viewer chronologically maintains and provides access to its own linear history of topics previously visited. By means of multiple viewers and topic histories users can individually

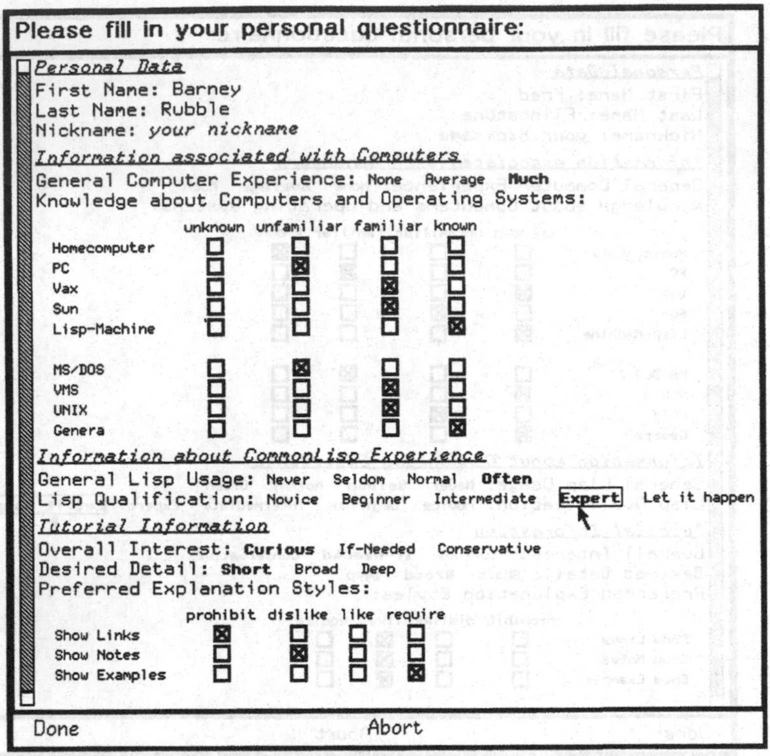

```
Please fill in your personal questionnaire:

□Personal Data
 First Name: Barney
 Last Name: Rubble
 Nickname: your nickname
 Information associated with Computers
 General Computer Experience: None  Average  Much
 Knowledge about Computers and Operating Systems:

                  unknown unfamiliar familiar known
   Homecomputer      □        □         □      □
   PC                □        ⊠         □      □
   Vax               □        □         ⊠      □
   Sun               □        □         ⊠      □
   Lisp-Machine      □        □         □      ⊠

   MS/DOS            □        ⊠         □      □
   VMS               □        □         ⊠      □
   UNIX              □        □         ⊠      □
   Genera            □        □         □      ⊠
 Information about CommonLisp Experience
 General Lisp Usage: Never  Seldom  Normal  Often
 Lisp Qualification: Novice  Beginner  Intermediate  Expert  Let it happen
 Tutorial Information
 Overall Interest: Curious  If-Needed  Conservative
 Desired Detail: Short  Broad  Deep
 Preferred Explanation Styles:

                  prohibit dislike like require
   Show Links        ⊠        □      □     □
   Show Notes        □        ⊠      □     □
   Show Examples     □        □      □     ⊠

 Done                        Abort
```

Barney identifies himself as an experienced Lisp expert. By giving an explicit "expert" qualification grade he assures that he is classified as an expert by the system initially. Barney is especially open to additional sources for help and potentially interesting information. Barney prefers concise presentations including programming examples that demonstrate the use of topics.

Figure 2. Barney's personal questionnaire.

arrange topics according to specific criteria, organize and maintain their private paths through the space of topics, backtrack to previously visited places, and explore alternatives.

Navigation by link-based browsing is the primary means for accessing information from the knowledge base. However, HYPADAPTER provides additional navigational support, addressing the well-known problems of disorientation and cognitive overload while browsing and encouraging information exploration without penalty (Conklin 1987) (see Figure 3):

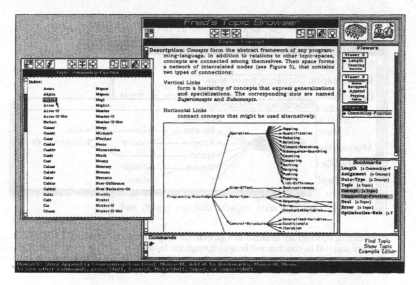

Figure 3. Topic browser with navigational facilities.

Topic browsers, as shown on the right side, integrate an embedded viewer, a graphical menu of viewers, a menu of bookmarks, and a command-based interface. The graphical menu of viewers offers a dynamic overview of all the viewers currently open together with parts of their current topic histories. By selecting an item from the menu the corresponding viewer can be popped up, hidden, or destroyed. Inside a viewer, control buttons (arranged in the middle of the header pane) can be invoked to step through the local history of topics. Besides offering embedded hypertext links within topic presentations, graphical knowledge maps (shown in the embedded viewer) and tabular indexes (shown in the viewer on the left side) can be used to directly access specific topics. The command-based interface complements navigation by allowing users to look up particular topics known by name. Completion for partial names is supported.

- Retrospective access to topics is provided by topic histories which record presentations of previously visited topics.

- Structure-oriented access to topics is supplied by *knowledge maps* which provide local or global graphical overviews of parts of the underlying knowledge base structure. Knowledge maps can be embedded in topic presentations (see Figure 3) or opened inside pop-up windows if needed (see Figure 4).

- Direct access to topics is provided by alphabetically sorted *indexes*.

- Personalized access to topics is supplied by user-defined *bookmarks*. Bookmarks provide a way to keep track of important points in a user's browsing session that can be accessed directly at a later time. By defining bookmarks users build a personal trail of important topics that have been visited already or might become interesting in the near future.

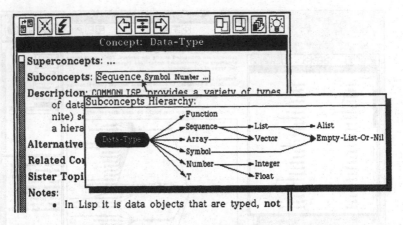

Programming concepts are arranged in a generalization/specialization heterarchy. Local knowledge maps are supplied to visualize and browse through the layers of super- and subconcepts. The map of subconcepts shown was activated by selecting the `subconcepts` field included in the topic presentation. By clicking on an item in the map the corresponding topic can be presented in a viewer

Figure 4. Local knowledge map for the programming concept `data-type`.

– Query-based access to topics partially known by name is provided by a
  command-based interface.

HYPADAPTER offers point-and-click navigation within the hyperspace of topics. To uniformly access the navigational facilities, links to topics are presented as active hypertext fields showing the topics' names. These visual references are either embedded in textual explanations within a topic or presented as sensitive items of topic histories, knowledge maps, index menus, or bookmark menus. By pressing different mouse buttons on a reference, the associated topic can be presented inside the current viewer, inside any other existing viewer, inside a new viewer, or it can be added to the menu of bookmarks.

2.1.3. *Individualizing the Presentation of Topics and Links*

An essential property of HYPADAPTER is its ability to adapt presentations of topics *and* links to individual users. Going beyond conventional hypertext systems like the Document Examiner (Symbolics 1988) – a help system that provides online access to the user manuals of Symbolics Lisp machines – the system acts as an adaptive visual information filter that dynamically highlights relevant information and puts less important aspects in the background. Thereby, the system not only adapts to different users but also takes the user's individual learning progress into account.

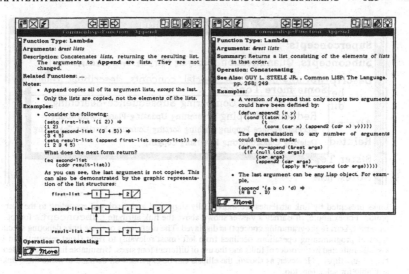

Regarding the topic append (a Common Lisp function) typical differences in presentation with respect to content and level of detail can be identified for Fred (left viewer) and Barney (right viewer). Fred, who visits the topic for the first time, is characterized as a Lisp beginner. Thus, the contents of descriptive attributes, such as *description, notes*, and *examples*, are tailored for beginners. According to his questionnaire, Barney is characterized as an experienced and curious programmer who likes concise presentations and prefers examples. Thus, Barney's view is mainly restricted to a short summary, expert-tailored examples, and a precise literary reference to external information sources. In any case, all less- or non-relevant attributes are "hidden" behind an icon which can be expanded on demand to selectively zoom into additional information left out in the initial presentation of the topic.

Figure 5. Individualized presentation of topics.

In HYPADAPTER, topics are represented as semistructured entities comprised of a set of attribute-value pairs describing inherent properties and functionality. Every topic includes *descriptive attributes* providing different kinds of textual and graphical explanations, examples, notes, and summaries. Semantic relations between topics are represented by *link attributes* which, for example, refer to content-related topics, superior topics, alternative topics, or sister topics that should be learned together.

Whenever a topic is presented at the user interface the system dynamically determines an appropriate subset of attributes to be displayed depending on user characteristics. Figure 5 shows how individual differences affect the selection and visual order of attributes, as well as the presentation of their values.

HYPADAPTER not only supports the user-tailored selection and adaptation of descriptive attributes but also of link attributes. The reason for link adaptation is to

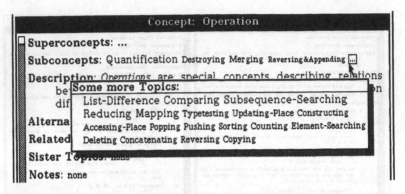

Figure 6. Individualized presentation of links.

Links presented by link attributes are individually suggested and displayed according to the user's profile. For example, in Barney's viewer shown above the link attribute subconcepts for topic operation (a programming concept) is displayed. The usefulness of these links denoting special types of programming operations declines from left (most relevant) to right (least relevant) and is visually reflected in the order of links and the use of different font sizes. Unsuitable links are "hidden" behind an ellipsis. However, as shown, the ellipsis can be expanded on demand to make these links available for selection, too.

suggest references to topics that might be relevant or interesting for users according to their current expertise (see Figure 6). The system tries to incrementally broaden users' knowledge horizons, taking care not to confront them with learning material that does not match their skills. To realize this kind of adaptation the system traces the progress of individual users.

2.1.4. Supporting Active Learning

Examples play a crucial role in learning and programming (Rissland 1984; Neal 1989). Beginners often reuse code examples from tutorials and manuals as templates for standard programming exercises. More advanced programmers tend to use code examples as structural frameworks for developing their own programs (Redmiles 1989). Moreover, code examples serve as reminders for syntactic language constructs.

HYPADAPTER emphasizes example-based and action-oriented learning strategies. Descriptive topic attributes may contain Lisp code that can be evaluated and manipulated by the user (see Figure 7). By supporting a motivating "learning by doing" mode users are encouraged to get hands-on experience with stated problems and develop and test solutions on their own to gain a deeper understanding of the programming domain.

The seamless integration of editing and programming tools into the hypertext learning environment has been achieved straightforwardly. Common Lisp not only

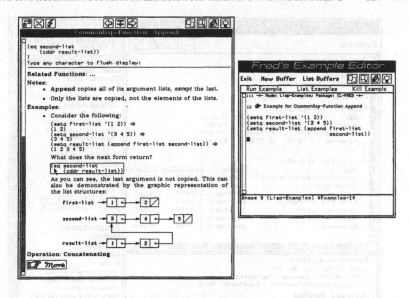

HYPADAPTER supports example-based learning by supplying topics with attributes that contain examples, especially Lisp code. Code examples are active: by clicking the mouse on them, code can be evaluated (the results are displayed in a temporary pop-down window) or copied into an example-editor for further experimentation. The integrated example-editor provides a high-functionality Emacs-like environment for writing and testing lisp programs. This editor serves as a "playground" that motivates programmers to pose "What if . . . ?" questions easily.

Figure 7. Evaluating and editing programming examples.

provides the application domain but also the implementational platform for the HYPADAPTER system. It is composed of several subsystems for knowledge representation, user modelling, and user interface design that are built on the Common Lisp programming environment of a Symbolics Lisp machine. Thus, interactively evaluating or manipulating Lisp programs by calling the Common Lisp interpreter or an editor at run time is an easy matter.

2.1.5. *Making User Characteristics Transparent*

To avoid acceptance problems user characteristics modelled by the system must be made transparent to and controllable by the user. HYPADAPTER provides a *user model inspector* which gives users insight into the actual state of their model, discloses stereotypical classifications, and lets them customize certain aspects of their models (see Figure 8).

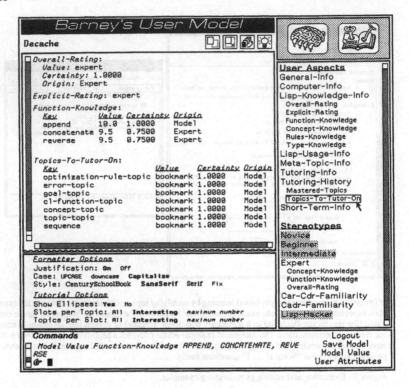

The user model inspector, shown here using Barney as an example, lets users query the values o individual model aspects, such as the actual knowledge level of topics, stereotypical properties, the user's current membership in stereotypes, and personal preferences with regard to presentations Models can be loaded on demand and saved for future sessions. As shown previously, certain mode aspects can be changed interactively by invoking a personal questionnaire from inside the mode inspector.

Figure 8. Barney's User Model Inspector.

2.2. INSIDE HYPADAPTER

In the following, we take a closer look at the conceptual and architectural underpinnings that characterize the adaptive behaviour of HYPADAPTER described previously. The implementation pursues an integrated approach to enhancing an elaborate hypertext environment with frame-based knowledge representation and user modelling techniques.

The architectural model of the system can be characterized as displayed in Figure 9: The available space of topics describing the Common Lisp applica-

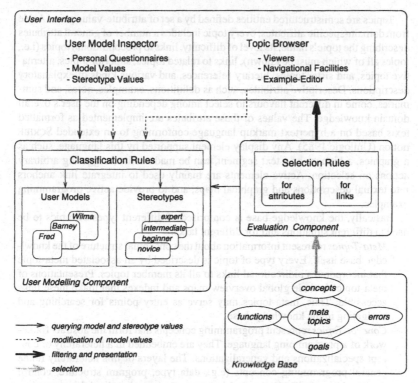

Figure 9. Architecture of HYPADAPTER.

tion domain is represented in a highly-structured *knowledge base*. Topic browsers provide navigational access to and individualized visualizations of topics. The presentation of topics is controlled by an *evaluation component* that identifies and filters topic attributes and links based on *selection rule sets* that refer to individual and stereotypical user characteristics maintained by a *user modelling component*. User models are dynamically adjusted or revised by analysing the navigational behaviour of individual users.

2.2.1. *The Knowledge Base*

The knowledge base models part of the programming knowledge relevant for Common Lisp programming. It is structured as a network of *topics*, the smallest chunks of information that signify or denote an understanding by a user and have meaning by themselves.

Topics are semistructured entities defined by a set of attribute-value pairs. Aside from domain-specific attributes, every topic includes a number of general attributes describing the topic's name, its level of difficulty, links to preconditional topics (i.e., topics all of which must be known), links to related topics, superior topics, alternative topics, and sister topics, literary references, and various kinds of explanatory descriptions. Descriptive attributes, such as definitions, examples, notes, and summaries, come in different flavours to select among depending on the user's overall domain knowledge. The values of these attributes are implemented as formatted texts based on a hypertext markup language conforming to an extended SCRIBE notion (Unilogic 1985). Any display element supported by this language, such as a graphics, a bitmap, or a text segment, can be made active, triggering arbitrary actions on selection. Active elements are mainly used to integrate link anchors into textual descriptions and graphical maps, and to provide active programming examples.

Basically, the knowledge base is comprised of different types of topics to be used in different situations and for different tasks:

- *Meta-Topics* represent information about the conceptual structure of the knowledge base itself. Every type of topic is described by an associated meta-topic that incorporates bidirectional links to all its member topics. Presentations of meta-topics include global overview maps and indexes that make these links accessible. Thus, meta-topics may serve as entry points for searching and navigating in the knowledge base.
- *Concept-Topics* represent programming concepts that form the abstract framework of a programming language. They are embedded in a heterarchy of concept specializations and generalizations. The layers of this heterarchy refine general programming concepts (e.g., data type, program structure, control structure) to specific Common Lisp concepts (e.g., list, lambda expression, macro, consing, mapping).
- *Function-Topics* describe information about built-in Common Lisp functions (including macros and special forms).
- *Goal-Topics* specify normative categories a Lisp programmer might adhere to, concerning stylistic characteristics, efficiency issues, and the preferential use of particular language constructs. These stereotypical aspects are intended to be part of user models that represent a programmer's preferred programming styles and intentions.
- *Optimization-Rule-Topics* describe transformation rules for optimizing program code according to the guidelines specified by goal-topics. These topics can be applied by code optimization components.
- *Error-Topics* describe typical programming errors concerning specific language constructs that can be detected by automatic program analysers, such as off-by-one offset errors and wrong order/type of argument errors.

For exploratory learning, users interactively explore the space of meta-topics, concept-topics and function-topics. The other types of topics are intended to be exploited by task modelling components, active help facilities, and code analysers that observe actual programming behaviour, help in breakdown situations, and provide active critiques and hints for code improvement.

2.2.2. The User Modelling Component

In HYPADAPTER, modelling the user's background and behaviour is the key to generating individualized presentations of topics and links. Typical user characteristics modelled by the system include personal data, programming competence and expertise, the actual knowledge states of topics, personal annotations, such as topics declared as bookmarks, and personal interests and preferences regarding presentational aspects, such as preferred explanation styles and detail levels.

The user modelling component of HYPADAPTER is based on MODUS, a general, application-independent user modelling framework described in (Schwab 1989). HYPADAPTER builds up and exploits *dynamic, individual user models* (Rich 1983) that can be characterized as follows:

- Each and every user is assigned a separate user model that, among other things, includes an overlay model representing the user's knowledge levels of individual topics.
- User models are initialized by stereotypes but evolve individually as users perform interactions.
- Various aspects of user models can be directly manipulated by their users during a session.
- User models are persistent between sessions; long-term user aspects will be reused in later sessions.

HYPADAPTER employs *stereotypes* (Rich 1983) to handle stereotypical knowledge about programming concepts and functions in Common Lisp. Currently, the system makes use of four stereotypes: *novice*, *beginner*, *intermediate*, and *expert*. They model four levels of expertise by differentiating relative to the user's current knowledge state of topics. Every stereotype masters topics up to a fixed level of difficulty, as shown in Table I. By *classification rules* each user is assigned to exactly one of these stereotypes based on the information already represented in the user model(see Figure 10). Initially, users are assigned to the *novice* stereotype by default, if no further information is available.

User models are dynamic. The known facts about each user may change during the dialogue and the user may acquire new expertise while working with the system. The system takes these changes into account by dynamically adjusting user models and re-classifying users with respect to stereotypes in the course of a session. These adaptations immediately affect future presentations of topic attributes and links. Thus, a topic presented on the user interface may look different not only for different users but also for a single user at different times.

Specifically, system-initiated adaptations are triggered automatically by user-invoked events:

Table I. Stereotypes in HYPADAPTER

Knowledge level of topic depending on stereotype and difficulty

| | Stereotype | | | |
Level of Difficulty	*novice*	*beginner*	*intermediate*	*expert*
mundane	familiar	known	known	known
simple	unfamiliar	familiar	known	known
advanced	unknown	unfamiliar	familiar	known
complex	unknown	unknown	unfamiliar	familiar
esoteric	unknown	unknown	unknown	unfamiliar

```
(def-classify-rule specified-explicitly
  (:stereotype = expert)
  (:conditions = (eq (model-value :specified-qualification) :expert)))
(def-classify-rule sufficient-topic-knowledge
  (:stereotype = expert)
  (:conditions =
     (and (eq (model-value :specified-qualification) :let-it-happen)
          (at-least-model-values
             :count 15
             :in :topic-knowledge
             :with
             (lambda (key value)
               (>=knowledge value
                            (stereo-value :topic-knowledge :key key)))
  ))))
```

Users are mapped onto stereotypes by classification rules. According to the rules displayed above users are classified as belonging to the *expert* stereotype if (1) they explicitly insist on being treated as experts (as stated in their questionnaires) or (2) they do not make self-assessments but provide knowledge levels for a certain number of topics (at least 15) that equal or exceed those defined for the *expert* stereotype.

Figure 10. Classification rules for the *expert* stereotype.

- By following a topic reference, such as an embedded link or an item in a map or index, the user causes the associated topic to be presented in a viewer. Each such interaction leads to a slight increment of the topic's knowledge level – a numerical value ranging from 0 (unknown) to 10 (well-known) – stored in the user model. Triggered by this adjustment the user is eventually re-classified with respect to stereotype membership going through a transition from novice to expert. This approach to tracing learning progress depends on the debatable assumption that by reading topic descriptions users come to know the underlying subjects.

- Whenever a topic is added to the menu of bookmarks by the user it is also put high on a list of topics of high priority maintained by the user model. These topics, which might become potentially relevant or interesting for the user in

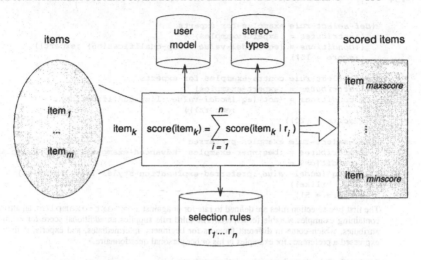

The process of evaluating topic attributes and links is based on a numerical relevance rating using selection rules. A set of items to be evaluated – either topic attributes or links – is transformed into a corresponding sequence ordered by relevance. For every item in the set all applicable selection rules are determined and applied. The total rating of an item is computed as the sum of the partial scores yielded by any single applicable rule with respect to the item. By ordering items according to their total ratings, an evaluation sequence is established that can be used by visualization components to visually order and filter topic attributes and links.

Figure 11. Evaluating topic attributes and links.

the near future, have a direct influence on the presentation of link attributes. This is described in detail in the following section.

2.2.3. *The Evaluation Component*

User models are exploited for dynamic topic and link presentation. Whenever a topic is presented in a viewer, an evaluation component identifies user-relevant topic attributes and links by applying *selection rules* to the topic-oriented model of the user's current knowledge state. Selection rules embody a model of teaching that is based on a scoring mechanism to determine those attributes and links that most closely match the user's needs and interests (see Figure 11). However, the user is never restricted to system-suggested information alone. Instead, the user may at any time zoom into additional information left out in the initial presentation of a topic.

To evaluate *descriptive attributes* a set of selection rules is defined according to the following aspects (see Figure 12):

```
(def-select-rule examples-for-experts
   (:attributes = :expert-examples)
   (:conditions = (eq (model-value :lisp-qualification) :expert))
   (:score = 15))

(def-select-rule contra-examples-for-experts
   (:attributes = :expert-examples)
   (:conditions = (not (eq (model-value :lisp-qualification)
                            :expert)))
   (:score = -20))

(def-select-rule examples-preferred
   (:attributes = :beginner-examples :advanced-examples :expert-examples)
   (:conditions =
      (eq (model-value :preferred-explanation-styles :key :examples)
          :like))
   (:score = 5))
```

The first two selection rules are defined to rate for or against :expert-examples, an attribute containing examples suitable for experts. The third rule supplies an additional score for example-attributes, which come in different flavours for beginners, intermediates, and experts, if the user expressed a preference for examples in his or her personal questionnaire.

Figure 12. Selection rules for descriptive attributes.

- The contents of attributes should correspond to the user's overall qualification. For example, explanations should be tailored to the user's current stereotype classification, ranging from novice to expert.
- The user's overall learning style and behaviour should be considered, presenting, for example, additional information to curious users.
- The user's preferences for certain attributes, such as examples or notes, should be taken into account.
- For explanations, different levels of detail, such as short summaries or in-depth descriptions, should be supplied according to the user's preferences.

To evaluate *link attributes* the system applies selection rules to topic references according to the following criteria (see Figure 13):

- Topics that are more or less mastered should be avoided.
- Topics requiring unknown previous knowledge should be avoided.
- Topics that are needed immediately should be preferred.
- Topics declared as bookmarks should be preferred because they might become potentially useful in the near future.
- Topics that closely relate to topics already known should be preferred.
- The topic's level of difficulty should match the user's qualification. For example, beginners should be protected from sophisticated topics.

The goal of these rules is to protect users from being confronted with information that is not consistent with their expertise and to support the incremental expansion of the user's knowledge space by topics that are ready to be learned. Learning material demanding too much or too little of the user is avoided in favour of

```
(def-select-rule easy-topic-for-beginners
  (:conditions =
     (and (eq (model-value :lisp-qualification) :beginner)
          (member (instance-value :level-of-difficulty)
                  '(:mundane :simple))))
  (:score = 10))

(def-select-rule avoid-known-topic
  (:conditions =
     (>=knowledge (model-value :topic-knowledge
                               :key (instance-value :self))
                  :known))
  (:score = -20))

(def-select-rule stress-high-priority-topic
  (:conditions = (member (instance-value :self)
                         (model-value :high-priority-topics)))
  (:score = 5))
```

The first selection rule provides a score for topics whose level of difficulty is suitable for beginners. The second rule provides a negative score for topics that are already known. The third rule provides an additional score for topics of high priority, such as topics that are contained in the user's menu of bookmarks.

Figure 13. Selection rules for link attributes.

topics that easily integrate new knowledge into the user's own understanding of the programming domain.*

3. Related Research

This section compares the HYPADAPTER approach with similar or alternative work in the field of adaptive systems focusing on two domains: programming support and information exploration.

3.1. ADAPTIVE APPROACHES TO PROGRAMMING SUPPORT

COgnitive Adaptive Computer Help (COACH) is an adaptive advisory system that supports Lisp programmers (Selker 1994). COACH watches the user's actions to build an explicit user model that records user-demonstrated experience and proficiency to create personalized interactive help. As the user is writing code, the system might choose to provide appropriate advice in the form of explanations, examples, usage and syntax information at four different levels of expertise. To this end, COACH models knowledge about the skill domain in terms of *learnable*

---

* This behaviour corresponds to the concept of "increasingly complex microworlds" described by Fischer (1988): The learning environment adapts to the learner's progress by incrementally disclosing valuable functionality of the application domain.

things, such as language elements, tokens, and concepts. User expertise with respect to learnable things is expressed in terms of *experience* (frequency of use), *latency* (how long it has been unused), *goodness* (user's overall performance), and *slope* (rate of change of goodness). Coaching knowledge is contained in *update rules*, *consistency rules*, and *presentation rules* that create and control the user model and determine the specific kind of help that will be provided to the user.

Viewing programming as a cooperative problem-solving process between user and computer, the work of Böcker (1988) identifies possible creative roles the computer could take on, such as constructively criticizing and commenting on user programs. The OPTIMIST system (Fischer 1987) assesses Lisp code written by the user and provides individualized suggestions for improvement. Based on *transformation rules*, program code is not only optimized according to global criteria, such as code efficiency, readability, and maintainability, but also with regard to individual programming styles, conventions, and preferences represented in a user model.

Systems such as COACH and OPTIMIST have taken the approach of providing adaptive agents that work in place of human coaches or assistants to give personalized instruction or advice while a programmer is actually working out solutions. Currently, HYPADAPTER does not support non-intrusive "teach while doing" approaches such as these. Instead, we utilize adaptation technologies to encourage and support exploration of domain knowledge by identifying and suggesting useful information sources. However, integrating active advisory-style help elements into HYPADAPTER – by exploiting the available domain and user modelling facilities – seems to be a promising approach towards a personal programmer's assistant that supports multiple, context-specific strategies for exploratory learning and programming.

3.2. ADAPTIVE APPROACHES TO INFORMATION EXPLORATION

In the last few years, adaptive hypertext systems have emerged that provide individualized presentations of information spaces by employing user modelling techniques (Brusilovsky 1996). In general, developments either focus on the adaptation of the contents of information nodes or on the adaptation of links.

As far as we know and according to a recent state of the art report on adaptive hypermedia systems by Brusilovsky (1996), HYPADAPTER to date is the only adaptive hypertext system that exploits user modelling for different purposes, namely for adaptive presentations of information nodes and for adaptive navigational support.

Systems such as that of Boyle and Encarnaçion (1994) and Beaumont (1994) concentrate on the adaptation of the textual contents of information nodes, composing differential descriptions or tailoring explanations to the expertise of individual users.

METADOC by Boyle and Encarnaçion (1994), an adaptive hypertext reading system in the domain of technical documentation, is typical of this category. META-

DOC explicitly represents knowledge about concepts in the UNIX programming domain. Driven by a user modelling component, document contents are tailored to the user's knowledge level of individual concepts. Based on a *stretchtext metaphor* adaptive textual descriptions featuring different levels of detail and explanation are generated. Stretchtext can be selectively expanded by the user to access further details.

Approaches to link adaptation are based on different information filtering techniques, providing individualized navigational support by filtering (presentations of) large-scale information spaces according to user characteristics.

Kaplan *et al.* (1993) present HYPERFLEX, an adaptive hypertext system that suggests information nodes by monitoring the navigational behaviour of other users that pursue similar goals and interests. Using associative matrices, the system records nodes typically visited by users showing specific interest profiles. By matching user profiles, the system identifies and suggests those nodes which closely correlate with the user's actual interests.

Nielsen (1990) suggests a similar approach to automatically generating filtered graphical overview diagrams. Based on a statistical analysis recording the frequency of path traversals by a group of users, well-travelled links are emphasized in the diagram while paths less frequented are candidates for pruning.

Not only presentations of information spaces but also the underlying information structures themselves may be subject to dynamic adaptation. The work of Stotts and Furuta (1991) is concerned with adapting hypertext structures to the behaviour and preferences exhibited by users while following links. As the user traverses the hypertext structure, hyperlinks are added or deleted dynamically, shortening, for example, the distance of traversal based on statistics of frequently travelled paths by individual users.

4. Conclusions and Future Directions

The basic contribution of HYPADAPTER to the field of exploratory learning and programming environments is the integration of dynamic, individual user modelling techniques with adaptive techniques for presentation and exploration. The HYPADAPTER system is a first step towards personalized programming assistants that simultaneously support learning as well as working processes. The following characteristics mainly influenced the design of the prototype system:

- The knowledge base of topics not only models the proper space of learning themes but also reflects its own conceptual structure explicitly by meta-topics. These meta level representations can support users by providing overviews and appropriate starting points for browsing. Additionally, meta-topics could be provided defining guided tours, tutorial elements, or instructional assistance for introductory Lisp programming.
- The system represents and reflects the different needs, knowledge levels, and the progress of individual users. For beginners the system may be useful as

an exploratory learning environment; for expert programmers the system may serve as an adaptive on-line manual for directly looking up expert-tailored descriptions of concepts and functions of Lisp.

- Learners incrementally explore the conceptual structure of the application domain. The individualized presentation of topics and links aims for disclosing useful domain knowledge step by step, explaining new concepts in terms of concepts already known and used.
- The system supports different inductive learning strategies in the context of exploratory programming: Learning by exploration, learning by examples, and learning by active experimentation and simulation. Other learning strategies, such as guided tours or tutorial lectures, can be integrated easily.
- Adaptive systems should not leave the user with a feeling of loss of control. Also, since adaptive systems cannot self-adapt appropriately in any situation, it is essential to provide flexible means for user-initiated customizations and corrections (Fischer 1993; Oppermann 1994). The controllability and acceptance of user modelling systems can be enhanced by giving the user insight into model values and making system-inferred classifications and assessments visible and subject to user-specific modifications. HYPADAPTER makes user models and stereotype classifications visible and accessible to their users through a direct-manipulation interface. Moreover, users are always in control of browsing through the hyperspace, deciding which link to follow on the basis of system-suggested references.

Currently, the domain model of the HYPADAPTER prototype is restricted to an important subdomain of Common Lisp, namely collection and list processing. In this context, preliminary system evaluations have posed questions and revealed prospects for future developments of the system addressing the following issues:

- The startup user models are rather primitive; more realistic ones can be seeded by feeding in information gathered from external information sources. For example, diagnostic code analysers that evaluate users' already existing programs can yield valuable input for differential initial user models and stereotype classifications.
- Currently, the system traces learning progress by straightforwardly incrementing the knowledge level of any *visited* topic. More realistic models of knowledge ratings could be arrived at by integrating a tutoring component that tries to figure out from tests whether a topic has been really understood. An alternative approach to tracing the user's level of experience is taken by Vassileva (1996): The user's navigation actions are recorded and checked for patterns which imply that his or her proficiency has increased. When there is evidence the user's level of experience is changed by the system after interactively obtaining the user's consent.
- User modelling should integrate a theory of forgetting. The longer domain topics have not been used, the easier they can be lost from memory. Instead of continuously incrementing the knowledge state of any visited topic, the rate of

change of user's overall performance with respect to this topic and the period of time the topic has been unused should be taken into account.

- Up to now, knowledge maps provide uniform graphical views of topics and their interconnections. The adaptation mechanisms could be used to provide not only individualized presentations for link attributes but also for local and global knowledge maps. We are currently investigating approaches to visual information filtering of knowledge maps by graphical fisheye views, extending Furnas' original idea (1986) to graph layouts with multiple focus points (Hohl *et al.* 1993). The motivation for incorporating fisheye views of knowledge maps is to provide users with a balance of local detail and global context according to their individual knowledge levels. Valuable "knowledge islands", including relevant topics related to user-specified points of interest, are visualized in great detail while less relevant domains are abstracted or omitted entirely.

- Currently, multiple views of the knowledge base are utilized and provided by different access mechanisms. It would be reasonable to "synchronize" these multiple views, so that a user's focal point of activity is reflected in all related views. For example, while looking at a concept description, the concept-tree representation would adjust automatically to bring the relevant section of the tree into focus.

- The knowledge base of topics was built up "by hand". For every topic appropriate definitions for descriptive attributes, coming in different flavours depending on the user's overall knowledge state, and link attributes were formulated explicitly. Topics are currently restricted to Lisp programming concepts and functions for manipulating lists and sequences. It would be helpful to develop and integrate authoring and editing support tools that make use of semi-automatic knowledge acquisition operating on external information sources to generate a full-fledged knowledge base for Common Lisp.

- When scaling up the system to realistic large knowledge bases, detailed internal and formal evaluations will have to be performed. Empirical work should especially address the following issues: Does the measure realized in HYPADAPTER reduce the presented information sufficiently and in a manner such that no crucial information becomes suppressed? Do users learn "better" (e.g., faster, less mistakes, more and longer lasting learning gains, . . .) with the system than without it (or with adaptation turned off)? Is their learning qualitatively different (e.g. less problems with and more satisfaction from exploratory learning than under other conditions)?

- Authoring and editing tools would also become helpful if we were to apply the system to problem domains different from Common Lisp. To do this, we would build up a new knowledge base and define new selection rules as well as domain-dependent stereotypes for the user modelling component. The user interface components and the basic user modelling framework could be ported unchanged. Progress in this direction is linked to the evolution of general client-server architectures for adaptive hypertext shells which are applicable to different domains (Kobsa *et al.* 1994).

- The way the stereotype mechanism is used by HYPADAPTER leaves some room for improvement. Currently, the system defines generic stereotypes for user modelling (*novice, beginner, intermediate, expert*) which are mutually exclusive. To some extent this contradicts the very idea of stereotypes (Kay 1994) and the way users acquire specific expertise in different subdomains of Common Lisp. It would be more appropriate to augment or even replace the overall stereotype classification scheme by *domain-oriented* stereotypes that relate to the user's experience with respect to different contexts and subdomains of Lisp. It seems reasonable, for example, to dissect the space of Common Lisp functions into certain subdomains and to associate stereotypes accordingly (e.g., *expert for numerical processing, beginner for list processing*).

Acknowledgements

Numerous people have contributed to HYPADAPTER. We would especially like to thank Thomas Schwab for valuable suggestions and for developing the general user modelling framework MODUS. We are also grateful to Matthias Ressel who worked on the Common Lisp knowledge base and implemented an initial version of the topic evaluation component. Thanks to Susanne Reicherter for building an initial version of the user modelling component. Finally, we would like to thank the reviewers of this paper for their useful comments and hints.

References

Beaumont, I.: 1994, 'User Modelling in the Interactive Anatomy Tutoring System ANATOM-TUTOR'. *User Modeling and User-Adapted Interaction*, 4(1), 21–45 (reprinted in this volume, pp. 91–115).

Böcker, H.-D.: 1988, 'OPTIMIST: Ein System zur Beurteilung und Verbesserung von Lisp-Code'. In: R. Gunzenhäuser and H.-D. Böcker (eds.): *Prototypen benutzergerechter Computersysteme*, chapter 9. Verlag Walter de Gruyter, Berlin - New York, pp. 151–168.

Boyle, C. and A. O. Encarnaçion: 1994, 'MetaDoc: An Adaptive Hypertext Reading System'. *User Modeling and User-Adapted Interaction*, 4(1), 1–19 (reprinted in this volume, pp. 71-89).

Brusilovsky, P.: 1996, 'Methods and Techniques of Adaptive Hypermedia'. *User Modeling and User-Adapted Interaction*6(2-3), 87–129 (reprinted in this volume, pp. 1–43).

Conklin, J.: 1987, 'Hypertext: An Introduction and Survey'. *IEEE Computer*, 20(9), 17–41.

Fischer, G.: 1987, 'A Critic for Lisp'. Proceedings of IJCAI-87, Milano, pp. 177–184.

Fischer, G.: 1988, 'Enhancing Incremental Learning Processes with Knowledge-Based Systems'. In: H. Mandl and A. Lesgold (eds.): *Learning Issues for Intelligent Tutoring Systems*. Springer-Verlag, New York, pp. 138–163.

Fischer, G.: 1993, 'Shared Knowledge in Cooperative Problem-Solving Systems'. In: M. Schneider-Hufschmidt, T. Kühme, and U. Malinowski (eds.): *Adaptive User Interfaces: Principles and Practice*, Human Factors in Information Technology 10. North-Holland, pp. 49–68.

Fischer, G.: 1995, 'New Perspectives on Working, Learning, and Collaborating and Computational Artifacts in Their Support'. In: H.-D. Böcker (ed.): *Software-Ergonomie '95*. Teubner, Stuttgart, pp. 21–41.

Fischer, G., A. Lemke, and T. Schwab: 1985, 'Knowledge-based Help Systems'. CHI '85 Conference Proceedings: Human Factors in Computing Systems, New York. ACM SIGCHI/HFS, pp. 161–167.

Fix, V., S. Wiedenbeck, and J. Scholtz: 1993, 'Mental Representations of Programs by Novices and Experts'. INTERCHI '93 Conference Proceedings: Human Factors in Computing Systems, New York. ACM SIGCHI, IFIP TC 13, pp. 74–79.

Furnas, G. W.: 1986, 'Generalized Fisheye Views'. CHI '86 Conference Proceedings: Human Factors in Computing Systems, Boston, MA. ACM SIGCHI/HFS, pp. 16–23.

Hammond, N. and L. Allinson: 1989, 'Extending hypertext for learning: An investigation of access and guidance tools'. In: A. Sutcliffe and L. Macaulay (eds.): People and Computers V. Cambridge University Press, pp. 293–304.

Hohl, H., J. Herczeg, and M. Ressel: 1993, 'An Interactive Design Environment for Graphical Browsers'. HCI International '93: Proceedings of the Fifth International Conference on Human-Computer Interaction, Orlando, Florida. Elsevier Science Publishers, pp. 585–590.

Jonassen, D. H. and H. Mandl (eds.): 1990, Designing Hypermedia for Learning, volume 67 of NATO ASI Series F. Springer-Verlag.

Kaplan, C., J. Fenwick, and J. Chen: 1993, 'Adaptive Hypertext Navigation based on User Goals and Context'. User Modeling and User-Adapted Interaction, 3(3), 193–220 (reprinted in this volume, pp. 45–69).

Kay, J.: 1994, 'Lies, damned lies and stereotypes: pragmatic approximations of users'. UM '94: Proceedings of the Fourth International Conference on User Modeling, Hyannis, MA. The MITRE Corporation, pp. 175–184.

Kobsa, A., D. Müller, and A. Nill: 1994, 'KN-AHS: An Adaptive Hypertext Client of the User Modeling System BGP-MS'. UM '94: Proceedings of the Fourth International Conference on User Modeling, Hyannis, MA. The MITRE Corporation, pp. 99–105.

Neal, L. R.: 1989, 'A System for Example-Based Programming'. CHI '89 Conference Proceedings: Human Factors in Computing Systems, New York. ACM SIGCHI, pp. 63–68.

Nielsen, J.: 1990, Hypertext and Hypermedia. Academic Press.

Oppermann, R.: 1994, Adaptive User Support. Lawrence Erlbaum Associates.

Redmiles, D. F.: 1989, 'Case-Based Programming: Understanding Examples for Software Reuse'. Technical report, Department of Computer Science and Institute of Cognitive Science, University of Colorado, Boulder, CO.

Rich, E.: 1983, 'Users are individuals: individualizing user models'. International Journal of Man-Machine Studies, 18, 199–214.

Rissland, E. L.: 1984, 'Explaining and Arguing with Examples'. AAAI '84: Proceedings of the National Conference on Artificial Intelligence, University of Texas at Austin. W. Kaufmann, Inc, pp. 288–294.

Schneider-Hufschmidt, M., T. Kühme, and U. Malinowski (eds.): 1993, Adaptive User Interfaces: Principles and Practice. Human Factors in Information Technology 10. North-Holland.

Schwab, T.: 1989, 'Methoden zur Dialog- und Benutzermodellierung in adaptiven Computersystemen'. Dissertation, Fakultät Informatik der Universität Stuttgart.

Selker, T.: 1994, 'COACH: A Teaching Agent that Learns'. Communications of the ACM, 37(7), 92–99.

Steele Jr., G. L.: 1990, Common Lisp: The Language, Second Edition. Digital Press.

Stotts, P. D. and R. Furuta: 1991, 'Dynamic Adaptation of Hypertext Structure'. Proceedings of the ACM Hypertext '91, San Antonio, Texas, pp. 219–231.

Symbolics: 1988, 'Document Examiner'. In: Genera User's Guide, chapter 16. Symbolics, Inc., Cambridge, MA.

Unilogic: 1985, SCRIBE Document Production Software – User Manual. Unilogic Ltd., Pittsburgh, PA, fourth edition.

Vassileva, J.: 1996, 'A Task-Centered Approach for User Modeling in a Hypermedia Office Documentation System'. User Modeling and User-Adapted Interaction 6(2-3), 185–223 (reprinted in this volume, pp. 209–247).

VisualWorks: 1992, VisualWorks User's Guide. ParcPlace Systems, Inc.

Wender, K. F., F. Schmalhofer, and H.-D. Böcker (eds.): 1995, *Cognition and Computer Programming*. Ablex Publishing Corporation, Norwood, New Jersey.

Authors' Vitae

Dr. Hubertus Hohl
Siemens AG, Dept. ZFE T SN 5, D-81730 Munich, Germany
Dr. H. Hohl received his Masters (Diplom) degree and his Ph.D. (Dr. rer. nat.) in Computer Science from the University of Stuttgart. As a member of the research group DRUID, he has worked in the fields of adaptive systems, information visualization, knowledge-based design of graphical user interfaces for object-oriented programming environments, and hypermedia systems for cooperative work environments. Since April 1995, he is doing research in the field of CSCW environments at the Corporate Research and Development Department of Siemens AG.

Dr. Heinz-Dieter Böcker
GMD IPSI, Dolivostr. 15, D-64293 Darmstadt, Germany
Dr. H.-D. Böcker is doing research at the Integrated Publication and Information Systems Institute (IPSI) of the German National Research Center for Computer Science. Dr. Böcker received his Masters (Diplom) degree in Psychology from the University of Hamburg and his Ph.D. (Dr. rer. nat.) in Computer Science from the University of Stuttgart. He has worked and published in several areas of human-computer interaction, including programming environments, visualization, and educational uses of computers. The joint work with Hubertus Hohl and Rul Gunzenhäuser described in this volume reflects his long standing interest in adaptive and adaptable systems.

Prof. Dr. Rul Gunzenhäuser
Department of Computer Science, University of Stuttgart, Breitwiesenstr. 20-22, D-70565 Stuttgart, Germany
Prof. Dr. R. Gunzenhäuser is Full Professor of Computer Science at the University of Stuttgart and head of the Human-Computer Interaction group. He studied Mathematics, Physics, and Philosophy of Science at the Universities of Stuttgart and Tübingen (Germany) and received his M.S. and Ph.D. degrees from the University of Stuttgart. R. Gunzenhäuser was then Assistant Professor at the University of Stuttgart Computer Center, Associate Professor at the State University of New York and the State University Teachers College at Esslingen (Germany). His present interests lie in the areas of knowledge-based man-machine communication, interactive user-oriented systems, computer-aided instruction, computer assistance for blind users, and education in computer science.

A Glass Box Approach to Adaptive Hypermedia

KRISTINA HÖÖK,[1] JUSSI KARLGREN,[1] ANNIKA WÆRN,[1],
NILS DAHLBÄCK,[2] CARL GUSTAF JANSSON,[3] KLAS KARLGREN[3] and
BENOÎT LEMAIRE[4]

[1] Swedish Institute of Computer Science, Box 1263, S-164 28 Kista, Sweden, Email: push@sics.se,
www: http://www.sics.se/humle/; [2] Department of Computer and Information Science, Linköping
University, S-581 83 Linköping, Sweden, Email: nda@ida.liu.se; [3] Department of Computer and
Systems Sciences, Stockholm University and The Royal Institute of Technology, Electrum 230, S-164
40 Kista, Sweden, Email: calle@dsv.su.se and klas@dsv.su.se; [4] University of Grenoble II,
Department of Education Sciences, BP 47, F-38040 Grenoble Cédex 9, France, Email:
lemaire@shm.grenet.fr

(Received 22 June 1995; in final form 5 August 1995)

Abstract. Utilising adaptive interface techniques in the design of systems introduces certain risks.
An adaptive interface is not static, but will actively adapt to the perceived needs of the user. Unless
carefully designed, these changes may lead to an unpredictable, obscure and uncontrollable interface. Therefore the design of adaptive interfaces must ensure that users can inspect the adaptivity
mechanisms, and control their results. One way to do this is to rely on the user's understanding of
the application and the domain, and relate the adaptivity mechanisms to domain-specific concepts.
We present an example of an adaptive hypertext help system POP, which is being built according to
these principles, and discuss the design considerations and empirical findings that lead to this design.

Key words: adaptive hypermedia, plan inference, multimodality, user modelling

1. Introduction

Utilising adaptive interface techniques in interactive systems introduces certain
risks. An adaptive interface is not static, but will actively adapt to the perceived
needs of the user. Unless carefully designed, adaptation and the changes it occasions
may lead to an unpredictable, obscure and uncontrollable interface.

As is frequently pointed out it is important that users feel to be in control of the
systems they work with. This becomes increasingly important when systems act
autonomously: e.g. read and sort our mail, choose which news items to read, book
our meetings. Systems that act too independently, e.g. knowledge-based systems or
systems with adaptive interfaces have not always been acceptable to users (Berry
and Broadbent 1986; Meyer 1994; Vassileva 1994). One reason for this is that
complex problem solving should not be implemented as a system task alone, but
rather be approached as a joint task of the system and the user, to be solved in
interaction (Pollack et al. 1982).

P. Brusilovsky et al. (eds.), Adaptive Hypertext and Hypermedia, 143–170.
© 1998 Kluwer Academic Publishers.

Giving users a sense of control can be achieved only if the systems' internal workings are *transparent* to users or if the systems' actions are *predictable* to users. Adaptive interfaces sometimes make very bold assumptions of user characteristics, and adapt accordingly. It is not to be expected that such adaptation always will be correct. We believe that virtually all adaptive interfaces will at times make mistakes resulting in erroneous adaptations (see e.g. Kay (1994)). This is a strong argument for ensuring that an adaptive interface provides mechanisms for control, again on an appropriate level of abstraction, in order not to confuse the user with technical details of the adaptivity mechanism.

Transparency gives the user a view of the internal workings of the system. Ideally, users should see a system as a glass box, within which the lower level components act as black boxes (du Boulay *et al.* 1981; Karlgren *et al.* 1994). The view given can be very abstract: Maes (1994), e.g., represents the internal state of a personal meeting booking agent as a facial expression – the form of visualisation and the level of abstraction must be chosen carefully in order not to lead the users' expectations astray.

Predictability can be more difficult to achieve in an adaptive interface. Meyer (1994) describes this requirement as a requirement of a stable relation between stimuli and response, that is, the same input in the same context (or what the user perceives as being the same input in the same context) should always give the same output. There is an inherent contradiction between this requirement and the general idea of adaptive interfaces, that of changing presentations according to the perceived needs of the user. The design of adaptive interfaces must thus aim at achieving predictability in some alternative way than a strict adherence to the stable stimuli – response requirement. One solution is to split the interface into a stable unchangeable component, which is carefully designed to be predictable, and one which does change, as, e.g. an interface agent.

In this paper, we present an example of an information seeking application, for which we have developed an user-adaptive hypertext solution. This solution does not rely on an agent metaphor to achieve transparency, predictability and control in an adaptive interface, but instead focuses on finding a *domain specific* design of the interaction. The (generic) adaptive functionalitites are made visible to users by means of language and functionalitites inherent in the particular domain of information. The example application, an adaptive information seeking assistant, enhances interaction and control through multimodal interaction including unconstrained text input, and utilises task adaptation for information selections. Task adaptation is made controllable both through explicit task selection and user-verified plan recognition. We briefly describe each of these mechanisms, and describe how they are designed to deal with transparency, predictability and control.

In general, domain-dependent solutions allow users to communicate with the system in the domain language. Most other approaches to transparent and controllable user modelling are generic. An example are the adaptive prompts by Kuhme *et al.* (1993). This design allows a user, or a program analyst, to tailor the mechanisms for adaptivity, but in order to do this, the user must learn a new, complex vocabulary which distinguishes between sets of terms such as e.g. "goal", "action", and "interaction". Furthermore, it is unlikely that users will be able to predict the *effects* of this tailoring, as the different parameters interact in a complex way to achieve adaptiveness. Still, the architecture of our solution aims to separate the domain specific information from the general inference mechanisms, and both from the interface design. This should make it possible to transfer our solution to other information seeking applications with little effort.

We first describe our studies which underlie the design (Section 2), followed by a description of the non-adaptive hypertext system (Section 3). We then describe the multimodal interface chosen (Section 4.1) and the adaptivitiy mechanisms (Sections 4.3 and 4.4).

1.1. PROJECT BACKGROUND

The Plan- and User Sensitive Help (PUSH) project aims at developing and testing intelligent help solutions to information seeking tasks. The domain is a method for development of large telecommunications software systems, SDP-TA. The method itself is documented in a huge information space, about 500 documents consisting of 5–20 pages each SDP-TA is structured in *objects* and *processes*. Objects denote results produced when applying the method, e.g. code, documentation and similar. The work performed in a project using SDP-TA is organised in processes, e.g. defining the requirements on the system, performing design, etc. Processes are related to one another, objects are also related to one another, and finally, objects are produced and refined in certain processes.

The design solution discussed in this paper is currently being implemented, and a prototype named POP (PUSH Operational Prototype) runs on SUN workstations. POP is implemented in an object-oriented extension of Sicstus Prolog; Sicstus Objects (SICStus User's Manual 1995).

2. Studies Which Underlie the Design

Adaptivity in hypermedia is proposed as a means to meet users with different needs, background knowledge, interaction style, and cognitive characteristics (Kobsa *et al.* 1994). In order to do so, we must have ways of knowing more about the targeted group of users and their needs, related to the domain of the information system that we are developing.

Acquiring knowledge about users in order to build an intelligent help system is similar to, but distinct from the problem of gathering knowledge for knowledge-based systems: when developing knowledge-based systems, the focus is on the *domain expert* and the problem of how to "extract" the expert's knowledge, whereas in the case at hand, where we design an adaptive information system, we must focus on the *users* and their needs. While the area of knowledge-based systems has had a fair amount of research done on system development methods, methodology for domain analysis from the adaptive system perspective remains largely a field in its infancy. Often claims are made about user needs that have very little to do with what will actually be of real use to users in a particular domain. For instance, a common claim is that explanations must avoid concepts unfamiliar to the particular user reading the text, or that they should be provided with less details (Kobsa *et al.* 1994). This may be true in some cases, but not in the general case: for instance, if the user is attempting to *learn* more about a particular issue, the contrary might just as well be true (Höök 1995).

The most challenging goal in the PUSH project has been to find which adaptive techniques in fact do improve the interaction, given the side constraint that the knowledge representation and reasoning strategies must be scalable and easy to update, to accommodate new releases and changes in the very large target system.

2.1. KNOWLEDGE ACQUISITION METHODS UTILISED IN PUSH

The PUSH project was fortunate in that SDP-TA already is well documented in a large on-line manual, and that the project was given access to a large number of users for whom the documentation of SDP-TA was a crucial issue in their daily work situation. This has enabled us to set up a series of studies where we could find what users' needs are, what support they have currently, what supports need to be added, when users turn to the manual, etc. In this work, we have followed the principles of Cognitive Task Analysis (Roth and Woods 1989). We first tried to understand the problem area, focusing on the types of tasks that users typically were involved in when addressing the manual information. This was done to avoid ending up with a solution that would only solve an example scenario, but not scale up to the whole problem area.

During our initial work, we found several problems that could not be solved by a help system on the process itself. The main reason was that the user's specific problems arise from their current *project task* rather than from difficulties in understanding the development method. Essentially, the tasks of different projects using SDP-TA are all unique. We also found some problems with SDP-TA that could not be addressed by a help system alone. Some of these problems originated from the SDP-TA process itself, others from a mismatch between the process and the organisation in which it was applied. This is not surprising; it is a frequent result in the development of help systems, that you end up wanting to make changes to the underlying system or the environment in which it is applied (Breuker 1990). These findings have proved useful in the subsequent development of SDP-TA, but they lie outside the scope of the help system – the help system is supposed to give help on the method as it is, not compensate for it. For these reason, our latter studies have concentrated on extracting the users *information seeking needs*, as these are the primary reason for addressing the help system, as opposed to their project tasks.

Our initial interviews (we interviewed about 20 persons) did point to a number of problems that were directly connected to the method and its documentation. When using help, users felt a problem of information overload, they had difficulties in finding information, and once they found information they had problems in interpreting and making use of the text and graphs they had found. User suffered from the classical bind of too much and yet too little information! (McDermid and Ereback 1994).

We then went on to the more focused study on users information seeking needs in their daily work. This study was based on interactions with 23 users in their daily work during a quite long period of time. The purpose was both to collect a "corpus" of questions from users, to test which answers would have been most satisfying and also to look beyond the surface level and extract a hierarhcy of *information seeking tasks*, depicted in Figure 1 (Bladh and Höök 1995).

In the task hierarchy, we may observe that learning about SDP constitutes quite a large part of the tasks. This caused us to make a study on the novices and experts conceptual understanding of the ideas behind SDP-TA (18 novices and 10 experts paticipated in this study). The purpose was both to see whether we could apply any theories of learning that could influence the design of our help system, but also to get a general grip of how difficult it is to grasp this domain for the users. The theory of learning that we applied was from Micki Chi's work (Chi *et al.* 1994), and it turned out to be quite hard to apply. Our hypothesis is that her theory works well for learning "natural concepts", while the more abstract concepts in SDP-TA are not as easy to classify according to her theory.

We did find that there were quite some confusion about fundamental concepts in SDP-TA among the novices. The primary explanation for this is that a lot of the concepts are fuzzy and users are expected to get an intuition about the whole concept of object-oriented thinking rather than being able to find precise, formal definitions of the concepts. We cater for some of this concept communication in our POP system.

Finally, we have made a set of evaluative studies on some of our design choices. In particular, we have produced a set of explanations that differ in how they meet the perceived needs of users and tasks they engage in, and tested these explanations on users (Höök 1995), also described below. Seven persons participated in the first of our controlled evaluative studies. We have also continuously shown our prototypes to real users.

3. The Basic System

The knowledge acquisition phase has been intertwined with the design and development of a prototype help assistant, the POP system. In order to understand how our adapivity and multimodal interface has been designed, we first need to describe the basic hypertext system that we have developed. First, we describe an example

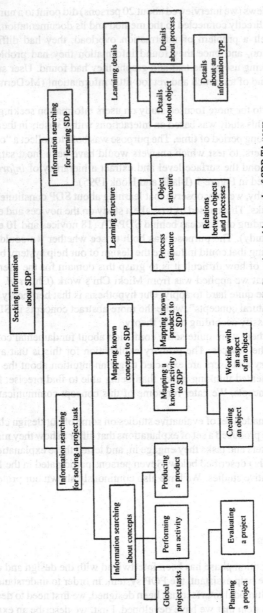

Fig. 1. Parts of the domain-dependent task hierarchy of information seeking needs of SDP-TA users.

scenario (without adaptivity) and the basic interaction principles of POP. We then describe the underlying knowledge representation with information entities.

3.1. EXAMPLE SCENARIO IN THE POP PROTOTYPE

A software developer at Ellemtel that has been assigned the task of producing a specification of a subsystem in the software her project is developing. The software developer has quite extensive knowledge of the application domain, but is fairly unfamiliar with the SDP-TA method. Her project manager has informed the project members briefly about where in the method they should start working, let us name that part of the method "process X".* She enters the on-line help system, POP, through entering Netscape (a World Wide Web (www) viewer) and enters an unspecific question about process X: "describe process X". The system then provides her with some information about process X, see Figure 3.1, in what we shall name an *answer page*. The answer page consists of both some graphics and also some text under different headings.

As shown in the graphs, the process is part of the general process SuperX, and process X has seven activities: a, b, c, d, and e. There is a set of input objects and another set of output objects. This information helps the software developer to see how the method is structured with the focus on process X. The user can click on any of the symbols causing the graphic displays to change, putting the object that was clicked on in the centre. She may, for example, click on one of the input objects. This object is then displayed in the centre of the object graphics window and any objects which are related to it are also shown in that window.

In the page, there is also some textual information. Some fairly basic information about the process X is provided and the underlying purpose behind process X is also shown. There are also some headers without associated texts. These indicate that there is some more information available. Our user decides to click on the header titled "Purpose". A description about the underlying purpose behind the process X is is inserted into the page below the header she clicked on.

When reading through the text some terms are quite unfamiliar to our software developer, she gets confused by: "perform and document an object-oriented analysis?". This text is displayed in bold style, indicating that it is possible to ask follow-up questions on those concepts, which she does, and the information is also inserted into the page, see Figure 3.1. The follow-up questions are currently available trough first "opening" the bold word (i.e. clicking on the Query-symbol next to the hotword (Kobsa *et al.* 1994)), which makes a set of alternative follow-up questions available marked as links. (Once www allows it, we aim to turn these into pop-up menues.)

When our user feels satisfied with the information about process X, she can turn to other processes in SDP-TA, or gain information about the objects in SDP-TA.

---

* The SDP-TA method is proprietary to Ellemtel. Only minimal information about the method itself is given in this paper.

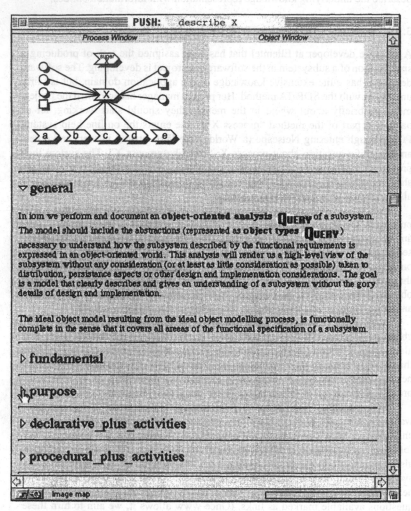

Figure 2. The interface of the current version of POP.

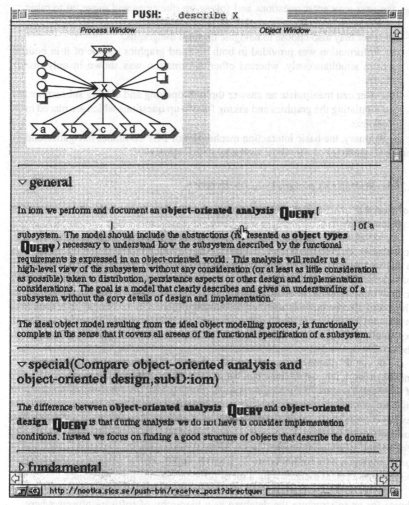

Figure 3. The interface after "opening" the purpose-description and posing a follow-up query on "object-oriented analysis".

The new object or process is then presented in it's own, dynamically generated, answer page in www.

In summary we can observe that:

- the user may enter questions and follow-up questions and move on to other processes or objects.
- the user may also choose to navigate through the graphs.
- the information was provided in both text and graphics - some of it in both modes simultaneously, whereas other information was shown in only one mode.
- the user can manipulate an answer through opening and closing subsections, manipulating the graphics and asking follow-up questions which are placed in a context.

In summary, the basic interaction mechanism of POP combines navigation and search (Lemaire *et al.* 1994) through a hypertext space.

3.2. HYPERTEXT AS INFORMATION ENTITIES

Let is now discuss how the information is organised in the underlying knowledge representation.

As we could see from the example, the processes and objects and their relationships in SDP-TA do not by themselves convey much information. In addition to this structure, a lot of mainly textual information is available. This information may concern why a certain object is produced, how a process is carried out, hints on how to produce good quality output, entry and exit criteria and similar issues. There will also be information that is not tightly related to any single object, such as comparisons between similar process steps with slightly different purposes, or explanations of commonly used terms (as "object-oriented analysis" in our example above).

In the POP prototype, we divide all available information about processes and objects into typed *information entities*. Each information entity is a piece of hypertext (possibly including a static picture), that in turn can contain semantic links to related information. Links are formulated as follow-up questions to the text. For example, a short description of a process step may contain a link to a comparison between this process step and another. The object relationships are also represented as information entities, where the type denotes the type of relationship: for example, an information entity such as "input objects" is a list of the names of the input objects, associated with a set of possible queries for each object.

Since SDP-TA is structured in an object-oriented fashion, it was a natural choice for us to structure the database as a hierarchy of software objects where the information entities constitute attributes of the software objects, see Figure 4. In this hierarchy, we can associate some information entities (as comparisons) to generic classes (or superobjects) to be inherited by all objects sharing the same information. Similarly, the explanation operators consistute inherited methods of each software object. Each software object therefor has knowledge about what it "knows" about itself and can explain itself through using an inherited explanation method (Lemaire 1995).

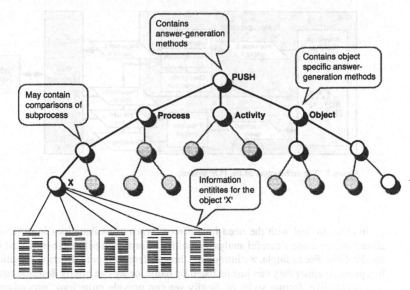

Figure 4. The knowledge representation and explanation operators in POP.

When a question is posed about one of the objects in our knowledge base, the object itself will know which information entities it should return as an answer, and it will also know how to provide the necessary information that is used for constructing the graphs in the interface, i.e. the graphs are not predefined pictures, but generated on the spot. In fact, the whole answer page is generated dynamically as a response to the question.

4. Multimodal Interaction and Adaptivity

Our hypertext system is carefully designed to enhance the understanding of the SDP-TA domain and the structure of it. However, the empirical investigations point towards difficulties that are not addressed by this solution alone. Some users immediately get lost and do not know where to search or what to ask, other users will need a specific explanation style to understand the information, and finally users in general suffer from "getting more than they asked for".

In order to support users with only a vague understanding of the content and organisation of the information system, we provide the possibility to pose vague questions using text input. Users with very specific information needs are also helped by the free text input possibilities. This solution is further described in Section 4.1.

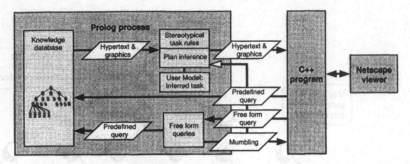

Figure 5. The architecture of the POP system.

In order to deal with the need for different types of explanations in different situations, we made a careful analysis of which information entities should exist in the database. For example, we introduced three different ways to describe activities in a process: either they can just be listed by name, or we can briefly describe each in a declarative, factual style, or, finally we can provide quite long, procedural, description that are full of hints on how to think and what to do (Höök 1995). Each description style is represented by a hypertext information entity. We describe our work in this area in Section 4.2.

In order to deal with the information overflow, answers are tailored using knowledge about the user's current task. Each information entity has an associated list of tasks which is provides to fulfilling. Our system can then choose which information entities are best fitted given that we know which task the user is performing. How to know about the users task and how we provide this kind of adaptivity is further described in Sections 4.3 and 4.4.

In all of these solutions, it is very important to allow the user to inspect and control the functionality. In the following sections, we shall describe in detail how this is achieved in POP.

In Figure 4 we see a picture of the basic architecture of POP. The knowledge database consists of the objects of the domain and their information entities. It also has all the methods for explanations inherited down into each domain object. The free form queries are transformed into the set of standard queries that the system is able to understand. This sometimes require a dialogue - this is further dicussed below. The answer in turn, is altered by the inferred task of the user. This process might affect the explanation so that certain information entities are hidden and others are opened – the task inference and adaptation of explanation is further described below.

The whole result of the query is finally sent to a C++ program which turns our extended html-format (with information about what is "hidden" in the page and which follow-up menues to display if requested) into a proper www-page which is shown to the user in, e.g. Netscape.

4.1. ISSUES IN MULTIMODAL INTERACTION

The interface is multimodal – meaning that it produces both graphics and text, and accepts both text, menu choice, and pointing and selection as input. Text and graphics (or, indeed, any combination of abstract and direct access representations) complement each other, in the sense that tasks of different types require different modalities (Cohen 1992), and that users have varying preferences for modalities or differing capacity to make use of them (Bretan 1995).

Text and language in an interface is often taken in opposition to the direct manipulation paradigm. The three main points noted of direct manipulation interfaces are (Shneiderman 1983):

1. continuous representation of the object of interest,
2. physical actions or labelled button presses instead of complex syntax, and
3. rapid incremental reversible operations, whose impact on the object of interest is immediately visible.

For points one and three, pictures and graphs show their strongest side: pictures or graphics can achieve the persistence sought for. At the same time, points one and three do not in any way contradict the possibility of using text or other language input – indeed, any interface at all, be it language based or point-and-click based would do well to follow the principles. We will use natural language, in our case typewritten text, as one of the mechanisms of interaction, thus relaxing the constraints posed by Shneiderman's second point, but continuing to observe points one and three.

Multimodal systems with strong cross-modal interactivity – where text input is but a component in an interface which otherwise behaves along Shneiderman's principles – show very encouraging results (Biermann et al. 1983, Bos et al. 1994, Capindale and Crawford 1990).

We find that in SDP-TA, which has structures that can be presented in graph form with little effort, some of the relations between objects and processes are of a type that need textual explication for users. Any relation that is semantically complex will need elucidation difficult to achieve in graph form. In addition, the user studies have also indicated that users do not want to rely on pointing and clicking to thread their way through a hypertext space, which is the way the manual is organised at present: they want more direct goal-oriented mechanisms, especially if they are not exploring the information but looking up something concrete. Users in the study expressed frustration at not finding a correct answer a few clicks away: hypertext somehow raises the expectations of users to the point that the information they seek should be immediately available. By not only using 'point and click' but also allow the user to make use of the abstractions possible in natural language we can at least partly overcome these drawbacks.

Another reason to include a free-form text input is that the standard queries only have been designed to answer a specific set of foreseen questions, and users of a help system almost by definition are at odds with the information structure

```
I have no clear picture of which .hh files and
.cc files belong to an II or an OU
respectively.
POP interprets your query as:
1 compare II and OU.
2 describe hh.
3 describe cc.
```

Figure 6. A query which cannot be generalised without extensive inferencing. POP simply catches the referents and proposes queries to describes them. In this case, where multiple queries result, the user will be given a chance to choose which ones to process.

of the target system – e.g. when the user really is novel to the subject and knows too little of the domain to be able to use the predefined queries, or when the user has a specific information need which has simply not been anticipated in the set of queries. Affording text input provides these users with a way to enter queries and needs that were unexpected.

The system is designed to accept all queries, and map them on to the set of internal query templates. If no exact match is found, the least general query that is consistent with the query representation will be chosen: the entities that have been identified as reasonable references are assumed to be the topic of the query, and a general query which includes the identified references is constructed. This is displayed to the user, who thus will see what assumptions the system is capable of making together with the answer. An example is shown in Figure 6. This means that users are always given answers, but that the answers may well be inconsistent with the gist of their queries; this will still give the user an idea of what POP handles, better than error messages would.

A well-known problem for natural language interfaces is reference resolution (Cohen 1992). Our system allows the user to refer to previously mentioned entities by using pronouns and definite references: "Compare it to IOM". This is done keeping track of a *focus stack* where referents are stored together with a score indicating how salient for subsequent mention they are. This salience score is composed by a weighted sum of scores from recent actions, linguistic as well as non-linguistic. The system will certainly make inappropriate weightings at times – but as Bos *et al.* (1994) found, users will accept the occasional error if the error itself is understandable. The top elements of the focus stack are displayed to the user to make focusing explicit (Karlgren *et al.* 1995; Bretan 1995, Bretan *et al.* 1995), which adds to the permanence of referents, and displays the results of focus calculation. Together with the dialogue history this gives the users transparency to the system view of the discourse situation, thus addressing Cohen's point above.

4.2. ADAPTATION TO THE USER'S INFORMATION SEEKING TASK

The main problem we faced in the PUSH application was the vast amount of information available. The information connected to a single domain object may well exceed more than twenty pages. In the initial studies, we found that users were likely to read only the first page of information they found relevant to their purposes (Bladh and Höök 1995). This made it necessary to find rich mechanisms for information extraction, so that the individual user initially would be presented with the information that was deemed most relevant for him or her.

In line with the work of Kaplan (Kaplan *et al.* 1993), we can identify several possible "parameters" which could be relevant for determining whether a certain piece of information is relevant to a particular user. The object-oriented structure of the domain itself is such a parameter: if the user is reading about a specific object, he or she may be interested in information about objects related to this one. The knowledge base is structured according to the domain, into objects, information entities belonging to objects, and semantic links between information entities.

One potential usage of this knowledge structure would be to construct all queries to be very specific (some of them represented by the navigational manœuvres in the interface), so that only a small fraction of all information would be relevant as an answer to any query. However, since the amount of information is so large, this solution would run the risk of users losing track of the *structure* of the domain in their search for the right information – users may get "lost in hyperspace". Furthermore, this solution will not provide users with any sense of *how much* information they have found and what is still available.

Instead, in answers to precise queries about a specific object, we include all information around the object, although the information that is not directly relevant for the query is "hidden" from the user's immediate view: in the example above, Section 3.1, the hidden parts are the ones under the headings that are not yet opened, and also the follow-up questions associated with hotwords. This way, users will know that if they decide to open all the hidden information in a page, they will have accessed all information related to this object. Furthermore, we allow users to ask "open" questions, such as "compare **object1** and **object2**". The answers to these imprecise queries will be very large, but if users read the entire answer, they can be certain of having exhausted the information around a certain subject (represented by the query).

An important concern of ours has been to define what textual information entities each domain object should have. It is important to plan for information entities that cover all available information in the current system, as well as the additional needs of users that we found during our knowledge acquisition work. But another concern is that the domain experts who will eventually write these texts, must be able to understand the purpose of each information entity, to write text answers to the needs of a user addressing this entity. In other words, several different writers must *keep user models in their heads* while writing the text.

Initially we started out with a small set of identified information entities, and a small set of stereotypical user models, intended to capture a variation of user backgrounds and user roles. Our idea was that each information entity was to be written in several versions, one for each user stereotype. However, this approach is unfeasible in practice, since it grows intractable in this large domain. Furthermore, it proved very hard to grasp what a stereotype really meant, and how it would affect the formulations of a certain information entity. The stereotypes also modelled aspects of user background that turned out not to affect the discourse. Much the same critique was put forward by John Self (Self 1988) in the area of student modelling in tutoring systems. Self expresses this as "don't diagnose what you cannot treat". We can paraphrase this in the area of user modelling as "don't model user characteristics that do not affect interaction": in our case this meant that we should not try and write different information entities when in fact, they did not turn out to be sufficiently different.

Instead, we have chosen to further refine our division of information into information entities that describe some aspect of an object or a concept where the description is geared to a specific purpose. It turns out that the classification by task subsumes both the level of expertise and the role: for example, a person who is trying to "learn structure" is a novice (at least in the area of SDP-TA which he or she is working with), and a person who is "planning a project" at least nominally is a project leader.

This structure has proven very useful. Each information entity is large enough to be self-contained and internally consistent, which makes it possible to combine several of them into one answer. Coherence is further enhanced by only selecting such texts for presentation, that have been written with either the same or closely related tasks in mind. The structure also provides flexibility for design and maintenance of the help assistant: if a novel information need is detected, this can be handled either by defining a novel combination of information entities relevant to this need, or through adding entirely new information entities geared specifically to the novel need.

The different typical task descriptions will in a specific situation determine the choice of information entities to display. For instance, an explanation of a process for a user engaged in a "Follow activity" task will display a "How To Do It" text (a procedural description replete with practical tips); whereas an explanation for a user engaged in "Product Planning" will include an "Activities" text which is a more declarative description of a process, similar to the difference proposed by Paris (1988).

The mapping between tasks, queries and information entities is rule-based, see Figure 4.2.

The information presented to users is affected in two ways by the selection of a task:

— The information entities that are deemed relevant for the current task are opened at the time an answer is generated.

Learning structure →
    Fundamental, Purpose, Activities, Input objects, Output objects,
    Information model, Relations to other processes, Simple example

Projectplanning →
    Project planning, Activities, Information model, Simple example

Producing a product →
    General, How to do it, Release, Input objects, Output objects, Entry,
    Exit, Information model, Advanced example, Frequently asked questions

Reverse engineering →
    Information model, Activities, Release

Figure 7. Four rules for the query "describe **process**", describing which information
entities should be displayed if the user is pursuing a certain task.

- Follow-up questions are organised into two-level menus, where the first level
  contains only a few questions, relevant to the current task, and the second level
  contains all follow-up questions. This solution is inspired by the "adaptive
  prompts" in (Kuhme *et al.* 1993). A similar approach to dynamic menus is
  described by Mittal and Moore (1995).
- The acronyms in SDP-TA are expanded into full terms for some tasks; for
  example, SDP-TA can be spelled as "System Development Process for Telecommunications Applications".

In accordance with our fundamental glass-box approach, the system must display its task knowledge to the users in order to allow them to inspect and control
the adaptation. In the POP prototype, we have decided to investigate two parallel
approaches to do this, namely *plan recognition* and *explicit task selection*. The
interface design allows us to use both mechanisms in combination or separately
from each other. The motivations for and detailed form for these two approaches
are described further below.

4.3. TRANSPARENT TASK STEREOTYPES

One approach to making the task knowledge of POP transparent to the users,
is simply to allow the users to choose which task they themselves think that
they are performing. As indicated in the introduction, dynamic adaptation has
some drawbacks. In particular, user modelling cannot be anything but a guess if it
attempts to model the user's knowledge (Kay 1994). In a hypertext application the
input from the user may be quite limited; we know which texts the user chooses to
see and whether any links are followed from those texts. These manœuvres provide
very little information about the user.

As discussed in the introduction, the requirements on transparency, control, and predictability make it less desirable to keep a separate and generic user model, since users will have great difficulties in inspecting and controlling such a model. Even if users are allowed to alter the user model, it might be very difficult for them to foresee what the effects of a modification would be. Furthermore, in our domain, and indeed in most applications, users are likely to spend very little time modifying the adaptive components, since this does not immediately provide mileage for their main task. This leads to a behaviour where users are forced to use unnatural and lengthy sequences of interactions geared to "circumventing" the adaptivity when it goes wrong (Woods 1993).

So, with our solution where the users are allowed to choose which task they think they are performing, we avoid some of the problems inherent in user modelling, but we also introduce some new ones. Firstly, if there are too many tasks to choose from it will become very difficult for the user to predict what an alternation of the task will result in. Second, even with a small set of tasks, the users might not be willing to always restate which tasks they are performing as their goals and needs change during a session with our system. Users might start out trying to do some reverse engineering task, and then discover that they need to learn more about some aspect, i.e. a move to the learning details task. As shown by (Oppermann 1994), the best solution seems to be somewhere inbetween system-controlled and user-controlled adaptation, which is why we think that allowing the user to choose among a small set of predefined, stereotypical tasks, should be combined with a dynamic change of user task in response to the users actions (see the plan inference approach described below).

Our users are therefore required to state which out of a small set of tasks that the think they are adhering to. Currently, we are experimenting with four tasks: "Learning the structure of SDP-TA", "Project Planning", "Reverse engineering", and "Following an activity". The task stereotypes were selected to allow users to predict which explanation will satisfy their need in a particular situation, and are based on the empirically established task hierarchy in Figure 1. These tasks are expressed in domain concepts, and are understood by users of SDP-TA. They know the meaning of "reverse engineering" and they also know whether they are working this way or not. So, as said in the introduction, we are not forcing the user to learn and understand an abstract language with words as "goal", "action", etc., instead they express their needs for adaptation in the domain language.

In order to establish that users would be able to choose among these four tasks and then be able to predict or somehow understand what their choice would result in, we performed a small study where we asked 7 subjects (with varying familiarity with SDP-TA) to couple four tasks with four explanations and to provide motivations for their choices. Five subjects did a correct coupling and 2 did a partially correct coupling. More important were their comments on our explanations, which we have used to improve the mapping rules from task to explanation. That made us add, for example, one information entity specifically geared towards the needs of project planners explaining the purpose of a certain step in the SDP-TA process. This new information entity was needed in order to help the planners to determine what in SDP-TA their projects absolutely have to do, and what they can skip in certain circumstances. Other similar alternations where made.

A critique of our user-controlled task adaptation, could be that the explanations we provide will be too static to be a good approximation of what kind of explanations our users need. But, since we allow users to change the explanation through opening and closing parts of it and through clicking on hotwords and receiving explanations to concepts that are unfamiliar to them, we have in fact introduced what Moore and Swartout have raised as a requirement on explanations (1989):

> Explanation is an interactive process, requiring a dialogue between advice-giver and advice-seeker. Yet current expert systems cannot participate in a dialogue with users. In particular these systems cannot clarify misunderstood explanations, elaborate on previous explanations or respond to follow-up questions in the context of the on-going dialogue.

Instead of drawing the conclusion that Moore and Swartout does, namely that explanation systems must engage the user in a text dialogue, we have a direct-manipulation, multimodal, hypertext solution to the same problem. We see many advantages with this approach: it does not require text dialogue, it builds on direct-manipulation techniques and simple queries in a multimodal setting. Finally, the appearance of the system as that of a familiar direct-manipulation interface (with the addition of our free form queries) will not cause users to false expectations of its conversational competence.

In a way, the direct-manipulation and the follow-up queries provide the user with ways in which they can alter the explanations that the task stereotypes provide.

4.4. USER VERIFIED TASK RECOGNITION

The proposed solution with static task stereotypes still runs into some problems, that instead may be addressed by *dynamic* adaptation to the user's task. As said above, the first problem is that the set of task stereotypes must be rather small, in order for the user to select among them and learn to understand their effects on explanations. As seen in Figure 1, the complete set of empirically identified tasks is large, and this analysis is not exhaustive. The second problem is that in our prestudies, we found that users very often *move between* tasks. Typically, a user may start using the system in order to get help to develop a particular object. But while reading the detailed description of this object, he or she comes across a term that is not understood, and starts looking for information explaining this term. This represents a shift in task to the task of "learning a concept". It is unlikely that users will go through the effort to always mark these new tasks explicitly – especially since users are unlikely to actively reflect on the focus shift. Rather, they will open new information entities or pose new queries to cover their needs. This is of course perfectly possible, but this means that the user must go through the extra effort of searching for the right information entities when posing new questions or moving around in the information domain. We discussed earlier that a dynamic interface may require unnecessary manœuvres to circumvent erroneous adaptations. Here, we have the opposite situation: users may also perform unnecessary manœuvres to circumvent an unnecessarily *static* nature of the interface.

To deal with these problems, we have decided to utilise plan recognition techniques to allow the system to actively adapt to the users' tasks. The plan recognition mechanism is the only intelligent technique we have included that actively adapts the presentation. In order to keep the interface transparent and controllable, we have selected to let plan recognition affect only the answers to queries, while the navigation in the information structure still is done through direct manipulation.

The answer to a user question will be affected in one additional way by the plan recognition. As for explicit task selection, the information entities that are deemed relevant for the current task are opened at the time an answer is generated, and the menus with follow-up questions are organised to show the queries first, that are most relevant for the current task. But in addition to this, the plan recognition method generates a textual phrase in the beginning of the answer, that reads "This answer is assuming that your current information seeking task is X". X is a mouse sensitive hotword, with an associated menu containing a list of alternative tasks. Both the statement itself and the menu of alternatives are generated dynamically. The menu is tailored to include only such tasks that actually would alter the presented information.

4.4.1. *Plan Recognition Characteristics in the PUSH domain*

Plan recognition can be interpreted as the task of recognising, or guessing at, an agent's *intention* underlying its actions and utterances. The reason this is usually called plan recognition is that the most widespread approaches to the problem try to follow an agent's actions or utterances, and match these to some more or less procedural description of a plan, corresponding to a particular intention (Kass and Finin 1988, Kautz 1987).

The plan recognition problem appears in three different forms: plan recognition when the actor is aware and actively co-operating to the recognition, for example by choosing actions that make the task easier (intended plan recognition), plan recognition when the actor is unaware of or indifferent to the plan recognition process (keyhole plan recognition),* or plan recognition when the actor is aware of and actively obstructs the plan recognition process (obstructed plan recognition).

Applications of plan recognition in human–machine interfaces are to some extent almost always keyhole. There are several reasons for this: firstly, users are not always provided with means to communicate their intentions, they do not find

---

* Keyhole plan recognition has got its name from the analogy to "looking through a keyhole" – the system is observing the user's actions, but the user is not aware of this happening, or indifferent to it.

any reason to communicate their intentions, but foremost, they are not enough *aware of the plan recognition abilities* of the system to aid the plan recognition process. It is highly desirable that whenever plan recognition is utilised in an interface, users should be provided with means to inspect, understand and control the plan recognition process, to achieve a situation where users actually intend the system to perform plan recognition. Pure keyhole plan recognition in direct manipulation interfaces can be extremely difficult, since the user's goal usually is at a very high level compared to the individual interactions with the system, and since users may frequently change task, or adopt a novel strategy for the same task, without in any way signalling this to the system.

One way to do better the odds for intended plan recognition is to provide the user with *co-operative task enrichment* (Wærn 1994). An interface provides co-operative task enrichment if

- it adapts responses to individual user interactions on the user's task, that is, plan recognition is an *integral part of* the dialogue,
- it communicates its assumptions to the user, and
- it allows the user to explicitly interact with the plan recognition mechanism.

The POP interface is a characteristic example of a point-and-click interface that combines features both of intended and plan recognition by providing co-operative task enrichment. There are several keys available for inferring a user's task: his or her moves between different information pages, the way of selecting the page (navigation or direct query), the opening and closing of information entities within a page, and finally the explicit selections of tasks. The plan inference also is an integral part of the dialogue, as it selects what information to present and what to hide, at each time a new page is generated.

Still, this system shares a lot of properties with other direct-manipulation applications of plan recognition: the individual actions are at a low level compared to the user's task, and users may frequently move between different strategies for a task, and even between tasks. For example, we cannot draw any definite conclusions about a user's task from his or her way of selecting a page of information – some users will always navigate to the sought information, whereas other will prefer search commands. In our prestudies on an existing information system in the domain, we also found that users that started out with one particular task, frequently would move over to other tasks.

The most interesting aspect of this application is that since plan recognition is an integral part of the human - system interaction, we cannot determine the plan patterns that users will exhibit prior to the implementation of the plan recognition component! Clearly, a kind of bootstrapping procedure is needed, where machine learning techniques are used to gradually build up the system's plan knowledge.

In the second version of POP currently under development, we utilise an extremely simplistic plan recognition algorithm called "intention guessing", that can be described as a probabilistic plan parsing approach with a limited "attention span" (Wærn and Stenborg 1995). This algorithm is useful in this domain since it requires little or no declarative knowledge about user plans, and instead it can be trained from examples. It is also inherently forgetful, making it suited to deal with users changing intentions. More advanced approaches to plan recognition such as the plan parsing approach by Kautz (1987) have problems with recognising when users move between tasks. Furthermore, the intention guessing algorithm only keeps track of such tasks that are likely to be performed at the time of observation, and no more is really needed to produce answers to a specific query.

5. Example Extended with Adaptivity

Turning back to the example introduced above, Section 3.1, in which ways would the adaptivity have changed the interaction with the user? Assuming that we combine the sterotypical tasks with the plan inference mechanism, the following scenario is possible:

- When the user first entered the system she is encouraged to choose among a set of stereotypical tasks.
- The choice of task then affects the first answer page, making certain informations entities open and others closed, and affecting which follow-up questions (on hotwords) are immideately available.
- As the user starts manipulating the answer page, and asking follow-up questions, the plan inference component might decide to alter the assumed task, and that in turn then affects the answer page.
- The user may at this point, disagree with what the system has inferred and decide to change the task back to what it was orignially or to some other task. This can be done through clicking on the hotword in the answer page which displays which task the system has inferred that the user is trying to complete. Only those alternative tasks that actually will alter the presentation will then be shown to the user.
- In addition to this, the free form questions will allow the user to search for specific information, or to pose a vague question.

In other words, the adaptivity will try and make the answer page as short as possible given the demands inherit from the information seeking task, and it will furthermore affect the navigation from this answer page to other pages through affecting the follow-up queries available from the page. The free form questions will also affect the navigation and search aspects of the system, allowing both experienced and inexperiences users to express their questions.

6. Conclusions

The focus of this paper has been to discuss how user adaptive techniques can be integrated with direct manipulation in an interface design to achieve an inspectable, controllable and predictable interface. In particular, we have pointed out the need for several integrated modes of interaction, and the need for means of inspection and control of adaptive functionalities. In order to make these means understandable by users, we advocate that they are presented in *domain-specific* terms, and not by system-internal terms that may be difficult for the user to understand, and predict the effects of alterations.

This consideration has affected in particular the design of linguistic interaction in the system, and the means for inspection and control of adaptivity. The linguistic interaction may lead to obscure results for users: we remedy this by giving users *query paraphrases* and a visible dialogue history which will add to the transparency of the interface behaviour. To inspect and control task adaptation, users are provided either with *task stereotypes* that can be actively selected, or with *user verifiable task presumptions* and a menu of other candidate tasks for the user to choose from.

Deliberately, we have introduced *two* means for users to control the system's adaptation to the user task, both task stereotypes and user verified plan recognition. We have voiced arguments for and against both approaches, and we plan to perform a comparative study of these two techniques, aiming to determine which of them that provides the best user performance and acceptance. However, one should note that it is perfectly feasible to include them both in the same interface, and let the user chose the level of self-adaptiveness from the system. In our prototype system, users are provided with a separate window dealing with "task information", in which they can select from a small set of task stereotypes. If one of these are selected, the generated answers are tailored to this task. If none is selected, plan recognition is used to determine the user's task. Again, this provides the user with a high-level and domain-specific control of the adaptivity of the system, in accordance with our general glass-box approach to adaptiveness.

The hypertext solution selected for the POP help system is an example of the balance between finding intelligent and flexible techniques for aiding users, and the requirements on maintainability and tractability in a large real-world domain such as SDP-TA. The singular hypertext items are written for users seeking information for specific purposes. Each item is a self-contained coherent piece of text, that still can be combined with other texts to provide answers to more general queries. This gives a modular and extendible solution, which still is understandable for the text writer who has to write, and update, the hypertext.

Since the interface design of POP entirely relies on domain-specific terms, an obvious question that arises is to what extent our solution carries over to other domains. However, even though the particular realisation is domain specific, the fundamental concepts used are generic. In particular, this concerns the object-oriented structure of the domain information, and the definition of a task hierarchy. This generality is mirrored in a clear division of generic and domain-specific information in the implementation of POP. It is our current belief that the POP system currently under development will be fairly easy to transfer to other information seeking applications, and we aim to attempt this within a close future.

Acknowledgements

The authors wish to thank all the anonymous subjects who took part in our studies. PUSH is funded jointly by Ellemtel Utvecklings AB, SICS and NUTEK. Ellemtel, SICS, Stockholm University and Linköping University participate in the project.

References

van Beek, P. and R. Cohen: 1991, 'Resolving Plan Ambiguity for Cooperative Response Generation'. Proc. IJCAI-91, Sydney, Australia, Morgan Kaufmann.

Berry, D.C. and D.E. Broadbent: 1986, 'Expert Systems and the Man Machine Interface: Part 2: The User Interface'. *Expert systems: The International Journal of Knowledge Engineering* 4.

Biermann, Alan W. , Bruce W. Ballard and Anne H. Sigmon: 1983, 'An Experimental Study of Natural Language Programming'. *International Journal of Man-Machine Studies* 18, 71–87.

Bladh, Malin and Kristina Höök: 1995, 'Satisfying User Needs through a Combination of Interface Design Techniques'. Proceedings of INTERACT'95, Lillehammer, Norway, 1995.

Bos, Edwin, Carla Huls and Wim Claassen: 1994, 'EDWARD: Full Integration of Language and Action in a Multimodal User Interface'. *International Journal of Human-Computer Studies* 40, 473–495.

du Boulay, Ben, Tim O'Shea and J. Monk: 1981, 'The Black Box inside the Glass Box: Presenting Computing Concepts to Novices'. *International Journal of Man-Machine Studies* 14.

Bretan, Ivan: 1995, 'Natural Language in Model World Interfaces'. Licentiate Thesis, Department of Computer and Systems Sciences. Stockholm: The Royal Institute of Technology and Stockholm University.

Bretan, Ivan, Niklas Frost and Jussi Karlgren: 1995, 'Using Surface Syntax in Interactive Interfaces'. Paper presented to the 10th Nordic Conference of Computational Linguistics. Helsinki: University of Helsinki.

Breuker, Joost (ed.): 1990, *EUROHELP: Developing Intelligent Help Systems.* EC, Copenhagen, Report on the P280 ESPRIT Project EUROHELP.

Capindale, Ruth A. and Robert G. Crawford: 1990, 'Using a Natural Language Interface with Casual Users'. *International Journal of Man-Machine Studies* 32, 341–362.

Chi, Michelene T. H., James D. Slotta and Nicholas de Leeuw: 1994, 'From Things to Processes: A Theory of Conceptual Change for Learning Science Concepts'. *Learning and Instruction – The Journal of the European Association for Research on Learning and Instruction* 4(1), 27–43.

Cohen, P: 1992, 'The Role of Natural Language in a Multimodal Interface'. Proceedings of the ACM Symposium on User Interface Software and Technology (UIST), Monterey, 1992, pp. 143–150.

Höök, Kristina: 1995, 'Adaptation to the User's Task', SICS Research Report R95:08, Sweden.

Kaplan, Craig, Justine Fenwick and James Chen: 1993, 'Adaptive Hypertext Navigation Based On User Goals and Context'. *User Modeling and User-Adapted Interaction* 3(3), 193–220 (reprinted in this volume, pp. 45–69).

Karlgren, Jussi, Ivan Bretan, Niklas Frost and Lars Jonsson: 1995, 'Interaction Models, Reference, and Interactivity for Speech Interfaces to Virtual Environments'. Proceedings of Second Eurographics Workshop on Virtual Environments – Realism and Real Time, Monte Carlo. Darmstadt: Fraunhofer IGD.

Karlgren, Jussi, Kristina Höök, Ann Lantz, Jacob Palme and Daniel Pargman: 1994: 'The Glass Box User Model for Filtering'. 4th International Conference on User Modeling, Hyannis, ACM.

Kass, Robert and Tim Finin: 1988, 'Modeling the User in Natural Language Systems'. *Computational Linguistics* 14(3), Special Issue on User Modeling, eds. A. Kobsa and W. Wahlster.

Kautz, Henry A: 1990, 'A Circumscriptive Theory of Plan Recognition'. In: P. R. Cohen, J. Morgan and M. E. Pollack (eds.): *Intentions in Communication.* Cambridge, MA: MIT Press, pp. 105–133.

Kay, Judy: 1994, 'Lies, Damned Lies and Stereotypes'. 4th International Conference on User Modeling, Hyannis: ACM.

Kobsa, A., D. Müller and A. Nill: 1994, 'KN-AHS: An Adaptive Hypertext Client of the User Modeling System BGP-MS'. Fourth International Conference on UM, Hyannis, MA, ACM.

Kühme, T., U. Malinowski and J. D. Foley: 1993, 'Adaptive Prompting'. Technical Report GIT-GVU-93-05, Georgia Institute of Technology.

Lemaire, Benoit: 1995, 'Object-Oriented Explanation Planning'. In: W. Hoeppner and H. Horacek (eds.): *Principles of Natural Language Generation – Papers from a Dagstuhl Seminar*, Report SI-12 of the University of Duisburg, Germany.

Lemaire, Benoit, Catriona McDermid and Annika Wærn: 1994, 'Adaptive Help by Navigation and Explanation'. SICS technical report T94:05.

Maes, Pattie: 1994, 'Agents That Reduce Work and Information Overload'. *Communications of the ACM* 37, 7.

McDermid, Catriona and Anna-Lena Ereback: 1994. Initial application evaluation and help requirements for SDP. PUSH working paper WP94:01/01.

Meyer, B: 1994, 'Adaptive Performance Support: User Acceptance of a Self-Adapting System'. 4th International Conference on User Modeling, Hyannis, ACM.

Mittal, V. O. and J. D. Moore: 1995, 'Dynamic Generation of Follow Up Question Menus: Facilitating Natural Language Dialogues'. SIGCHI '95 (Denver Colorado, May 7-11, 1995) Human Factors in Computing System Proceedings 1995. New York: ACM SIGCHI, pp. 90–97.

Moore, J D and W. R. Swartout: 1989, 'A Reactive Approach to Explanation'. 11th Int. Conf. on AI, pp. 1504–1510.

Oppermann, Reinhard 1994, 'Adaptively supported adaptability'. *Int. J. Human-Computer Studies* 40, 455–472.

Paris, Cecile: 1988, 'Tailoring Object Descriptions to a User's Level of Expertise'. *Computational Linguistics* 14(3), 64–78.

Pollack, M. E., J. Hirschberg and B. L. Webber: 1982, 'User Participation in the reasoning processes of expert systems'. In: Proceedings of the Second National Conference on Artificial Intelligence, Pittsburgh, Penn.

Raskutti, B. and I. Zukerman: 1994, 'Query and response generation during information-seeking interactions'. 4th International Conference on User Modeling, Hyannis, ACM.

Roth, E. M. and Woods, D. D: 1989, 'Cognitive Task Analysis: An Approach to Knowledge Acquisition for Intelligent System Design'. In: G. Guida and C. Tasso (eds.): *Topics in Expert System Design*, Elsevier Science Publ. B.V. (North-Holland).

Self, J: 1988, 'Bypassing the Intractable Problem of Student Modelling'. Proc. of the Conference on Intelligent Tutoring Systems ITS-88, pp. 107–123.

Shneiderman, Ben: 1983, 'Direct Manipulation: A Step Beyond Programming Languages." *IEEE Computer* 16(8), 57–69.

SICStus Prolog User's Manual (Release 3#0). Swedish Institute of Computer Science, Box 1263, S-164 28 Kista, Sweden. ISBN 91-630-3648-7.

Julita Vassileva: 1994, 'A Practical Architecture for User Modeling in a Hypermedia-Based Information System'. Fourth International Conference on UM, Hyannis, MA, ACM (An updated version of this paper was published as Vassileva, J.: 1996, 'A Task-Centered Approach for User Modeling in a Hypermedia Office Documentation System'. *User Modeling and User-Adapted Interaction* 6(2-3), 185–223. The latter paper is reprinted in this volume, pp. 209–247).

Wærn, Annika: 1994, 'Cooperative Enrichment and Reactive Plan Inference – Applying Plan Inference Outside Natural Language Dialogue'. Presented at the UM-94 workshop on applied planning and plan recognition, available from SICS.

Wærn, Annika and Ola Stenborg: 1995, 'Recognizing the Plan of a Replanning User'. To be presented at the IJCAI workshop on Plan Recognition, Montreal, Canada.

Woods, David D: 1993, 'The price of flexibility'. In: W. D. Gray, W. H. Hefley and D. Murray (eds.): *Proc. of the 1993 Workshop on Intelligent User Interfaces*. ACM Press, pp. 19–25.

Authors' Vitae

Ph. Lic. Kristina Höök
SICS, Box 1263, S-164 28 Kista, Sweden, kia@sics.se

Kristina Höök is a researcher in the HUMLE (HUMan Computer Interaction and Language Engineering) group at SICS, and the project manager of the PUSH project described in this article. Kristina Höök is a Ph.D. candidate in Computer Science at Stockholm University. She received her M.Sc. in computer science from Uppsala University in 1987 and a Licentiate of Philosophy in Computer Science from Stockholm University in 1991. She has worked with adapting explanations to users, and has applied the work in both the area of route guidance systems and documentation of software methods, as presented in this article. Other research interests include methods for interface development, spatial cognition and its relation to navigational ability, and in general individual differences and their effect on interactions with computers.

Ph. Lic. Jussi Karlgren
SICS, Box 1263, S-164 28 Kista, Sweden, jussi@sics.se

Jussi Karlgren is a researcher in the HUMLE (HUMan Computer Interaction and Language Engineering) group at SICS. Jussi Karlgren is a Ph.D. candidate in Computer Science and Computational Linguistics at Stockholm University. He received his B.A. in Computational Linguistics in 1988 and his Licenciate of Philosophy degree in Computer Science in 1992. His primary interests are dialog and communication, taken broadly enough to include human computer dialog design, information retrieval, and language typology. This paper has been influenced by his interests in flexible input and transparent interaction.

Tech. Lic. A. Wærn
SICS, Box 1263, S-164 28 Kista, Sweden, annika@sics.se

Annika Wærn is a researcher at SICS, and manager of the HUMLE (HUMan Computer Interaction and Language Engineering) group. She received her M.Sc. in Computer Science from Uppsala University, and her Tech. Lic. from Stockholm University, and is currently a Ph.D. candidate in Computer Science at Stockholm University. Annika Wærn has previously published work in the area of program analysis for parallel logic programs, but is now working within the field of adaptive interfaces. Her Ph.D. work deals with plan recognition in human-computer interaction, some of it summarized in the published article.

Dr. Nils Dahlbäck
Department of Computer and Information Science, Linköping University, S-581 83 Linköping, Sweden, nda@ida.liu.se

Dr. Dahlbäck is Assistant Professor in Cognitive Science at Linköping University. He received a B.A. in Psychology from Lund University in 1973 and a B.S. in Speech Therapy from Lund in 1978, and his Ph.D. in Communication Studies from Linköping University in 1992. He has worked with communication disorders as a speech therapist and family therapist. Dr. Dahlbäck's main line of research has been the development of empirically based computationally tractable dialogue models for natural language interfaces. Other research interests are adaptable user interfaces, psychological models of discourse coherence, spatial cognition, and individual differences in cognition.

Professor Carl Gustaf Jansson
Department of Computer and Systems Sciences, Stockholm University/The Royal Institute of Technology, Electrum 230, S-164 40 Kista, Sweden, calle@dsv.su.se

Carl Gustaf Jansson received a M.Sc. in Engineering Physics at KTH in 1975 and a Ph.D. in Technical Computer Science at KTH in 1986. He is currently acting professor and deputy head of the Department for Computer and Systems Sciences at Stockholm University/The Royal Institute of Technology. He was appointed Associate Professor in Artificial Intelligence in 1993. Jansson's field of research is Artificial Intelligence, in particular Knowledge Representation (thesis work) and Machine Learning (managing a research group in the area since 1987). Current interests include the application of artificial intelligence techniques in human-computer interaction, in particular adaptive interfaces.

Klas Karlgren
Department of Computer and Systems Sciences, Stockholm University/The Royal Institute of Technology, Electrum 230, S-164 40 Kista, Sweden, klas@dsv.su.se

Klas Karlgren is a Ph.D. student at the Department of Computer and Systems Science at Stockholm University. He holds a degree in psychology and philosophy and a degree in information processing and computer sciences, both from Stockholm University. He has studied cognitive aspects of human-computer interaction, e.g., orientation problems, when using hypermedia applications and the interpretation of graphic models. His current work focuses on conceptual change in learning and understanding.

Dr. Benoît Lemaire
Department of Education Sciences, University of Grenoble II, BP 47, F-38040
Grenoble Cédex 9, France, lemaire@shm.grenet.fr

Dr. Lemaire is an Associate Professor in Education Sciences at Grenoble University. He received his Ph.D. in Computer Science from the University of Orsay, France in 1992. In 1993, he got a postdoctoral fellowship from I.N.R.I.A. to work at the Learning Research and Development Center at the University of Pittsburgh under the supervision of Johanna Moore. In 1994, he worked at the Swedish Institute of Computer Science where he contributed to the research described in this paper. His primary interests lie in the area of artificial intelligence, explanation generation and educational software.

User-Centered Indexing for Adaptive Information Access

NATHALIE MATHÉ and JAMES R. CHEN*
NASA Ames Research Center, Mail Stop 269–2, Moffett Field, CA 94035, U.S.A.
E-mail: mathe@ptolemy.arc.nasa.gov, jchen@ptolemy.arc.nasa.gov

(Received 2 March 1995; in final form 13 March 1996)

Abstract. We are focusing on information access tasks characterized by large volume of hypermedia connected technical documents, a need for rapid and effective access to familiar information, and long-term interaction with evolving information. The problem for technical users is to build and maintain a personalized task-oriented model of the information to quickly access relevant information. We propose a solution which provides user-centered adaptive information retrieval and navigation. This solution supports users in customizing information access over time. It is complementary to information discovery methods which provide access to new information, since it lets users customize future access to previously found information. It relies on a technique, called Adaptive Relevance Network, which creates and maintains a complex indexing structure to represent personal user's information access maps organized by concepts. This technique is integrated within the Adaptive HyperMan system, which helps NASA Space Shuttle flight controllers organize and access large amount of information. It allows users to select and mark any part of a document as interesting, and to index that part with user-defined concepts. Users can then do subsequent retrieval of marked portions of documents. This functionality allows users to define and access personal collections of information, which are dynamically computed. The system also supports collaborative review by letting users share group access maps. The adaptive relevance network provides long-term adaptation based both on usage and on explicit user input. The indexing structure is dynamic and evolves over time. Learning and generalization support flexible retrieval of information under similar concepts. The network is geared towards more recent information access, and automatically manages its size in order to maintain rapid access when scaling up to large hypermedia space. We present results of simulated learning experiments.

Key words: user-centered indexing, long-term adaptation, adaptive information retrieval, adaptive navigation, user feedback, shared information access

1. Introduction

1.1. HUMAN PROBLEM

We are interested in facilitating access to reference information contained in large volume of on-line technical and operational manuals. Technical reference information is used in many fields by professionals like lawyers, doctors, power plant controllers, airplane mechanics, pilots, astronauts, flight controllers, etc. These professionals need to access a large amount of technical information to perform their

---

* Dr. Mathé and Dr. Chen are contractors with Recom Technologies, Inc.

P. Brusilovsky et al. (eds.), Adaptive Hypertext and Hypermedia, 171–207.
© 1998 *Kluwer Academic Publishers.*

everyday job. Moreover, technical information is usually highly cross-referenced, creating a huge space of hypermedia connected documents.

For these users, the context of the information access task is different from the one assumed by traditional information retrieval tasks. In general, they already know most of the information they need and where it is stored. However to prevent human errors, they are usually required to quickly access information relevant to specific tasks they are performing. They rarely need to search for new information. When they do find new interesting information, they need to memorize where to find it for future reference. For example, this type of information access is of great importance to Space Shuttle flight controllers at NASA Johnson Space Center (JSC). It takes years of training to become a flight controller in the Space Shuttle Mission Control Center. As part of this training, controllers learn to use a large corpus of documentation to solve problems. They develop a deep knowledge of the organization and content of these manuals in order to access the proper sections as quickly as possible. This knowledge, developed as part of a situational and task-oriented process, is highly context-dependent and user-dependent (Boy, 1991). Contextual factors such as frequency of access, date of last use, relative relevance to a task, and individual user preferences have been shown to be very important to classify, organize and access information from an individual point of view (Barreau, 1995). Therefore there is a need to support information access based on contextual use and individual user preferences.

Another aspect of the problem is the time span of the information need: technical information access is a long term process, in the sense that information pertaining to a particular task needs to be accessed each time this task is performed. However, human memory of information organization and content does not persist very long unless the same information is accessed often under the same conditions. Users therefore develop artifacts to support their memory, like hand-written annotations, Post-It notes, bookmarks; or they create condensed representations of important information, like cue cards, quick access guide, abbreviated checklists. For example, each flight controller develops a personal collection of information selected from existing Shuttle operations documents, which is referred to as a "goody book". A personal "goody book" is used to access critical or often-used information faster. Therefore there is a need to support customization of information access by individual users.

Another problem related to the long term aspect of this information task, is due to frequent updates and revisions of technical manuals. Users have to continuously revise what they know, as well as manually update their personal annotations and quick-access collections. This is time consuming, and creates a potential safety risk. Therefore there is a need to support persistence and incremental modification of customized information access.

To summarize, technical information access task is characterized by a large volume of hypermedia connected documents, the need for rapid and effective access to already known information, and long-term interaction with evolving information.

The problem for technical users is to build and maintain a personalized task-oriented model of the information in order to quickly access information relevant to specific tasks at hand.

1.2. TECHNICAL PROBLEM

Two main ways of accessing on-line information are querying and browsing. Querying consists in providing a description (query) of the information being sought, and having an information retrieval system locates information that matches the description (Salton, 1989). Browsing assumes that the information has already been organized (usually in a hierarchical structure like a table of contents, or with cross-reference hyperlinks), and a hypertext system provides means for the user to navigate within this structure (e.g., World Wide Web browser like Mosaic).

Many useful techniques in traditional information retrieval have been developed in the past few decades (van Rijsbergen, 1979; Salton, 1989). Inverted index has long been used for fast and effective retrieval. Boolean retrieval models compare Boolean queries with term sets used to identify document contents. Extended Boolean systems employ query and document term weights to generate ranked output documents. Vector Space models represent both queries and documents by term sets and computes similarity measures between them (Salton et al., 1975). Latent Semantic Indexing uses singular value decomposition to encode compressed representation of a term-document matrix in vector space, which facilitates both efficient and generalizable retrieval (Dumais et al., 1988). Probabilistic indexing models (Fuhr, 1992) follow the Probability Ranking Principle to achieve better retrieval performance (Robertson, 1977). A Bayesian Inference Network retrieval model regards information retrieval as uncertain inference (Turtle & Croft, 1991). It provides a unified representation framework of different models, and allows the integration of multiple sources of evidence and the combination of different queries and query types. These information retrieval systems require significant pre-processing to extract indexing information from the content of a relatively static set of documents. These information retrieval techniques are very effective, but with huge spaces of documents, they might still retrieve too many relevant documents based on content only. There is a need to further discriminate among relevant documents based on tasks users are engaged in and individual user preferences, which evolve over time.

On the other hand, hypertext systems provide user-driven navigation. Their main strength relies on a fixed structure to support navigation, but this is also their main weakness, since the structure is usually authored by someone else than the user (or automatically generated by a software program), and cannot be easily modified. Knowledge-based hypertext systems add a second-level structure (often referred to as a thesaurus, semantic net, domain knowledge, or index space) on top of the basic document hypertext structure, in order to provide more flexible and intelligent navigation (Agosti et al., 1995; Belkin et al., 1993; Tudhope et al., 1995).

Concepts in the index space are assigned to hypertext nodes in the document space. Navigation in the document space is performed indirectly through navigation in the index space, and hyperlinks can be dynamically computed. Constructing the index space and associating concepts to hypertext nodes is usually performed manually by domain experts, and/or automatically pre-computed from existing thesaurus. As for the document-level structure, this second-level structure is usually pre-computed and authored by someone else than the user. With large hypermedia systems, users might however "get lost in hyperspace" without intelligent navigation support adapted to each user's needs.

In term of customization at the document level, most hypertext systems let users add their own annotations and sometimes hyperlinks on top of the existing hypertext structure. They usually offer a mechanism to create a quick-access list of user-selected information (Hotlist or Bookmarks list in WWW browsers), hierarchically organized under unique headings. However, these customization techniques do not scale up with large hypermedia spaces. There is a need to automatically filter and adapt pages and links for different users and different tasks. The work presented in this paper focuses primarily on customized information access for individual users and groups of users. Other papers in this issue (Vassileva, 1996; Höök et al., 1996) focus on task-oriented information access, and are discussed in the related work section (Section 2), since the two approaches are related and complementary.

1.3. PROPOSED SOLUTION

A solution to the problem of quickly accessing information contained in large volume of hypermedia connected documents relies on providing user-centered adaptive information access, both for querying and browsing; as well as on providing tools to continuously let users customize information access over time. We consider three ways of adapting information access (Brusilovsky, 1994): (1) adaptive information retrieval, (2) adaptive hypermedia presentation, and (3) adaptive hypermedia navigation.

Adaptive information retrieval allows users to access information using personal conceptual descriptors, in addition to usual keywords. For example, given a query containing a list of keywords and a list of personal concepts, an adaptive information access system retrieves a ranked list of information units relevant to the query. Depending on particular applications, information units might correspond to entire documents, pages, or hypertext nodes. Conceptual descriptors might correspond to tasks, problems, goals, topics explicitly specified by the user, or automatically deduced by the system.

Adaptive hypermedia presentation changes the set of visible links displayed to the user. For example, given a hypertext node selected by the user, and a set of personal concepts, the system filters existing hyperlinks associated to the selected node, and displays only existing links relevant to the set of personal concepts.

Adaptive hypermedia navigation changes the layout of links (by re-ordering existing links, or by generating new links) to provide intelligent guidance to the user. For example, given a selected hypertext node, and a set of personal concepts, the system dynamically generates a list of hypertext nodes destinations likely to be relevant to the set of personal concepts, given the starting hypertext node. Such adaptive hyperlinks are computed on the fly, and are dynamic instead of static links.

We propose a technique, called Adaptive Relevance Network (ARN), which supports adaptive information retrieval, as well as adaptive hypermedia presentation and navigation, based on a second-level user-centered indexing structure. Information access is customized to individual user' needs. ARN supports users in creating and managing personalized information access maps, which are organized by concepts. Each concept is user-defined and is described by a descriptor, corresponding to a task, a problem, a goal, a topic, etc. Our approach is complementary to information discovery methods which provide access to new information, since it lets users customize future access to previously found information.

The adaptive relevance network creates and maintains a complex indexing structure to store individual user's information access maps (Mathé & Chen, 1994) (see Sections 4.1 and 4.2). Adaptation is based both on usage (automatic adaptation), and on explicit user input (adaptation prompted by user) for assigning user-defined concepts to information units, and for updating relevance weights between concepts and information units (see Section 4.3). Direct adaptation by the user is also supported with tools for editing concept descriptors. Flexible retrieval is provided by the ability to compute relevant information from incomplete relevance knowledge stored in a network (see Section 4.4). The network maintains a balance between memorization and generalization, to support retrieval of information under similar sets of concepts. The indexing structure is dynamic: ARN incorporates incremental user input and dynamically adjusts the indexing structure and relevance weights over time. It is geared towards more recent information access, and can adjust the speed at which it forgets, as well as the number of inputs after which it forgets (see Section 4.5).

To store user's information access maps, we chose an indexing structure rather than a hierarchical structure, since it is generally recognized that multiple information access points are needed (Barreau, 1995). We chose a complex structure (a composite-index network), rather than a flat index structure, to be able to capture non-linear aspect of conceptual knowledge, such as exceptions (Boy, 1991). In the context of this paper, non-linear means that a portion of relevant information units cannot be derived from information units relevant to individual concepts, but only from information units relevant to a specific set of concepts, representing a complex concept. These complex concepts are represented by composites nodes in a network. Relations between single and complex concept nodes denote a sub-set relationship, rather than a hierarchical relationship. Lastly, we implemented the adaptive relevance network so that it provides rapid information access, and automatically manages its size in order to maintain rapid access when scaling up to large hypermedia space (see Section 4.5).

We integrated our adaptive relevance network technique into the HyperMan hypermedia system (Rabinowitz et al., 1995). Space Shuttle flight controllers at NASA/JSC use HyperMan to access operations documents in mission control. Adaptive HyperMan builds upon the hypertext features of HyperMan, and helps users organize and access large amount of information. It lets users select and mark any part of a document as interesting, and index that part with user-defined concepts, corresponding to particular flights, simulations, problems, systems, tasks, goals, or topics. Users can then do subsequent retrieval of marked portions of documents by concepts. This functionality allows users to define and access personal collections of information, which are dynamically computed, thus providing a virtual "goody book" facility to individual flight controllers. Adaptive HyperMan provides user-driven and long-term adaptation: it lets users build their individual information access maps, and automatically keeps them up to date. The system also supports collaborative review by letting users build group information access maps using a shared list of concepts.

Lastly, our adaptive relevance network technique is independent of any particular information system or document format. It is complementary to other information retrieval and hypermedia systems which support querying and browsing, and discovery of new information. In fact it has also been successfully integrated with the Boeing Portable Maintenance Aid system for airplane mechanics, and with the World Wide Web for organizing and sharing personal pages collections. These applications are at the prototype and testing stage, and are not described in this paper.

In the following section, we present an overview of related approaches to adaptive information access. In the third section, we describe the Adaptive HyperMan system and illustrate its use with an example scenario. The fourth section describes in details the structure of the Adaptive Relevance Network, its learning method based on user input, and its adaptive information access method. Results of simulated learning experiments are presented in the fifth section. We propose future directions of research in the sixth section, and then conclude.

2. Related Work

In Section 1.2, we reviewed traditional information retrieval techniques and knowledge-based hypertext systems, and their limitations in adapting to individual users' needs. We now briefly compare our proposed solution to these techniques, and then review related work on adaptive information retrieval, adaptive information filtering, and adaptive hypermedia.

While traditional information retrieval systems are very effective at retrieving information from large set of documents based on content, they are not geared towards building customized personal indices, nor supporting incremental modifications by users over time. The ARN technique we propose supports a customizable and sharable, personal index system, which is complementary to existing information retrieval systems. It is similar to an inverted index with a more complex composite index structure. Simple probabilistic estimates are used to quickly represent and compute relevance measures. Although ARN does employ a network architecture and probabilistic relevance estimates similar to those of a Bayesian Inference Network, it is different. ARN focuses on maintaining a dynamic and effective indexing structure, instead of on optimizing probabilistic estimates. Lastly, some techniques like logical queries and/or queries with weighted terms, which are not currently supported in our application interface, could be integrated to accommodate more complex queries.

Short-term adaptive information retrieval systems provide relevance feedback mechanisms to help users formulate queries, and improve retrieval. User feedback is used to modify the current query, either query terms and/or weights (Harman, 1992; Haines & Croft, 1993; Robertson & Sparc Jones, 1976). Our work primarily uses user feedback to capture user-centered indexing information over time and across several queries, instead of refining the formulation of a single query. Standard relevance feedback method, however, is also applicable to our personal indexing system. Another approach of adaptive information retrieval uses a connectionist network to learn the information space structure over time from users' combined input (Belew, 1989; Rose & Belew, 1991). These systems usually require a long training period before reaching a state of fertility (Chen, 1995).

Adaptive information filtering examines a continuous stream of incoming documents and display only these that are relevant to a user's long term interests (Callan et al., 1992). Most information filtering methods rely on modeling and learning user interests over time. Although we are not modeling users' interests, but rather modeling information access and organization, we face similar issues in modeling changes over time, and in sharing information access maps with other users. Jennings and Higichi have embedded a connectionist model of long-term user interests into a system for reading Usenet news (Jennings & Higichi, 1993). They apply supervised learning to manage large search space without extensive knowledge engineering. Fischer and Stevens apply a rule-based technique to suggest boolean search agents for reading Usenet news (Fischer & Stevens, 1991). Sheth and Maes (1993) use a genetic algorithm to evolve boolean search agents parameters. The main problem is to model changes and persistence in user interests, as well as interaction between interests. This often requires combining machine learning techniques with interest management through user interaction. Collaborative filtering methods go one step further by involving the explicit advice of other users (Pargman, 1994). Collaborative filtering might be based on other users' actions (to search information read by another user (Goldberg et al., 1992)), or based on other users' evaluations (to search information that has received positive feedback from other types of users, or from users with similar interests (Bergstrom & Riedl, 1994)). Maes and Kozierok apply memory-based learning and learning by example from both individual user and similar users' agents (Maes & Kozierok, 1994).

Adaptive hypermedia systems have been developed to tailor information content and hyperlinks to different classes of users with different goals and knowledge, and to provide individual guidance through large hypermedia spaces (Brusilovzky, 1994). Typical application domains are educational and tutoring systems, advanced help and explanations, and on-line documentation. Most adaptive hypermedia techniques in tutoring systems rely on a domain model, implemented as a more or less complex semantic net, and on relations between hypertext nodes and concepts in the domain model. The individual user model is usually an overlay model of what the user knows about the domain, or a simpler stereotypical model. The systems are complex and require extensive knowledge acquisition and modeling, which does not scale up easily.

Simpler approaches have been developed for on-line documentation. Adaptive hypermedia presentation automatically changes the information displayed, or the set of visible links (by hiding irrelevant information or links, or by highlighting relevant ones). Armstrong et al. have proposed a learning by example apprentice, which help users locate desired information by highlighting recommended links in a Web document (Armstrong et al., 1995). Recommendations are based on the user's information goal, and the content of the previously selected hypertext node, its surrounding sentence and its parent headings. The user provides feedback by accessing or not the suggested nodes. This system requires pre-processing a set of training data first, and does not learn in an incremental manner. Vassileva proposes to limit the browsing space according to the current task performed by the user and her level of experience (Vassileva, 1996; Vassileva, 1994). The system utilizes pre-defined tasks hierarchies, which are acquired by empirical analysis of the domain. Hypertext nodes are associated to tasks under which they are relevant (indexing done a priori by a knowledge engineer). Users manually select a current task, which provides a starting point for browsing as well as a filter by providing access only to nodes relevant to the current task. User's level of experience is automatically adjusted by the system based on analysis of previous user navigation actions. The system also supports users in directly modifying the task hierarchy, creating new tasks or changing their level of experience. This approach is similar to ours, the main difference being that the task model is pre-defined by a knowledge engineer, instead of being incrementally learnt from the user. This is appropriate for small domains with relatively stable hierarchical task models.

Adaptive navigation automatically changes the layout of links to provide guidance, by re-ordering links, augmenting links with dynamic comments, or suggesting most relevant links to follow. Kaplan et al. proposed a model to memorize user preferences about relevance between topics in an associative matrix (Kaplan et al., 1993). The system is based only on user input, and does not generalize the information for different usage. Other adaptive navigation methods utilize learning by observation techniques to automatically learn patterns of navigation based on frequency of nodes accesses (Kibby & Mayes, 1989; Monk, 1989). Similar to Vassileva's and our approaches, Höök et al. propose to adapt hypermedia using knowledge about the user's current task (Höök et al., 1996). They developed a help assistant system which provides both adaptive presentation of content, and adaptive navigation with follow-up questions most relevant to user's task. The current task is either directly selected by the user, or automatically selected using . This approach assumes relatively stable hierarchical task models, and a priori knowledge acquisition of a task hierarchy might become a problem for large domains.

At the other end of the spectrum, fully user-driven customization systems, which don't rely on any a priori knowledge, have been developed to help users organize their personal information space. The Warmlist system is a personal Internet assistant which lets users build their own collections of interesting WWW documents, organize them hierarchically, index them with a full-text indexing engine, and share them with other users (Klark & Manber, 1995). The Active Notebook system lets users label WWW documents with conceptual classifications, and organize these documents into a semantic taxonomy, which can be shared with other users (Torrance, 1995). Because they are fully manual, these systems do not provide any intelligent support to users in creating hierarchies and taxonomies, and their approach might not scale up to large information spaces.

To summarize, we propose to use a second-level conceptual indexing structure, similar to the one used in knowledge-based and adaptive hypertext systems. But, instead of being manually acquired from experts or pre-computed, this structure is incrementally learnt over time from user input, and therefore customized to individual user's needs. Compared to personal information space organizers, our approach is automated: users assign concepts to information units, and our system automatically builds a conceptual network structure, which is used for adaptive information access. The problem of sharing complex taxonomies among users is tackled by combining input from multiple users into a group network structure.

3. Adaptive HyperMan System

This section illustrates our user-centered indexing approach to adaptive information access with the Adaptive HyperMan system (AHM). AHM lets users select and mark any part of a document as interesting, and index that part with user-defined concepts, corresponding to particular flights, simulations, problems, systems, tasks, goals, or topics. Users can then do subsequent retrieval of marked parts of documents by concepts. This functionality allows users to define and access personal collections of information, which are dynamically computed, thus providing a virtual "goody book" facility to individual flight controllers. The system also supports collaborative review by letting users build group information access maps using a shared list of concepts.

3.1. THE HYPERMAN VIEWER

HyperMan is a software tool for document viewing and parsing, developed as part of the Electronic Documentation Project (EDP) at NASA/JSC (NASA JSC–26679, 1994). The goal of the EDP project is to provide an electronic capability to support authoring, distribution, viewing, and controlled revision of crew and ground controller operations documents, for use in Mission Control Center and in their office environment. EDP integrates the state-of-the-art hypertext document viewer, HyperMan, with JSC flight planning and scheduling tools, and commercial workflow automation tools. Starting with a literal representation of the current paper-based system, HyperMan extends that metaphor with hypertext capabilities. HyperMan is a full blown wysiwyg PDF (Adobe's Portable Document Format) viewer designed for hundreds of simultaneous users. HyperMan is being used by flight controllers in support of Space Shuttle missions since July, 1995.

To answer flight controllers' need for intensive customization of documents, HyperMan provides the ability for end-users to create and store various types of visual markers in a document (Figure 1). User create visual markers on a page by first selecting a tool in the tools palette, then selecting a portion of the page, or a location in the page. Different types of visual markers are available: *color highlight* (changing background color of selected text or graphical region), *colored text* (changing foreground color of selected text), an *anchor icon*, a *bookmark icon*, a *notepad icon* (hidden note), or a *sticky note* (visible note). Users can also create hyperlinks between any markers (both inter- and intra-book, and uni- or bi-directional) by selecting the linking tool in the tools palette and selecting two markers. To support collaborative work, users can publish their markers and links, and subscribe to published markers and links from various user groups.

Other useful features include full text search, automatic hyperlinking at parsing time, version control (to retain user markers and hyperlinks between versions of documents), and transportable hypertext layer (each user's markers and links are stored separately from the documents, so that the document itself is never altered by the creation or deletion of markers or links). We do not have space to describe the HyperMan system in full details, and will focus in the next sections on the adaptive functionality we added to the system.

3.2. ADAPTIVE HYPERMAN

Adaptive HyperMan (AHM) builds upon the hypertext features of HyperMan by allowing users to create markers on a page to mark any part of a document as interesting, and to assign conceptual descriptors to selected markers in documents. Users can then retrieve markers that are relevant under particular conceptual descriptors. These conceptual descriptors are called *topics* in AHM user interface.* Topics cor-

---

* This supplements full text search by keyword capability, as markers may have been indexed under topics that never appear as words on that page, or markers may be associated with graphics.

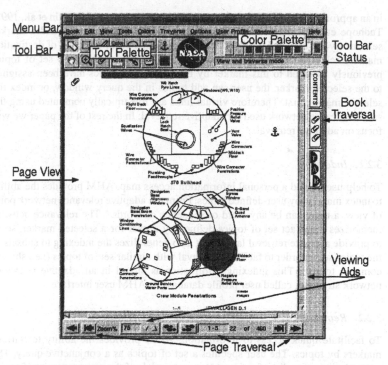

Figure 1. HyperMan book window. The annotation tools palette is shown at the top left, below the menu bar. Various visual markers are shown on the page. The User Profile menu has been added for the adaptive version of HyperMan.

respond to particular flights, simulations, problems, systems, tasks, goals, or any concept relevant to facilitate information access. They are either offered by the user, or chosen from the system-defined list, which is used to facilitate sharing of indexing information among groups of users. AHM also lets users provide feedback over time to update the relevance of markers to topics. The system utilizes the Adaptive Relevance Network mentioned in Section 1.3 (and fully described in Section 4) to store these users' personal information access maps. AHM supports both adaptive retrieval of markers, and adaptive navigation. Adaptive presentation of markers has not been implemented.

For *adaptive retrieval*, given a particular user and a query containing a list of topics, the system computes a ranked list of markers relevant to the set of topics for this user, by accessing his/her personal information access map stored in a relevance network structure. For *adaptive navigation*, navigation in the document space is performed indirectly through navigation in the relevance network structure, in an approach similar to those proposed in (Agosti et al., 1995; Belkin et al., 1993; Tudhope et al., 1995). More specifically, given a particular user and a marker selected by the user, the system dynamically computes a ranked list of destination markers relevant to the selected marker, by using as a query the set of topics previously assigned to this marker by the user. If no topics have been assigned to the selected marker, the user can add topics in the query window, or index the selected marker first. Therefore virtual links are dynamically computed using the same relevance network used for adaptive retrieval. In the rest of the paper we will focus on adaptive retrieval.

3.2.1. *Indexing*

To help users build a personal information access map, AHM provides the ability to index markers by user-defined topics. From the adaptive relevance network point of view, a topic can be any word or sequence of words.* The relevance network memorizes the exact set of topics defined by a user for a selected marker, so as to provide accurate retrieval later on. It also generalizes the indexing to subsets of the topics set, in order to facilitate retrieval with similar sets of topics (i.e., sharing common topics). This indexing information is stored in an adaptive relevance network structure, called user profile database in AHM user interface.

3.2.2. *Retrieval*

To facilitate quick access to information, AHM provides the ability to retrieve markers by topics. The user specifies a set of topics as a conjunctive query. The network retrieves a list of markers by exact match, if the exact same set of topics was previously assigned to some markers (memorization); or by derivation from previous queries (memorized or generalized) which contain subsets of the current query.

3.2.3. *Learning*

To help users maintain an accurate information access map, as the information is updated or the user knowledge evolves, AHM offers users the ability to give feedback in order to modify the relevance of markers to given topics over time (users can always add new topics through the indexing capability). When users give positive or negative feedback to markers retrieved with given topics, the adaptive network automatically adjusts its relevance measures for these markers and topics, and propagates feedback to all proper topics subsets (generalization). The adaptive network also learns to improve its retrieval performance by usage. It automatically analyzes co-occurrence statistics of topics over a collection of previous queries,

---

* We do not currently represent semantic relationship between topics, but plan to do it in our future work.

then selects and memorizes sets of topics with high co-occurrence value to improve the generalization process.

3.2.4. *Collaborative work*

To facilitate sharing of information among a group of users (e.g., flight controllers with the same console position), and to facilitate training of novice users, AHM combines inputs from all users in a separate network, called system profile database (in addition to each user's profile database). Only system-defined topics are used. This supports the creation of a corporate memory over time, which can be shared by all users, or used as a starting point to their individual indexing.

3.3. A SAMPLE SCENARIO

This section describes how users interact with Adaptive HyperMan. An explicit design goal was to change the HyperMan user interface as little as possible, so as not to confuse novice HyperMan users. The only visible difference we made to the book window is the additional *User Profile* menu (Figure 1), which provides access to four new windows: *Categorize Marker* (Figure 2), *Markers Basket* (Figure 3), *Marker Retrieval* and *Marker Retrieval Results* (Figures 4 and 5).

3.3.1. *Assigning topics to markers*

Initially, a user starts by identifying information of interest and assigning topics to it. This is performed by first creating and selecting a marker in the HyperMan book window ("crew module penetrations" text highlight on top of Figure 1), then choosing the Categorize Marker option from the User Profile menu. The Categorize Marker window is displayed with the selected marker at the top (Figure 2). The selected marker is described by its name ("crew module penetrations"), library name ("SWYearLib"), book name ("IFM GC2"), and page number ("Page 1-5"). Each user has the choice to store associations between topics and markers into a personal User Profile database (private), or into a Shared Profile database (shared by a group of users). The user then selects topics from the lists of topics on the right and assembles a list of topics to be assigned to the selected marker on the left. Topics might for example correspond to particular flights, simulations, problems, systems, tasks, or preferences. Topics are either personal and defined by each user (User Topics), or shared by all users and pre-defined (Author Topics). To assign topics that are not in the User Topics lists, users can directly type them into the Add User Topic field. These new topics will automatically be added to the User Topics list and saved for future use. When the user clicks on the Categorize button, the selected marker is automatically indexed under the list of topics specified by the user, and this customization is stored in the selected profile database.

For example in Figure 2, the highlighted text marker "crew module penetrations" is indexed into the user profile database under the user-defined topics "STS-75",

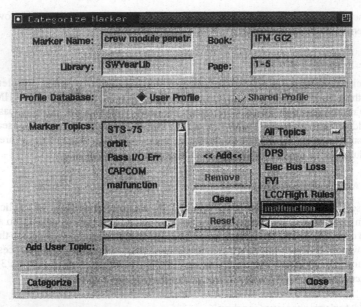

Figure 2. Categorize Marker window. The user selects from the list of topics on the right and assembles on the left a list of topics to be assigned to the marker shown on top.

"orbit", and "malfunction", corresponding to a mission name, a phase of the mission, and a task of handling a malfunction; and under the pre-defined topics "Pass I/O Err" and "CAPCOM", corresponding to a problem description, and a system name.

3.3.2. *Setting aside interesting markers*

After marking interesting information, users might not always have time to categorize markers during a mission, or they might prefer to mark information for a while, then come back and categorize it. The Markers Basket is a place where users can store a list of markers belonging to any book (Figure 3). This list is personal and saved from one session to the next. To add a marker to this list, a user first selects a marker in the HyperMan book window (Figure 1), then chooses the Markers Basket option from the User Profile menu. To later categorize a marker stored in the list, a user first selects this marker in the list, then clicks on the Categorize button at the bottom (Figure 3): the Categorize Marker window is displayed with the selected marker in at the top (Figure 2).

The Markers Basket can also be used as a quick access tool, like Bookmarks in Netscape or the Hotlist in Mosaic. Users can directly go to markers attached to

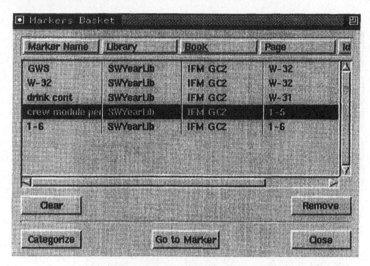

Figure 3. Markers Basket window stores a list of markers for quick access or future indexing.

specific pages in books, by simply double-clicking on a marker in the Basket, or selecting it and clicking on the Go to Marker button.

3.3.3. *Retrieving markers by topics*

Once a user has categorized a few markers, he/she can search all books in any given library for markers relevant to specific topics. The user opens the Marker Retrieval window (Figure 4a) from the User Profile menu. This window provides several options specifying how to perform the retrieval. The top portion of the Marker Retrieval window allows users to select the library to retrieve markers from. The middle portion of the Marker Retrieval window allows users to select the profile database to retrieve markers from, either User Profile or Shared Profile, and the topics to be used to retrieve markers. The bottom portion of the Marker retrieval window lets users select the matching mode and the maximum number of markers to be retrieved (Max Hits option). The Matching Mode option specifies whether to retrieve markers which are categorized under all selected topics on the left (All Topics), or which are categorized under any one of the selected topics (At Least One). For example in Figure 4a, the user specifies to retrieve markers he/she personally indexed under all three topics "orbit", "Pass I/O Err", and "STS-75".

After the user submits the search, the system displays a ranked list of retrieved markers in the Marker Retrieval Results window (Figure 4b). Retrieved markers are listed by order of relevance to the retrieval topics, the more relevant marker being displayed at the top of the list. In this example, only two markers were

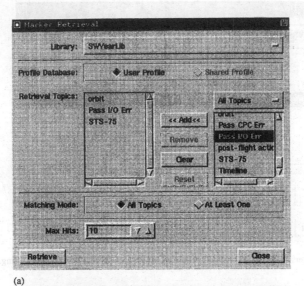

(a)

(b)

Figure 4. Marker Retrieval and Marker Retrieval Results windows. The user assembles a list
of topics describing the markers they are looking for (a), and the system displays a ranked list
of markers relevant to the retrieval topics (b).

indexed under all three topics. However these markers were originally indexed under a more specific set of topics ("STS-75", "orbit", "malfunction", "Pass I/O Err", and "CAPCOM" in Figure 2), and the system used a derivation algorithm (see Section 4.4.2) to retrieve these markers under a more general set of topics ("orbit", "Pass I/O Err", and "STS-75").

Users can double-click a marker and directly go to that marker in a book, or select a marker and click on the Go to Marker button. Users can also associate additional topics to a marker using the Categorize button, which displays the Categorize Marker window with the selected marker. The same marker can be categorized with different sets of topics as many times as needed. Finally, users can provide feedback regarding the relevance of markers to specifics sets of topics, as described in the next paragraph. Feedback buttons (Success and Failure) are used to adjust the ranking of a particular marker, which will move the marker up/down the list.

Indexing and retrieving markers by topics lets flight controllers create personal collections of markers. A personal collection corresponds to a list of markers retrieved under specific topics in the Marker Retrieval Results window. Flight controllers call it a "virtual goody book". (A paper "goody book" is a personal collection of selected paper pages from existing Shuttle operations documents, assembled by each flight controller to perform their task more efficiently.) This list is dynamically computed, and always kept up to date. Moreover, flight controllers can create markers for multiple purposes: quick access, highlighting critical information, writing down comments during a mission. Therefore being able to index markers under multiple topics is very valuable, as it gives them capabilities to retrieve markers for a given flight or simulation, for a particular problem, for a particular system, and to combine these topics to narrow down the list of markers.

3.3.4. *Providing feedback*

In the following example we illustrate more sophisticated capabilities for customizing information access. After categorizing more markers, the user decides to retrieve all markers relevant to both "orbit" and "STS-75" (Figure 5a), which is more general than the previous query "orbit, Pass I/O Err, STS-75" (Figure 4a). The user has previously categorize the markers named "crew module penetrations", and "1-6" with the set of topics "STS-75", "orbit", "malfunction", "Pass I/O Err" and "CAPCOM". Because of its generalization algorithm, the relevance network has also propagated the relevance of these two markers to each individual topic, with a lower relevance weight. Therefore the system retrieves these two markers, together with five other relevant markers, when the user submits the query "orbit" and "STS-75". The user however decides that these two markers are not relevant for this general query, since they correspond to very specific malfunctions. The user decides to tell the system about this exception by selecting each marker and clicking on the Failure button. The list of retrieved markers is automatically resorted upon feedback. As a result, the system first moves them to the bottom of the retrieval list. The user continues to click on the Failure button until the system lower their relevance weight below the minimal threshold (see section 4.5.4), and removes these two markers from the retrieval list (Figure 5b). The two markers will still be retrieved by the query "orbit", "Pass I/O Err", and "STS-75" as in Figure 4, but won't be retrieved by the query "orbit" and "STS-75" anymore. This example illustrates the non-linear aspect of the Adaptive Relevance Network.

3.4. COLLABORATIVE REVIEW

Most markers are created by flight controllers prior to a mission, but they also write down comments during a mission whenever a problem is encountered. These comments, also called post-flight actions, are later used in collaborative reviews to revise procedures and update documents. With Adaptive HyperMan, flight controllers now have the ability to categorize their comments under the author-defined "post-flight actions" topic. After a mission and in preparation of a collaborative review, they can then access all annotated pages indexed under "post-flight actions" by other flight controllers, by retrieving markers from the shared profile database.

In the following section, we describe the structure of the relevance network, its learning method based on user feedback, and its information retrieval method. We finish the section with a discussion of the efficiency and computational cost of the relevance network.

4. Adaptive Relevance Network

An adaptive relevance network models user preferences on information relevance with respect to given tasks. This network provides a domain independent information architecture which facilitates incremental storage of both relevance information provided by users, and relevance information computed through other traditional retrieval techniques. The network memorizes information on the relevance of references based on user feedback for specific queries. It also aggregates and generalizes such information to facilitate future retrievals with similar queries.

4.1. RELEVANCE NETWORK

A relevance network records measures of relevance of output nodes with respect to input nodes. For information retrieval purposes, an *output node* corresponds to a reference, which can be a document or any marked location within a document. There are two types of input nodes: *basic nodes* and *composite nodes*. A basic input node corresponds to a descriptor. A descriptor can be a keyword in the index, a sequence of words in the text, or a user-defined task or goal. A descriptor can also be a reference, to retrieve other related references. A composite input node corresponds to a combination of query descriptors. Composite nodes are defined in Section 4.2.

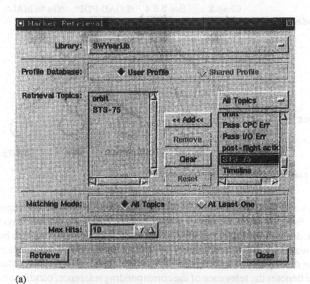

(a)

(b)

Figure 5. Providing Feedback. The user issues a fairly general query (a), and gets rid of non-relevant retrieved markers by giving negative feedback with the Failure button, until unwanted markers fall to the bottom of the list, or even disappear from the list (b).

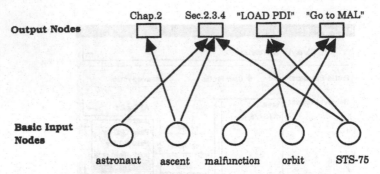

Figure 6. An example of a simple relevance network.

Figure 6 shows an example of a simple relevance network with only basic input nodes. Nodes in the top layer represent output nodes. Nodes in the lower layer represent input nodes. A user query is interpreted as an input activation pattern by the relevance network. A Boolean activation value of an input node denotes whether the corresponding descriptor is a member of the current query. An activation value on an output node denotes the relevance of the corresponding reference, conditioned by the current user query encoded in the input layer.

Associated with each connection from an input node to an output node is a relevance measure between the corresponding descriptor and reference. A network is initially empty.* As a user specifies queries and provides positive or negative feedback on the relevance of retrieved references, input and output nodes that do not exist yet in the network are created, and relevance measures associated with the connections are adjusted accordingly. A relevance measure, in its simplest form, is defined as the relative frequency of positive user feedback for a reference given a descriptor. Each relevance measure is maintained as two parts of a fraction: the number of positive feedback, S, over the number of total feedback, N. That is, a relevance measure R_{ij} of a reference j with respect to a descriptor i is

$$R_{ij} = \frac{S_{ij}}{N_{ij}} = \frac{\text{Number of (Positive Feedback)}}{\text{Number of (Feedback)}} .$$

Maintaining the total number of feedback in the denominator facilitates an accurate recording of both the relevance of the reference and the sampling precision of such relevance.

A relevance network can be built incrementally entirely through user feedback, starting from an empty network without any node and connection. For pragmatic purpose, however, a relevance network is often initialized with known relevance

---

* When the relevance network is empty, references relevant to a user query can be accessed through other retrieval means provided by the application interface. A relevance network can also be initialized using traditional information retrieval techniques.

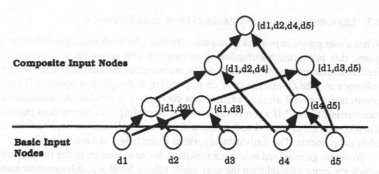

Figure 7. Input layer of a relevance network with composite nodes. Arrows denote subset relations. Output nodes and relevance connections are not displayed.

information. This can be done through various means. A user can borrow a personal relevance network from another user, or a shared network from a group, to create his/her own initial network. Information obtained from simple probabilistic indexing models can be used directly to initialize nodes and connections. For more sophisticated probabilistic or inference models, however, specific conversion algorithm will be needed to assign appropriate relevance measures to initial connections. Another way to initialize a relevance network is to submit a training set of queries with corresponding result references to the system. In this case the training set will be simulated as user feedback to derive appropriate relevance connections.

4.2. COMPOSITE NODES

The relevance model described thus far records only relevance information based on single descriptors. User preferences for particular composite queries cannot be saved, and non-trivial relations* between references and descriptors cannot be encoded. To retain better information from user feedback, the relevance network accommodates composite nodes in the input layer, as illustrated in Figure 7. It is assumed that the relevance information associated with a composite node is more specific than the information associated with its nested subset nodes or its basic input nodes (corresponding to its descriptors). Therefore, during retrieval, a user query is first matched against highest level composite nodes, rather than lower level nodes. The use of composite nodes enables the system to derive more accurate relevance measures learned from previous queries.

Composite nodes are added to the network in two ways. A new composite node, corresponding to a user query, is added to the relevance network when a user provides feedback upon retrieval. A second composite node addition method based on co-occurrence statistics of query descriptors is discussed in Section 4.5.3.

---

* E.g., a reference relates to {Apple, Computer} but does not relate to {Apple}.

4.3. LEARNING RELEVANCE MEASURES FROM USER FEEDBACK

When a user provides positive or negative feedback for a reference given the current query, this relevance information is memorized and generalized. To memorize feedback information on specific queries, relevance of the connection between the reference and the composite node corresponding to the query is updated. If such a connection does not already exist, a new connection is created and the relevance measure initialized.* If a composite node corresponding to the query does not exist, a new composite is created with associated relevance information derived from that of its components. The derivation algorithm is described in Section 4.4.2.

To derive generalized relevance measures for new queries in the future, nodes which are more general than the user query inherit feedback: relevance measures from all proper query subsets including basic input nodes are updated. We describe below how relevance measures are updated or initialized.

4.3.1. *Updating relevance measures*

As mentioned above, relevance measures from an input node can be adjusted either through direct user feedback from a query of the same composition as that node, or through feedback inherited from its superset composite nodes. Direct feedback provides more accurate information pertaining to the node than inherited feedback. To compromise between memorization and generalization, a weight constant integer $C >= 1$ is added to the relevance feedback adjustment: if $C = 1$, inherited feedback is as important as direct feedback; and the relative importance of inherited feedback decreases when C increases. Relevance measures are updated as follows:

$$R_{new} = \frac{S_{new}}{N_{new}} = \frac{S_{old} + \lambda * \delta}{N_{old} + \lambda}, \quad \text{where}$$

$$\delta = \begin{cases} 1 & \text{for positive feedback} \\ 0 & \text{for negative feedback} \end{cases}, \quad \lambda = \begin{cases} 1 & \text{for inherited feedback} \\ C & \text{for direct feedback} \end{cases}.$$

As mentioned in Section 4.1, maintaining relevance measure as a fraction provides additional information on the precision of the measure. To accommodate more recent changes into the relevance network, a maximal threshold on the denominator is specified. When the number of total feedback exceeds this threshold, the denominator is no longer incremented, instead, a momentum term is used in the calculation:

$$R_{new} = \frac{S_{new}}{N_{new}} = \frac{S_{old}}{N_{max}} * \alpha + \delta * (1 - \alpha),$$

where α is the momentum, $0 \leq \alpha \leq 1$, and N_{max} the maximal threshold

---

* The user can choose to give feedback on any reference s/he has access to (not only on these references retrieved from the network), thus automatically indexing this reference with the current set of query descriptors.

for number of total feedback. Since N_{new} must equal N_{max} in this case,
$S_{new} = S_{old} * \alpha + \delta * (1 - \alpha) * N_{max}$.

For consistency with the relevance adjustment formula where the denominator is smaller than the maximum threshold, the momentum is typically set accordingly as: $\alpha = (N_{max} - \lambda)/N_{max}$.

4.3.2. *Initializing relevance measures*

Relevance measure for a new connection is initialized with $S_{old} = 0$, $N_{old} = K$. K, a positive integer, corresponds to an initial negative bias. With this initial bias, the relevance measure asymptotically approaches one with the increase of the rate of positive feedback. The scale of relevance thereby provides better resolution for positive relevance information, and is biased against relevance measures with lower feedback frequency, which is assumed to indicate lower confidence of relevance accuracy.

4.4. RETRIEVAL OF RELEVANT REFERENCES

In response to a query, the network retrieves and displays a list of references with the highest relevance measures. A query is assumed to be semantically constructed as a conjunction of member descriptors. Relevance measures are derived from nodes most specifically related to the query. Equal importance is given to all query descriptors. And for each descriptor, relevance measures from composite nodes are pooled together according to their statistical accuracy. This retrieval algorithm is described in the following two subsections.

4.4.1. *Retrieval by exact match*

Upon presentation of a query, if a composite node corresponding to the query already exists in the network, the relevance measures from that node to associated references are directly used to generate a ranked list of relevant references.

4.4.2. *Retrieval by derivation*

If a matching composite node does not exist, relevance measures from other input nodes, corresponding to proper subsets of the query, are used to derive a list of relevant references. For a relevance network with only basic input nodes, a simplistic estimate of relevance of a reference with respect to a query can be taken as the product of the relevance measures of that reference with respect to the descriptors of the query. The use of multiplicative estimation assumes no weighting information among individual query descriptors, and gives higher relevance to references of uniform relevance to all query descriptors.

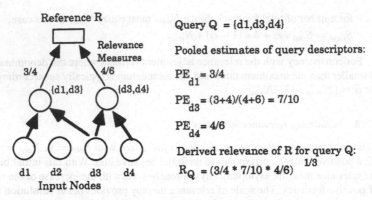

Query Q = {d1,d3,d4}

Pooled estimates of query descriptors:

$PE_{d1} = 3/4$

$PE_{d3} = (3+4)/(4+6) = 7/10$

$PE_{d4} = 4/6$

Derived relevance of R for query Q:

$R_Q = (3/4 * 7/10 * 4/6)^{1/3}$

Figure 8. An example of retrieval by derivation from subset query nodes for one reference.

With the presence of composite nodes corresponding to query subsets, relevance information is derived only from the top-level subsets, i.e., the ones not nested within other subsets. However, relevance measures for a query cannot be appropriately obtained by simply taking the product of top-level subsets' relevance measures. Top-level subsets of a query can be of different sizes, and are not necessarily disjoint. References connected from one composite node may not be connected from another. Multiplicative measures, therefore, can be biased toward certain query components. We propose a heuristic derivation algorithm intended to provide impartial relevance estimations. For simplicity, we describe the relevance derivation algorithm for a single reference R, hence subscript reference indices are neglected in the formulae that follow.

For each descriptor in a query, a pooled estimate (i.e., an average adjusted by the sample sizes of individual estimates) of the relevance between that descriptor and a reference, is obtained from relevance measures associated with the top-level subsets of the query which contain that descriptor. Let $Comp_j$ denote the set of descriptors in a composite index J, and S_{top} the set of top-level subsets of a query Q. The pooled estimate of relevance for a descriptor d_i in Q is

$$PE_i = \frac{\sum_j S_j}{\sum_j N_j}, \quad \text{where the sums are taken over all } j \text{ where } Comp_j \in S_{top}$$
and $d_i \in Comp_j$.

Relevance measure of reference R for the query Q is then computed as

$$Rel_Q = \sqrt[n]{\prod_i PE_i}, \quad \text{where } d_i \in Q, n \text{ is the size of } Q.$$

The derived relevance measures are then used to generate an ordered list of suggested references. An example of relevance derivation from query subsets is shown in Figure 8.

In a query derivation where no subset composite node is present in the network, the algorithm degenerates to simple multiplicative derivation over basic input nodes. When applied to a query with disjoint top-level subsets, the algorithm reduces to taking the root of the product of all top-level subsets, each to the power of its own size.

The use of multiplicative derivation of relevance described above is based on the design choice for our current application, that queries are semantically constructed as conjunction of member descriptors. This choice gives priority of relevance ranking to references more equally related to all components of a query. Other alternative aggregate functions can be used if deemed useful in future study. The relevance ratios associated with connections can be considered as probabilistic estimates, and can be combined with different Boolean operators. If weights associated with individual query descriptors are available, a weighted-sum of probabilities associated with descriptors can be used to estimate the probability of query-reference relevance.

4.4.3. *Partial match derivation*

The current implementation also supports retrieval with partial match of query descriptors, i.e., retrieving references which are indexed by some, but not all of the query descriptors. Users are given control of the level of partial match, i.e., the minimal number of query descriptors a suggested output reference must be related to. Partial match retrieval is similar to retrieval with a query of disjunctive descriptors. However, relevance estimates of partial match output references are still derived multiplicatively, to ensure consistent rank order display relative to full match results. A *missing relevance* value is used in the multiplicative derivation formula, as an estimate of relevance associated with a missing connection from a query descriptor to a reference. This missing relevance has very similar connotation as the default belief used by the inference network-based model in (Turtle & Croft, 1991). However, since the relevance network only deals with personal indexing independent of text information within the documents, our missing value is just a constant parameter which can be adjusted for better performance. In our current implementation, default value of the missing relevance is set at $1/2K$, where K is the constant initial bias discussed in Section 4.3.2. The value of missing relevance is also used in connection-trimming discussed in Section 4.5.4.

4.5. Managing network size and capacity

4.5.1. *Computing cost and the importance of capacity management*

The primary cost of computing time in the use of an adaptive relevance network is associated with the relevance derivation algorithm, which requires a search of composite nodes corresponding to all proper query subsets. In theory, this search can be computationally exponential with respect to the size of the query, due to the combinatorial large number of possible top level subsets. For pragmatic information retrieval purposes, however, the number of descriptors in a query is usually small, and only a very small percentage of all possible combinations of query descriptors is likely to be present in the network as subset composite nodes. Also, this cost of computing time is in the worst case linearly bound by the total number of composite nodes in the network. Thus the computational complexity of the derivation algorithm is not of realistic concern, provided that the number of composite nodes and the distribution of these nodes are well managed.

While the memorization capacity of a network increases with the number of composite nodes it contains, unnecessary composite nodes can potentially inhibit generalization of retrieval. Higher level large composites carry relevance information more specific to particular queries, whereas lower level smaller composites carry more general feedback information propagated from many queries. Relevance measures associated with larger composites, however, may also have less statistical accuracy since these composites receive less feedback from users. Managing the network capacity is therefore not only important in assuring control of the computing cost, but also important in maintaining a balance between the capacity of memorization and that of generalization.

4.5.2. *Cutting composite nodes*

A node cutting procedure is employed to control the size of an adaptive relevance network. A maximal number of composite nodes allowed in a network can be specified. When a new composite node needs to be inserted, and if the network has reached its specified size limit, an existing composite node with the least *frequency of usage* is removed to make room for the new one. The frequency of usage of a composite node is calculated by recording the number of times the node is used in query execution. In addition, it is also incremented when the composite node receives direct user feedback. The purpose of this feedback-based usage update is to give more weight to composite nodes which carry information that cannot be easily derived.

A portion (currently set at 20%) of the composite nodes most recently added to the network are left in a queue, excluded from the candidate list of nodes used by the cutting procedure described above. This ensures that a new composite node will have ample chance to accumulate usage statistics, thereby proving its usefulness. We are also planning to apply a decay formula on the frequency of usage to all composite nodes at regular intervals, so that previously useful composite indices that have become obsolete over time can be replaced.

The frequency of usage is a direct measure of how often a node is used for user queries. More subtly, it also serves as a measure of the *confidence level* of information accuracy associated with a node. The choice of removing nodes with the least frequency of usage ensures that the composites that remain in the network are the ones with most dependable relevance information.

Once a composite index node is removed, the relevance information it carries cannot be recovered. However, since much of the feedback information associated with this node had been propagated down to its lower level sub-composites and basic descriptors, only the information unique to this composite is lost.

4.5.3. *Adding composite nodes*

The query-based composite node creation method described in Section 4.2 is intended to ensure quick learning of user preference by memorizing relevance information. Ideally, these nodes would also become useful components of the relevance network information structure, to derive relevance information for new queries. Unfortunately, smaller composites are less likely to enter the network since the relevance information they are associated with may be too general for them to be used as specific queries by users. Yet these smaller compositions may be of great importance for a network to assure effective encoding of relevance information.

A node creation method based on co-occurrence of query descriptors is devised to extract compositions important to the relevance network information structure. The network maintains a record of recently submitted user queries, and periodically generates statistics on sets of descriptors that often appear together in different queries. A simple formula is currently used to calculate co-occurrence statistics of query descriptors over a collection of queries:

$$C_s = \frac{f_s}{\text{size\_of}(s)\sqrt{\prod_{i \in s} f_i}},$$

where C_s denotes the co-occurrence measure of descriptors in set S,

f_s denotes the frequence of set S appearing in queries, and

f_i the frequency of descriptor i in queries.

Composite nodes consisting of query descriptors of high co-occurrence statistics are then automatically added to the relevance network. Composite creation based on co-occurrence across queries facilitates effective encoding of non-trivial relevance information. It also helps generalize relevance information for future retrieval with similar queries.

4.5.4. *Trimming connections and the scale of relevance*

Another measure of the network size is the number of relevance connections from input nodes to output references. Relevance connections are indexed in a database by the nodes they are associated with, and only the ones related to a query need to be retrieved at a time. Unnecessary connections cause wasteful storage space, and can impact the performance of retrieval.

A connection with relevance value less than or equal to the missing relevance (described in Section 4.4.3), as a result of frequent negative feedback, is removed from the network. This connection *trimming* process prevents the network from unlimited addition of connections, and from keeping wasteful information of very low relevance. The relevance measure maintained by the network is therefore on a rational scale between the missing relevance and one, and it is non-linearly proportional to the ratio of positive feedback. The use of a positive scale does not deprive the network of its capability of encoding negative relevance information. By trimming relevance connections from a composite more specific to a query, i.e., a query subset composite node of larger size, positive information carried by more general, smaller subset composites will be ignored. Thus the effect of negation is supported by the dynamic architecture of the adaptive relevance network.

5. Experimental Results

The adaptive relevance network is designed to model subjective indexing based on user preference of information access. It is intended as an information framework which integrates indexing structure provided by users, with indexing information generated by other conventional indexing methods and/or retrieval methods specific to the domain of application. For application purpose, it has been designed to be incorporated into large-scale, complex information systems. It is therefore difficult to test the full functionality of the network independent of the application domain. As a first step, we focused on the validity of the proposed model and report on experimental results of the memorization capacity and generalization ability of the adaptive relevance network, with no attempt to simulate user behavior. Real-world usage study of Adaptive HyperMan by flight controllers is in progress.

5.1. SIMULATION SETUP

We used two test data sets of information retrieval from the SMART archive at the Computer Science Department of Cornell University. The first is a collection of 1963 Time Magazine news articles which consists of 425 articles and 80 queries. The second is the ISI collection of most highly cited articles and manuscripts in information science in the 1969–1977 period, with 981 articles and 76 queries. These experimental data sets were originally devised for the investigation of automatic indexing and document retrieval methods. Queries of the two sets employ large vocabularies, and different queries share very few similarities. These are therefore not ideal for the testing of adaptive indexing, where higher similarities among queries more specific to individual users and/or task domains, as well as non-trivial relevance structures between references and queries are expected. The collections, nevertheless, were used here in our simulation experiments to ensure objective evaluation of the adaptive relevance network.

Queries in these data sets are composed of common English phrases, e.g., "United Nation's efforts to get Portugal to free its African colonies". For our purpose, the queries are edited into sets of keywords with simplistic stemming, and common English words removed. Thus the above query becomes "unite, nation, portugal, africa, colony". The particular sequential order of words in a query is not utilized.

In simulation, a query is presented to the network as a set of descriptors, and the references retrieved by the network are compared with the target references listed in the original data set. Positive feedback is simulated for references that are in the target list but are not suggested by the network. Similarly, negative feedback is given to the network for suggested references not in the original data set. Although the adaptive relevance network is designed to accommodate other means of retrieval, all simulation trials were conducted with initially empty network, to demonstrate clearly the functionality of the adaptive engine.

It should be noted that the feedback simulation method of our study is very different from that of conventional information retrieval experiments. In our simulation, feedback information is not only given for references retrieved from the system, but also given for new references to be added to the system. The relevance network is designed as a personal index system to organize known information, not to retrieve unknown information. The experiments reported here are intended to verify the validity of the proposed indexing architecture and algorithm, not to measure real-world application performance.

We first tested the memorization capacity of the adaptive relevance network, i.e., the amount of relevance information a network can memorize with respect to the number of composite nodes. We then tested the generalization capability, i.e., the ability of a trained network to derive and suggest references for queries not previously presented to the network.

5.2. MEMORIZATION CAPACITY

The Time collection was first used to test the memorization capacity. Each query in this set should retrieve from one to 18 references. Query-based insertion of composite nodes was first disabled. Consequently the network did not contain any composite nodes hence could only encode and derive relevance information with the basic descriptors. This network was trained with the complete set of queries in random order. For each query, positive feedback was given for all relevant references not retrieved, and negative feedback given for irrelevant retrieval of references not in the target set. After one complete cycle of training, i.e., each

Table I. Comparison of ISI data set retrieval results with different numbers of co-occurrence based composite nodes. 100% recall of 2655 relevant references were attained in all cases.

Number of composites	Average precision in %		Total number of irrelevant references	
	1 cycle	3 cycles	1 cycle	3 cycles
0	78.1	78.1	2176	2176
23	85.2	86.1	1142	964
41	88.7	88.9	716	694
81	87.7	88.9	664	512
179	90.8	92.6	402	298

of the queries presented once, the relevance network was able to retrieve with 100% recall,* at a precision** of 93.1%. Specifically, all 321 relevant references, along with 37 irrelevant ones were retrieved. This result suggested that the data set is largely linear (i.e., relevance information associated with a query can be derived from relevance associated with its member descriptors), hence the addition of composite nodes could make limited retrieval enhancement. Without enabling the query-based composite node insertion algorithm, five composite nodes of the highest co-occurrence statistics among the queries were added to the initial network. The modified network was able to improve the precision slightly to 94.8%, with 34 irrelevant retrievals, without affecting the 100% recall. The performance could not be improved further with more composites of lower co-occurrences added.

With the query-based composite insertion enabled, the network achieved perfect performance of 100% recall and precision, by memorizing the target references with 80 composites corresponding to the query set. When the composite node cutting procedure is in effect, the network was able to maintain perfect performance with as few as 10 composites.

Similar studies were done with the ISI data collection. To better demonstrate the network's capacity to encode non-trivial information, for this data set we eliminated query descriptors which appear in only one single query. Two of the 76 queries were invalidated consequently, as they became empty. The resulting set consists of queries of sizes ranging from 2 to 15 descriptors. Each query is to retrieve from 3 to 125 relevant references.

In simulation runs using the ISI data set, different numbers of composite nodes based on levels of co-occurrence statistics were added initially. The results are shown in Table I. Precision and recall statistics were collected after 1 and 3 training cycles. 100% recalls were attained for all simulation runs. The network with 41 composite nodes had higher total number of irrelevant references, yet better average precision than the network with 81 composites. This is because an average precision

---

* Recall is defined as the proportion of relevant materials retrieved.
** Precision is defined as the proportion of retrieved materials that are relevant.

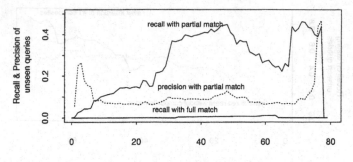

number of queries presented for training (out of 80 total)

Figure 9. Generalized retrieval results with unseen queries from the Time Magazine data set.

is taken over the precision measures of all queries, which is not the same as a pooled-average calculated directly from the total numbers of relevant and irrelevant references.

5.3. GENERALIZATION

We first tested the generalized retrieval capability of the network on the Time collection data. Since this data set is largely linear, no composite nodes were employed. Simulation tests were conducted in both full match mode and partial match mode (described in Section 4.4.3). Queries from the set are presented to the network one at a time for feedback simulation. At the end of each query simulation, the remaining queries in the set not yet presented to the network, were used to test the network's retrieval performance. The results are plotted in Figure 9. With full match only, the average generalized recall was only near 1%. This was not surprising since many queries in this data set contained unique descriptors. The precision was not available since for many queries no reference was retrieved. With partial match, the recall increased to 40% with half of the queries presented. Recall statistics had wider variations at the end of the curve, as the sample size of test queries became smaller. The average precision in partial match retrieval remained mostly stable at around 10%.

We then tested the ISI data set for generalized retrieval in partial match mode. The curve of generalized recall was similar to that of the Time data set, with a peak recall at 57.5%. Precision stayed low at around 10%. To see the effect of composites on generalization, we ran another test with 41 composites of high co-occurrences inserted to the network after 40 of the 74 queries were trained, and the generalization test continued afterward. The generalized recall performance in this case showed consistent improvement as training continued, with a peak recall of 86% at the end. Figure 10 shows the curves of generalized recall with and without

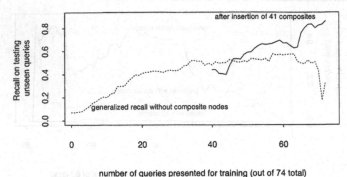

number of queries presented for training (out of 74 total)

Figure 10. Generalized recall with unseen queries from the ISI data, with and without added composite nodes.

added composite nodes. The low recall rate toward the end of the dashed-curve was partially caused by chance since only few unseen queries were left for testing.

5.4. DISCUSSION

Simulation tests have shown that with query-based composite insertion, an adaptive relevance network is capable of perfectly memorizing relevance information based on user feedback. Test results also suggested that, while a network without composite nodes cannot maintain good precision of retrieval for data sets which contain non-trivial relevance information, the precision can be significantly improved with the addition of only a small collection of composite nodes. Composite nodes help improve precision through the provision of more specific information in relevance derivation. In a real-world application, the query-based composite insertion facilitates the customization of relevance information for specific queries of frequent usage, whereas the co-occurrence-based composite insertion helps the establishment of efficient information structure for long-term usage. These two composition methods, together with the node cutting procedure, work like a genetic algorithm that governs the evolution of the relevance network architecture.

We have shown also in simulation that the network is capable of generalizing retrieval of relevant references for queries not previously seen, through its feedback propagation algorithm. Generalized recall is further enhanced with the addition of composite nodes, which helps direct feedback information to appropriate composite structures, thereby releasing capacity of other parts of the network to encode more accurate relevance information.

Simulation with partial match also incurred low precision for generalized retrieval. This is partially due to the wide variation of relevance information of the test queries. In addition, a complete list of references retrieved in partial match mode carries much additional relevance information, hence inhibits high precision. In practice, users are given flexible control of the amount of information displayed. Lastly, for simulation purpose, relevance information in a network was not initialized. The adaptive relevance network, for application purpose, should be initialized with traditional or other domain specific indexing retrieval information.

To summarize, the adaptive relevance network provides an information structure that facilitates integration of domain specific document indexing information and subjective user preferences. The adaptive architecture of a network, with associated relevance connections, supports a balance between customization and generalization. The control of balance between precision and recall is given to the users.

6. Future Work

A more sophisticated kind of adaptive hyperlinks based on previous path of traversal has been proposed in (Chen & Mathé, 1994). Instead of taking concept descriptors as input, the hyperlink traversal path to a current hypernode is defined as input to the system, and the filtered hyperlinks available from the current node is the suggested output. Like in the adaptive relevance network, composite nodes are used to construct relevance structure of adapted hyperlink information.

The current approach of network capacity management, in particular the composite node cutting procedure, is entirely usage based. An interesting direction of future research is to explore dependency among composite nodes in terms of their associated relevance information, and to utilize such information in the addition and deletion of composite nodes.

The employment of composite nodes to encode non-linear relevance information, like the use of hidden units in artificial neural networks, has the advantage of learning without assuming specific knowledge structure. On the other hand, given the vast complexity of information retrieval, it is likely that the incorporation of knowledge-based components into the network can greatly enhance pragmatic retrieval performance. One possible approach is to translate user queries with a knowledge-based system, into a set of internal input descriptors used exclusively by the relevance network. Another approach described in (Katsumoto et al., 1995) uses a user model to convert a user query to an "average user" query, which is then used by a knowledge base on textile design to retrieve relevant images.

In order to enable sharing of adaptations among a large number of users, it would be useful to have a common vocabulary for describing user-defined concepts. This could be done by acquiring a domain model and enforcing a fixed vocabulary on users; or we could learn this common vocabulary by applying machine learning techniques to the set of concepts defined by users after a period of time. Another extension to promote collaboration among users is to automatically find all users with similar concepts, in order to suggest them new documents found relevant by others with similar interests (Lashkari et al., 1994).

We plan to enhance the Adaptive HyperMan system in two major directions. First we will support collaborative work by providing a publish/subscribe mechanism to develop users group indices for markers. Second, we are studying the idea of a virtual goody book being displayed as a book (with pages to flip) instead of a list of markers, and of providing an authoring facility to let users edit this virtual book (adding their own new pages, or reordering pages).

Finally, we have been collaborating with Boeing on integrating the adaptive relevance network into the Portable Maintenance Aid prototype for airplane mechanics (Bradshaw et al., 1993; Bradshaw et al., 1996). We also integrated the adaptive relevance network into the World Wide Web for organizing and sharing personal pages collections. These applications are currently at the prototyping and testing stage.

7. Conclusion

We have presented a user-centered indexing approach to adaptive hypermedia and information retrieval. The adaptive relevance network technique supports users in creating and managing personalized information access maps, which are organized by concepts. This approach is extremely useful for technical information access tasks characterized by a large volume of hypermedia connected documents, the need for rapid and effective access to already known information, and long-term interaction with evolving information. We demonstrated adaptive retrieval and navigation with the Adaptive HyperMan system. The system provides sophisticated marking and hyperlinking capabilities to end-users, and allows them to assign user-defined and shared topics to markers, retrieve markers by topics, and provide feedback over time. We described the Adaptive HyperMan system, its user interface, and showed how it provides a virtual "goody book" facility for Space Shuttle flight controllers. The system also supports collaborative review by letting users share group access maps.

We then presented the adaptive relevance network which creates and maintains a complex indexing structure to represent personal user's information access maps. The model employs a simple adaptive algorithm embedded in a dynamic indexing architecture based on user feedback. It does not require any a priori specialized index structure, nor any a priori statistical knowledge or computation. We have shown that with query-based composite insertion, a relevance network with a limited capacity is capable of perfect memorization of relevance information based on user feedback. We have shown also that through its feedback propagation algorithm, a network is capable of generalizing retrieval of relevant references for queries not previously seen. While the query-based composite insertion facilitates the customization of relevance information for specific queries of frequent usage, the co-occurrence-based composite insertion helps the establishment of efficient information structure for long-term usage. The indexing structure is dynamic and evolves over time. A relevance network can adapt to specific user needs, or it can generalize over multi-user information requirements, supporting sharing and collaborative work. The network can easily be integrated with other information retrieval and hypermedia systems to provide user-centered, and rapid information access.

Acknowledgments

Many thanks to Peter Brusilovsky and the anonymous reviewers for very pertinent comments on this paper. Many thanks to Josh Rabinowitz and Shawn Wolfe for their help in implementing the Adaptive HyperMan system. Thanks to all members of the Electronic Documentation Project team at NASA/JSC and to Shuttle flight controllers for their support.

References

Agosti, M., Melucci, M., and Crestani, F.: 1995, 'Automatic Authoring and Construction of Hyper-media for Information Retrieval'. *Multimedia Systems* 3, 15–24.

Armstrong, R., Freitag, D., Joachims, T. and Mitchell, T.: 1995, 'WebWatcher: A Learning Apprentice for the World Wide Web'. *Proc. AAAI Spring Symposium on Information Gathering from Distributed, Heterogeneous Environments*, Stanford, California.

Barreau, D. K.: 1995, 'Context as a Factor in Personal Information Management Systems'. *Journal of the American Society for Information Science* 46(5), 327–339.

Belew, R. K.: 1989, 'Adaptive Information Retrieval: Using a Connectionist Representation to Retrieve and Learn about Documents'. *Proc. Twelfth SIGIR Conference*, Cambridge, Massachusetts, pp. 11–20.

Belkin, N. J., Marchetti, P. G., and Cool, C.: 1993, 'Braque: Design of an Interface to Support User Interaction in Information Retrieval'. *Information Processing and Management* 29(3), 325–344.

Bergstrom, P. and Riedl, J.: 1994, 'Group Lens: A Collaborative Filtering System for Usenet News'. MSc thesis.

Bradshaw, J. M., Richards, T., Fairweather, P., Buchanan, C., Guay, R., Madigan, D., and Boy, G. A.: 1993, 'New Directions for Comupter-Based Training and Performance Support in Aerospace'. *Proc. Fourth Int. Conference on Human-Machine Interaction and Artificial Intelligence in Aerospace*, Toulouse, France.

Bradshaw, J. M., Dutfield, S., Benoit, P., and Wooley, J. D.: 1996, 'KAoS: Toward an Industrial-Strength Open Agent Architecture'. To appear in: J. M. Bradshaw (ed.): *Software Agents*. AAAI/MIT Press.

Boy, G. A..: 1991, 'Indexing Hypertext Documents in Context'. *Proc. Third ACM Conference on Hypertext*, San Antonio, Texas, pp. 51–61.

Brusilovsky, P.: 1994, 'Adaptive Hypermedia: An Attempt to Analyze and Generalize'. *Proc. Workshop on Adaptive Hypertext and Hypermedia, Fourth Int. Conference on User Modeling*, Hyannis, Ma. URL:http://www.cs.bgsu.edu/hypertext/adaptive/Brusilovsky.html

Callan, J. P., Croft, W. B., and Harding, S. M.; 1992, 'The Inquiry Retrieval System'. *Proc. Third Int. Conference on Database and Expert System Applications*, pp. 78–83.

Chen, H.: 1995, 'Machine Learning for Information Retrieval: Neural Networks, Symbolic Learning, and Genetic Algorithms'. *Journal of the American Society for Information Science* 46(3), 194–216.

Chen, J. and Mathé, N.: 1994, 'Adaptive Dynamic Hypertext based on Paths of Traversal'. *Proc. Workshop on Adaptive Hypertext and Hypermedia, Fourth Int. Conference on User Modeling*, Hyannis, Ma. URL:http://www.cs.bgsu.edu/hypertext/adaptive/Mathe.html

Dumais, S. T., Furnas, G. W., and Landauer, T. K.: 1988, 'Using Latent Semantic Analysis to Improve Access to Textual Information'. *Proc. Sixth Conference on Human Factors in Computing Systems* (CHI'88), pp. 281–285.

Fischer, G. and Stevens, C.: 1991, 'Information Access in Complex, Poorly Structured Information Spaces'. *Proc. Eighth ACM Conference on Human Factors in Computing Systems* (CHI'91), New Orleans, Louisiana, pp. 63–70.

Fuhr, N.: 1992, 'Probabilistic Models in Information Retrieval'. *The Computer Journal* 35(3), 243–255.

Goldberg, D., Nichols, D., Oki, B. M., and Terry, D.: 1992, 'Using Collaborative Filtering to Weave an Information Tapestry'. *Communications of the ACM* 35(12), 61–70.

Haines, D. and Croft, W. B.: 1993, 'Relevance Feedback and Inference Networks'. *Proc. Sixteenth Int. ACM SIGIR Conference*, Pittsburgh, Pennsylvania, pp. 2–10.

Höök, K., J. Karlgren, A. Wærn, N. Dahlbäck, C. G. Jansson, K. Karlgren, and B. Lemaire: 1996, 'A Glass Box Approach to Adaptive Hypermedia'. *User Modeling and User-Adapted Interaction* 6(2-3), 157–184 (reprinted in this volume, pp. 143–170).

Jennings, A, and Higichi, H.: 1993, 'A Personal News Service Based on a User Model Neural Network'. *IEICE Transactions on Information* Systems 75(2), 198–209.

Kaplan, C., Fenwick, J., and Chen, J.: 1993, 'Adaptive Hypertext Navigation Based on User Goals and Context'. *User Modeling and User Adapted Interaction* 3(3), 193–220 (reprinted in this volume, pp. 45–69).

Katsumoto, M., Fukuda, M., and Shibata, Y.: 1995, 'Distributed Design Image Database based on Perceptual Link Method'. *Proc. of the 1995 Pacific Workshop on Distributed Multimedia Systems* (DMS'95), pp. 76–83.

Kibby, M. R. and Mayes, J. T.: 1989, 'Towards Intelligent Hypertext'. In: R. McAleese (ed.): *Hypertext Theory into Practice*. Albex, pp. 164–172.

Klark, P., and Manber, U.: 1995, 'Developing a Personal Internet Assistant'. *Proc. World Conference on Educational Multimedia and Hypermedia* (ED-MEDIA'95), Graz, Austria, pp. 372–377.

Lashkari, L., Metral, M., and Maes, P.: 1994, 'Collaborative Interface Agents'. *Proc. Twelfth National Conference on Artificial Intelligence*, Seattle, Washington, pp. 444–449.

Maes, P. and Kozierok, R.: 1993, 'Learning Interface Agents'. *Proc. Eleventh National Conference of Artificial Intelligence*, Washington, D.C., pp. 459–465.

Mathé, N. and Chen, J.: 1994, 'A User-Centered Approach to Adaptive Hypertext based on an Information Relevance Model'. *Proc. Fourth Int. Conference on User Modeling*, Hyannis, Massachusetts, pp. 107–114. The latter paper is reprinted in this volume, pp. 171–207).

Monk, A.: 1989, 'The Personal Browser: A Tool for Directed Navigation in Hypertext Systems'. *Interacting with Computers* 1(2), 190–196.

Pargman, D.: 1994, no title. *Proc. Workshop on User Modeling in Information Retrieval, Fourth Int. Conference on User Modeling*, Hyannis, Massachusetts.

Rabinowitz, J., Mathé, N., and Chen, R. J.: 1995, 'Adaptive HyperMan: A Customizable Hypertext System for Reference Manuals'. *Proc. AAAI Fall Symposium on Artificial Intelligence Applications in Knowledge Navigation*, Cambridge, Massachusetts. pp. 110–115.

Robertson, S. E.: 1977, 'The Probability Ranking Principle in IR'. *Journal of Documentation* 33(4), 294–304.

Robertson, S. E. and Spark Jones, K.: 1976, 'Relevance Weighting of Search terms'. *Journal of the American Society for Information Science* 27, 129–146.

Rose, D. E. and Belew, R. K.: 1991, 'A Connectionist and Symbolic Hybrid for Improving Legal Research'. *Int. Journal of Man-Machine Studies* 35(1), 1–33.

Salton, G.: 1989, *Automatic Text Processing: The Transformation, Analysis, and Retrieval of Information by Computers*. Addison Wesley, Reading, MA.

Salton, G., Wong, A., and Yang, C.S.: 1975, 'A Vector Space Model for Automatic Indexing'. *ACM Communications* 18(11), 613–620.

Sheth, B. and Maes, P.: 1993: 'Evolving Agents for Personalized Information Filtering'. *Proc. Ninth IEEE Conference on Artificial Intelligence for Applications*, pp. 345–352.

Torrance, M.: 1995, 'Active Notebook: A Personal and Group Productivity Tool for Managing Information'. *Proc. AAAI Fall Symposium on Artificial Intelligence Applications in Knowledge Navigation and Retrieval*, Cambridge, Massachusetts, pp. 131–135.

Tudhope, D., Taylor, C., and Benyon-Davies, P.: 1995, 'Navigation via Similarity in Hypermedia and Information Retrieval'. In: R. Kuhlen and M. Rittberger (eds.): *Proc. Conference on Hypertext*,

Information Retrieval, Multimedia (HIM'95), Universitätsverlag Konstanz, Konstanz, pp. 203–218.

Turtle, H. and Croft, W.B.: 1991, 'Evaluation of an Inference Network-Based Retrieval Model'. *ACM Transactions on Information Systems* 9(3), 187–222.

van Rijsbergen, C.: 1979, *Information Retrieval*. 2nd Edition, Butterworths, London.

Vassileva, J.: 1994, 'A Practical Architecture for User Modeling in a Hypermedia-Based Information System'. *Proc. Fourth Int. Conference on User Modeling*, Hyannis, Massachusetts, pp. 115–120.

Vassileva, J.: 1996, 'A Task-Centered Approach for User Modeling in a Hypermedia Office Documentation System'. *User Modeling and User-Adapted Interaction* 6(2-3), 185–223 (reprinted in this volume, pp. 209–247).

Authors' Vitae

Dr. N. Mathé is a research scientist at NASA Ames Research Center, employed through Recom Technologies, Inc. Dr. Mathé received her MS. degree in Physics from Paris VI University, France in 1986, and her Ph.D. in Computer Science from the National School of Aeronautics and Space Technology, France, in 1990. Since 1992, Dr. Mathé leads the Advanced Interaction Media group in the Computational Sciences Division at NASA Ames. Her research objective is to facilitate access to electronic information via the development of intelligent tools integrating hypertext, multimedia, collaborative learning, and knowledge-based systems capabilities.

Dr. J. R. Chen is a research scientist at NASA Ames Research Center, employed through Recom Technologies, Inc. Dr. Chen received his M.S. degree in Systems Analysis from the University of Wisconsin, Madison, and his Ph.D. in Computer Science from the University of California, San Diego. Dr. Chen is a member of the Advanced Interaction Media group at NASA Ames since 1993. His research interests include adaptive information retrieval, collaborative intelligent agents, and connectionist knowledge representation.

A Task-Centered Approach for User Modeling in a Hypermedia Office Documentation System

JULITA VASSILEVA
Institute for Technical Computer Science, Federal Armed Forces University Munich, 85577
Neubiberg, Germany
E-mail: julitav@faust.informatik.unibw-muenchen.de

(Received 9 November 1994; in final form 6 February 1996)

Abstract. The development of user-adaptive systems is of increasing importance for industrial applications. User modeling emerged from the need to represent in the system knowledge about the user in order to allow informed decisions on how to adapt to match the user's needs. Most of the research in this field, however, has been theoretical, "top-down." Our approach, in contrast, was driven by the needs of the application and shows features of bottom-up, user-centered design.

We have implemented a user modeling component supporting a task-based interface to a hypermedia information system for hospitals and tested it under realistic conditions. A new architecture for user modeling has been developed which focuses on the tasks performed by users. It allows adaptive browsing support for users with different level of experience, and a level of adaptability. The requirements analysis shows that the differences in the information needs of users with different levels of experience are not only quantitative, but qualitative. Experienced users are not only able to cope with a wider browsing space, but sometimes prefer to organize their search in a different way. That is why the user model and the interface of the system are designed to support a smooth transition in the access options provided to novice users and to expert users.

Key words: adaptation, adaptive interfaces, hypermedia and hypertext navigation, intelligent information retrieval, office/hospital documentation systems, task-based context for information retrieval, task-structures.

1. Introduction

Browsing is a useful technique for retrieving documents from data-bases (Thompson & Croft, 1989). It has been widely applied recently as hypertext and hypermedia systems have become increasingly popular (Begoray, 1990). The main cognitive advantage of this technique is that users in general are better able to recognize the information they want than to characterize it in advance. The disadvantages of browsing are that it is easy to get lost in a complex network of nodes representing documents and concepts and that there is no guarantee that browsing will be as effective as a more conventional search. If it offers a rich set of links, the system is responsible for helping the users understand what the links mean, how they might be used, and how to find their way in the network. Without this kind of help, browsing can take on the aspect of the user finding her way in a maze, where she can become hopelessly "lost in (hyper)space" (Conklin, 1987). User modeling can help in supporting the user's navigation and information retrieval. A user model is

P. Brusilovsky et al. (eds.), Adaptive Hypertext and Hypermedia, 209–247.
© 1998 *Kluwer Academic Publishers.*

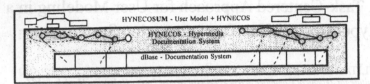

Figure 1. The "Russian doll" architecture of HYNECOSUM.

an explicitly represented collection of data about the user which allows the system to adapt its options to the needs of the user. The intensive development in the field of user modeling during the last decade (Kobsa & Pohl, 1994a) makes it possible to consider it as a practical approach for ensuring user-adapted information access in a hypermedia information system.

1.1. HISTORY OF THE PROJECT

Our work stems from an industrial project for creating a large hypermedia documentation system for hospitals. Four years ago, such a system was developed at the University Orthopedics Clinic of Heidelberg using a relational data-base (dBase). However, it was not well accepted by the hospital staff and hardly ever used.

This dBase information system was later integrated into HYNECOS (HYpertext Navigation on the Electronic patient reCord on the Orthopedic ward Section). The system was developed two years later at SIEMENS ZFE within the ESPRIT Project No. 6532 HIFI (Hypertext Interface For Information). The goal of the project was to demonstrate the applicability of the Hypertext Design Model HDM (Schwabe et al. 1990; Grazotto et al. 1991) for design of hypertext-based information systems from relational databases. HYNECOS contains textual and graphical data about patients (administrative data, reports, x-rays etc.), hospital staff (names, telephones and shift-information about all staff members), a medical encyclopedia (diseases, treatments, prognoses) and the location of the wards (room-plans, beds, occupancy etc.). It is implemented in ToolBook 3.0 and runs on an IBM PC 486. The third phase in the development of system was the application of user modeling to achieve a better user interface, adaptivity and adaptability. The resulting system, HYNECOSUM (HYNECOS + UM) is built on top of HYNECOS (see Figure 1), therefore its architecture reminds a "Russian Doll". The system was entirely developed and tested at the Federal Armed Forces University in Munich. In the next sections HYNECOSUM will be described and particular attention will be paid on the -UM part.

1.2. MAIN IDEA OF OUR APPROACH

We developed a task-based interface which ensures browsing support for users with different levels of experience. The main idea is to use task-hierarchies to restrict views of information; to define experience levels and to make some hypertext links accessible or not, based on the task hierarchy and the experience level of the user. In this way the interface allows a reduced choice according to the context provided by the user's current task. Since the users population can be characterized by clearly differentiated user types with specific tasks and rights to access information, it is necessary to tailor the interface in an optimal way to the needs of the different user classes. However, the users have also individual needs and preferences, different levels of experience with the information system, which also have to be taken into account. The solution we found (Vassileva, 1994) is to create a User Model (UM) based on a representation of the typical user tasks. Normally these tasks are characteristic of a given user class, so we designed several stereotype models which can be used as a kernel, default for initialization of individual UMs. However, tools are provided for the user to extend and modify her UM (adaptability). Every individual UM is automatically adapted during the user's work with the system to represent her level of experience. The task model, i.e. the kernel of the UM is designed to be an integral part of the interface, i.e. the user interacts with the system by means of selecting the task she wants to perform. In this way she communicates directly her intentions and the system does not have to infer them from the user's information retrieval activities. The requirement analysis showed that the differences between the information needs of novice and expert users are not only quantitative, but qualitative. Experienced users prefer sometimes to organize their search in a different way. That is why the UM should support a smooth transition in the options for access to information depending on the user's level of experience.

1.3. ORGANIZATION OF THE PAPER

This paper describes the whole cycle of development and testing of the system and discusses the UM and the main adaptive features of the system. It starts with analysis of the requirements (Section 2). Section 3 describes the task-analysis and -modeling. Section 4 describes the individual user model: the effect of the user's level of experience on the size of information space she is able to cope with and on her access strategy. Section 5 explains how the UM is coupled together with the information system. Section 6 discusses the adaptivity of the system to the user's level of experience, and Section 7 the tools for adaptability provided for the user. Section 8 presents and discusses the results of tests. Section 9 compares our approach with other work.

2. Analysis of the requirements

To analyze the requirements of the application we adopted three of the methods for acquiring cognitive models proposed by Anderson (1985): monitoring the user's data collection techniques, interviews and questionnaires. The results of our requirement analysis can be summarized as follows:

2.1. STANDARD USERS' TASKS

In the medical domain it is convenient to analyze typical task situations because many tasks arise from scheduled meetings and activities and are therefore well defined in time and have well defined information needs. After observing the work of the hospital staff at the ambulance and at one ward with HYNECOS we came to the same conclusion – that their interests in the information were comparatively short-term and strongly dependent on their current tasks. That is why we decided that it would be advantageous to use a task model as a basis for modeling the user's interaction with the information system.

2.2. ACQUIRING THE TASK MODEL (THE INFORMATION NEEDS OF TASKS)

The question of acquiring and eventually updating task models during the user's performance has to be decided bearing in mind several considerations. The first question to be answered is whether the users have unstable, frequently changing tasks, or tasks with unstable information needs. If the answer is yes, then the task model has to be designed so as to allow learning from the user's behavior. In this case it makes sense to perform a "deep" cognitive analysis of the user's activities in order to discover underlying goals, means and restrictions, so that the information needs can later be inferred from the user's feedback or by observation of the user's behavior. However, this is not necessary, if the set of possible tasks is known in advance, and every task has constant information needs, i.e. when the task provides a context in which the needed information (topic) is known in advance (Tyler & Treu, 1989).

In a medical application the tasks related to work with the documentation system have stable information needs which can be acquired at a design stage with standard knowledge engineering methods (Rasmussen et al., 1994). Of course, it can happen that the information needs of a certain task change. Such changes, however, are normally regulated and concern all the users performing the task. It would be far cheaper and more natural to provide options for a system administrator or for users to change directly the information needs of tasks when this is necessary, than to leave this out of users' control by providing the system with an incremental learning capability.

We do not claim that learning of the information needs of user tasks is in general too expensive and not necessary. As mentioned at the beginning of this section, for an application where the tasks performed by users are not well defined and standardized, i.e. there are no clear boundaries between them or not clearly definable relevance to specific information entities valid across all the users of a given class, it will be important to learn from the user's feedback and eventually change the information needs, the scope and relations between the tasks in order to reflect the individual user's cognitive model of the task. This, however, is too expensive and unnecessary for an application with relatively stable and well defined tasks. That is why in our UM the tasks are fixed in advance and they have pre-defined information needs.

2.3. USERS DESIGNATE THEIR CURRENT TASK

In order to suggest relevant information for the user, the system has to be able to recognize the user's current task from her behavior. Several interesting approaches exist for inferring the current task of the user from her information searching behavior. Most of them, however, concern query-based information retrieval from relational databases (Croft, 1984; Hoppe, 1992), and they cannot be used in our case. The problem of finding the current task or goal of the user in browsing is more difficult than in query-based information retrieval. The reason is that the contents and structure of the query may provide some indirect evidence about the user's goal or task, while the user's browsing activities can be chaotic and non-sequential and they are not necessarily related to a specific goal or task. In principle, one could build hypotheses of possible current tasks based on the user's selection of entities (having in mind the stable information needs of tasks) and then reduce the hypothesis set with every next selection of information entity* provided that the user is experienced and is able to select correctly needed for her task. However, the goal of the UM in our case is to support exactly the inexperienced users, who are not likely to browse systematically. Such a user would make mistakes, browse occasionally and therefore the system will make wrong conclusions about the user's current task from her browsing.

It is far more natural to organize the interface so that the users explicitly assign the task they are currently working on. Because the task-taxonomy and the users' understanding of their tasks in our application are very well standardized, it is not obscure or unnatural for the users to name what they are doing. That is why we decided not to infer the users' current task from their behavior, but to design the interface in such a way that the users select the task they want to perform directly from a graphical representation on the screen.

2.4. FIXED HYPERMEDIA SYSTEM

One of the main problems in hypertext and hypermedia design is creating the possible links between entities. From one side, it has to reflect the logical structure of the information and from the other side, it has to be rich in links to allow a wide variety of browsing behaviors. One way of supporting the user in her browsing is

---

* By "entity" we understand an elementary data type. Following the terminology adopted in HDM, an entity corresponds to the name of a column in a record in a relational database, i.e. a feature shared by a set of records. For example, the entity "diagnosis" is present in the records of all patients.

to enable or disable some of these links in order to restrict the user to a specific browsing behavior (Beaumont & Brusilovsky, 1995). In this way the chance of "getting lost" in hyperspace is reduced and the browsing space is tailored according to the user's goal/task or area of interest. For example, (Biennier et al., 1990; Kaplan et al., 1993) define a maximum connected graph as an underlying structure of their hypertext systems. By learning from user feedback about the relevance of the selected entities to other entities or to her goals some of the links increase their weights, i.e. the strength of association among the entities or goals. In this way an individualized version of the Hypertext is created for every user. However, in our particular case one of the requirements was that the hypermedia system is a "given" and it can be only "masked" or "viewed" by additional indexing of the links to the entities with respect to the user's current task. This implies that the UM can't be integrated into the hypermedia, but is added as an overlay "extra-index" on top of the hypermedia, to be coupled or decoupled, if needed. We believe this is an advantage, since it allows us to apply this approach not only to hypermedia, but also to any information system without changing its own indexing scheme.

2.5. USER CLASSES AND RIGHTS OF ACCESS

The communication structure connecting work situations and the actors is an important aspect of the design of integrated information systems. In a typical work situation in the hospital, several actors work in a team whose members are identified with relevance to roles and professional backgrounds, not to persons. Due to shift work requirements, most roles in the work at a hospital are not assigned to particular individuals. Therefore, a stable configuration is linked to work situations and roles (Rasmussen et al., 1994). We identified five different user classes characterized by different roles: doctors, nurses, administrators, students and patients. These main user classes can be refined further on the basis of their rank, location, and professional background. The different user classes perform different sets of tasks (of course, there can be partial overlapping) and have different rights of access to information. This clear identification of user classes in the hospital domain is an advantage for user modeling. It implies that the initialization of the UM can be done once for every user class (stereotype) and it can be used as a default for every individual user belonging to the class when she starts work with the system. Later on, this stereotype will be adapted, modified, extended or reduced and parametrized so as to account for the individual tasks, information needs and rights of access to the information.

2.6. INDIVIDUAL MODELS

During the knowledge acquisition phase it became clear that users performing the same tasks may have different information-access strategies and preferences. For example, experienced users who had been involved in the design of HYNECOS

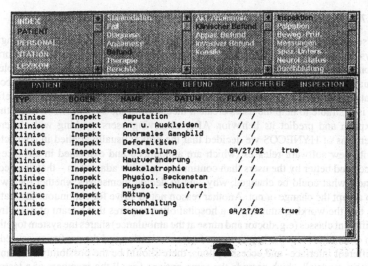

Figure 2. The semantic classification-based interface of HYNECOS.

preferred to be able to jump to the needed entity with a minimum of clicking and often used the direct access options of the underlying dBase. Users who had some experience, but were not experts with the semantic classification based interface of HYNECOS (see Figure 2, the upper part of the screen contains four menus organized according to the semantic classification of entities), occasionally complained that it is boring to click through so many menus in order to reach the needed entity. Novice users found it extremely difficult to understand the way the HYNECOS menus were organized and to find the needed information. They often made mistakes by selecting a wrong item in the first menu and went deep into the wrong branch of the classification, which made it impossible to find the needed entity. It became clear that a UM has to support the individual users in different ways according to their level of experience: for advanced or expert-users it has to ensure a fast, direct way of finding the information and to allow various access strategies. For novice users it is important to ensure that the user will always find the needed entity (possibly not directly and with a bit more clicking) and to teach her more advanced access options. Therefore an individual UM is needed, which must be able to recognize the transition from a novice- to an expert-level from the user's behavior and to adapt itself to more appropriate ways of supporting the user in her information access.

2.7. ADAPTATION AT DISCRETE POINTS OF TIME AND UNDERSTANDABILITY

Users need to have a coherent mental model of the system. A constantly changing system, even if this is supposed to happen for the benefit of the user, can bring confusion and decrease her confidence (Fischer, 1992), which is unacceptable in our application. In a medical domain sometimes it is of vital importance to access data quickly and the users want to be absolutely confident in the system. Therefore it is desirable to help the users create a metaphor of the system which helps them explain and predict its behavior. After observing users working with different versions of HYNECOS we decided that the policy usually applied in connection with new software releases (which are announced and explained in advance) is accepted better by the users than continuous invisible adaptation – they wanted to know what could be changed, why, and to decide themselves whether they want to accept the change or not. Another reason not to strive for continuous adaptation is that the working situation in a hospital often requires that a team of users from different classes (e.g. doctor and nurse at the ambulance) shares the system together. In order to prevent the impairment of communication and the confusion caused by different interface- and access-options, there should be the possibility of defining "team models" which provide the same options for all the members of a team, if they want it and agree about it.

3. User class stereotypes: task modeling

3.1. KNOWLEDGE ACQUISITION AND TASK ENGINEERING

At the beginning of the knowledge acquisition phase we carried out a series of unstructured interviews with the goal to find out the main user groups; to clarify the tasks different persons perform and the understanding of the task-needs and -boundaries shared by the users. The interviewers were trying to identify typical situations and tasks. We asked the users to name all functions and tasks in which they would work with the information system and thereafter the information needs of the tasks. In order to obtain a systematic insight we asked the users to describe the functions they participate in during the shift.

The results from the unstructured interviews showed that the tasks in a hospital environment in general are quite well standardized and characterized with stable information needs (forms, letters, tables etc.). This result is in agreement with (Rasmussen et al., 1994) who shows one possible time-model of the tasks performed at an operation wing of a hospital. Traditionally, the goal of a task analysis is to produce a description of the interaction between people and their work environment in terms of sequences of actions. Work in general, can be pragmatically decomposed into segments with respect to time, location, information needs or with respect to functional content, whichever is convenient for analysis and needed for the application. However, general modeling of the time-organization and the causal relations between the activities in the hospital was not interesting for us, since the information needs of the tasks were discrete (i.e. specific for every single task) and therefore not related to the temporal- and causal-aspects. Our goal was NOT to develop an expert system that assists the users in carrying out their tasks by advising them what to do next or how to do it, but only to ensure a task-based context for information retrieval. Modeling a cognitively plausible structure of tasks with respect to aggregation and generality is enough for this purpose.

In order to identify a set of typical activity elements for every user class which implies specific information needs we carried out a series of structured interviews. The main idea was that the first decomposition of general activity of every user class should correspond to the labels used by the (Rasmussen et al., 1994). Together with one highly motivated user (a doctor who had been involved in the design of HYNECOS) we developed a decomposition of the typical tasks he performs. Using this specific task decomposition as an example, we interviewed selected users, whom we considered typical user class representatives. They created variants of this scheme corresponding to their tasks. In this way we obtained several different task-decompositions, like those shown in Figure 3.

During the structured interviews the users spontaneously described their typical tasks (those involving work with the information system) as hierarchies. This is not surprising since the requirement to describe their activities systematically and independently from the time- and causal-relationships, resulted in isolating only the abstraction and aggregation links among the tasks. The validation of the prototype task-models showed that this hierarchical structuring is not occasional, but corresponds also to the abstract cognitive model the users have about their tasks. Once again, we have to say that this is not the only possible cognitive model which our users have. It is very probable that they have in the same time another, time-based cognitive model, which is linear (with loops). For example, if we had instructed them to show what they are doing in the course of the day including the temporal and causal relations, including those tasks for which they did not need the information system, we would have obtained far more complex structures. However, as mentioned before, our goal was not to develop a general task model of the hospital activities, but only a cognitively adequate user-focused subset of the tasks which involve work with the information system. The users found it reasonable to represent the tasks as hierarchies with upper nodes corresponding to more general tasks or tasks representing a set (sequence) of subtasks.

The prototypical task hierarchies obtained during the knowledge acquisition were, as expected, shared by the representatives of user classes taking different roles in the hospital work situation. These classes are defined by the work location (ward or ambulance), profession (e.g. doctor, nurse), and rank. Therefore the prototypical task hierarchies constitute the user-class models. They are the kernels (default initialization) of the individual UMs.

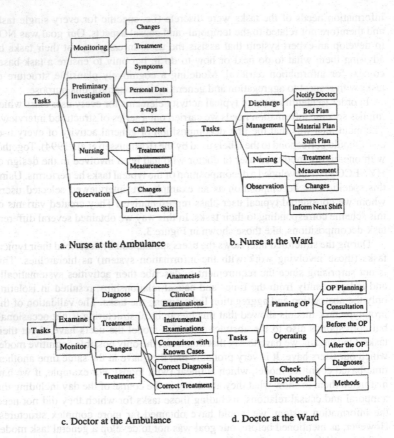

a. Nurse at the Ambulance   b. Nurse at the Ward

c. Doctor at the Ambulance   d. Doctor at the Ward

Figure 3. The prototypical task hierarchies of four user classes.

3.2. DEFINING THE INFORMATION NEEDS OF TASKS: VIEWS

Every task implies specific information needs, defined during the task analysis.
The hypermedia entities considered as necessary to carry out the task comprise
its "view". The user ideally should not be restricted to these entities only. That is
why the entities in a task view are actually the starting points for browsing in the
Hypermedia system.

The hierarchical organization of tasks with respect to aggregation and abstraction implies that more complex or abstract tasks require more information than their
subtasks. In all task hierarchies that we were able to configure, it turned out that
information needs (views) of higher level tasks include the sum of the information

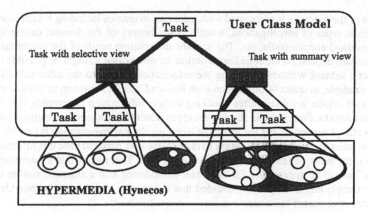

Figure 4. A selective view and a summary view from a higher level task.

needs (views) of all their subtasks. The generality of this result is debatable. We justify it with the following arguments.

Since the task-hierarchies are organized with respect to abstraction and aggregation links, every parent-task (more general task) may represent

– a task of selection among alternative subtasks, or
– an aggregation task which is performed by (a sequence of) all its subtasks.

An aggregation task is normally an abstract task which is introduced to name a group of subtasks and eventually to introduce some order in executing them. That is why it can be expected that its view can include some information specific to the parent-task concerning the decision of how to order or control the execution of the subtasks. Normally, the information needs of all the subtasks will be distributed along the time-axis, but still they all will be necessary for completing the parent-task. In the case where the user wants to perform the parent-task without specifying which subtask she wants to perform, she will need access to the information needed by the parent-task and to the information needed by all of the subtasks. We call this definition of the information needs of a parent-task "a summary view" (see Figure 4).

A selection parent-task represents a point of decision of which subtask to choose. Therefore, the information needs of such a parent-task are defined as the information needed for making the selection.

However, the user often takes the decision for selection of which subtask to perform next after investigating the information related to the subtasks. In these cases it would be convenient to have all the entities related to the alternative subtasks accessible directly from the parent-task. For example, let us say that the parent-task is "Diagnose" (see Figure 3c) and the subtasks are "Anamnesis", "Clinical Investigations", "Instrumental Investigations", and "Comparison with Known Cases".

Each of the subtasks is associated with information entities including results from different types of investigations, a table of the history of the disease, data from the medical encyclopedia, etc. The specific information needs of the parent-task (selection) depend on the selection criterion. In some cases it might be possible to select a subtask without consulting the information related to the other subtasks (for example, to select "Comparison with Known Cases"). However, in most cases the user selects a subtask after checking certain information concerning one or more subtasks. For example, she can decide to select "Instrumental Investigations" only after discovering that the results of a certain clinical investigation is doubtful. So, in order to decide which subtask to choose, the user needs to have this information at the point of selection, i.e. at the parent-task. That means that a "summary view" would be appropriate for this case. Considering that a situation similar to the example might happen, we decided that a summary view should be provided for selective-parent-tasks too.

The tasks define not only rights of access (by means of viewing the needed area of entities in the hypermedia), but also rights to modify the contents of these entities. One way, at least, of reducing the risk of data-corruption and loss, is to ascribe rights to modify data only to the tasks that are expected to change this data. For example (Figure 3c), during the task "Instrumental investigations", in the context of "Diagnose" the doctor needs to know the patient's results, but she is not supposed to change them. She is only allowed to modify the patient's diagnosis.

4. Individual user models: level of experience

An individual UM is based on a task hierarchy. It can be either the task-hierarchy of the corresponding user class, or a modification of it, created manually using the adaptability tools (see Section 7). Since the main characteristic which influences the individualization of information access in our application is not so much the task-hierarchy, which is more role (or user class) specific, but the level of experience of the user with the system, we shall concentrate mostly on it in this section.

The results of the requirement analysis showed that the user's experience in work with the system influences:

– the task-context i.e. the amount of information about the task, where the user can find her way;
– the access strategy, i.e. the ability to cope and the need to use alternative access strategies.

The user's experience level is represented by a parameter associated with every task in the user's task representation. It can have three values – novice, advanced and expert which define different characteristics of the task's view of the information entities. In this way the individual UM is an overlay model over the user's task hierarchy expressing the degree to which every task is mastered with respect to ability of the user to cope with the information space related to this task. The

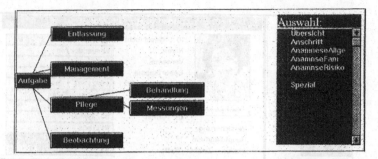

Figure 5. A task-dependent view. The selection menu (*Germ.* Auswahl) in the right part of the screen shows the names of the entities related to the current task "Treatment" (*Germ.* Behandlung). All of the entities are "read only" except one: "Domestic Situation" (*Germ.* Befund Soz Anamnese). The same task hierarchy in English case can be seen in Figure 3b.

degree of experience with a given task influences the size and the type of the view provided by the task.

4.1. Ensuring a Task-Based Context for Information Access

A task-defined "view" consists of all entities related to the task. It is realized by menu containing the names of all task-related entities which are used as starting points for browsing in the hypermedia. This menu is called "Selection" (*Germ.* "Auswahl")-menu (see Figure 5). Two types of task-relevant views over the hypermedia can be defined:

— "Restricted browsing" – by restricting the user's access only within the entities directly related to the current task. In this way the normal hypermedia links outside the current task-view are disabled ("masked").

— "Free browsing with an anchor" – by allowing browsing using the view – entities as starting points (Figure 6). The user can access all other hypermedia entities that are not explicitly forbidden to her or her user class.

The user of HYNECOSUM interacts with the system by selecting the task she wants to perform from a graphical representation of the user's task decomposition on the screen (Figure 5). Access to the Hypermedia is not allowed, if the user selects a higher-level task on which she is a novice. She has to specify subtasks until either she selects a task on which her experience level is advanced or expert or until she reaches a task that cannot be further decomposed. The corresponding view of the Hypermedia is then provided. If the user is advanced or expert on a higher level task in the task hierarchy, she will be provided with a summary view consisting of the views of all subtasks of this task. In this way she will get more starting points for browsing in the hypermedia. If the user is a beginner – she can only get a restricted browsing view, while if she has experience on the task, she can

Figure 6. Free browsing type of viewing. The screen-shot shows the contents of one information entity related to the user's current task (all patient data is fictitious). From here the user can browse following the Hypermedia links (the dark fields and buttons). For example, she can jump on the encyclopedia entity "Gonarthrose", click on the field "461" ("Room/Zimmer") to get a map of the room, where she can click on every bed to see which other patients lay in the same room and browse further to get more data about them. She can also search directly in the dBase using the search options in the left side of the screen, for example, to see the same data ("Stammdaten") for other patients. All these entities are not relevant to the current task, but they are accessible by browsing. In case that a "restricted browsing" was the current type of view all these files would have been unavailable for selection.

be provided with a free browsing type of view (if she wishes). In addition to the free browsing, an expert-user can use the access options offered by the underlying relational database (see Figure 6). For example, after selecting the entity "Main Data" (*Germ.* "Stammdaten"), the user can search the same entity of another patient by different criteria, e.g., name, ID, insurance company, ward name, diagnosis, bed number etc.

The observations made of users working with different sizes of task-defined views during the testing phase showed that in our application the users' degree of experience with the system determines the size of the view with which she is able to cope. Experienced users prefer to use wider summary views from higher-level tasks which allow them to select directly the needed information, since they know exactly where to find it. In contrast, inexperienced users prefer to select a specific subtask to get the corresponding smaller view where they cannot get lost.

We have now described how the local level of experience of the user on every task defines the information context of the task by means of the size of the information space and type of view which enables or disables the possibility of browsing. One can think also of a global level of experience of a user defined across the whole task-hierarchy which grows by propagating upwards through the hierarchy. The level of experience of a parent-task depends on the level of experience of its children tasks. More specifically, it is the minimum of the values of its children tasks. The assumption behind this is that the user is not able to cope with the broader view of a

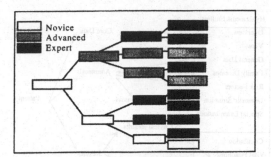

Figure 7. An individual user model: "global" level of experience. The model represents the user's task hierarchy where the color of every task represents the level of experience of the user on this task. The global level of experience is the proportion of the tasks with advanced or expert level over the number of all tasks (79% in this case).

general task, if she is not able to cope with the subsets of this view belonging to the single subtasks. After some time of work with the system, regions of the user's task hierarchy appear where she is experienced. They are initially closer to the leaf-tasks (see Figure 7). With the increasing experience of the user with HYNECOSUM, these regions spread up the task hierarchy towards the most general task (root task). How this happens will be explained in Section 6.

In summary, the task-based views depending on the user's level of experience provide an appropriate context for information retrieval. This is obtained by managing the size of the task-defined view of the information and the freedom of browsing. By gradually increasing the navigation space together with the user's global experience moving upwards toward the root of the task hierarchy, the user is always interacting with the system in an appropriate context.

4.2. ACCOMMODATING DIFFERENT ACCESS STRATEGIES

So far, our main assumption has been that the current task performed by the user always provides the needed context for browsing and the only difference between experienced and novice users concerns their ability to cope with wider task-dependent information context, i.e. to work on more general tasks (i.e. on several subtasks simultaneously). The requirement analysis, however, showed that the differences between the information needs of a novice and an expert concern not only the size of the browsing space, but also the access strategy.

Though the information needs of the users in our application domain are triggered in most of the cases by the standard tasks they are performing, there are cases when users approach the system with a different goal or attitude, not related to a specific task. For example, while performing the task "Nursing" (see Figure 3b), the nurse may want to know suddenly something not directly related with the

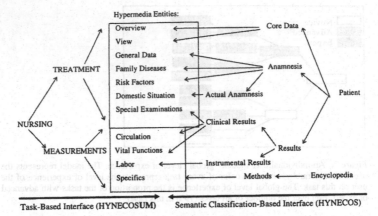

Figure 8. The two types of interfaces to hypermedia entities.

current task – the amount of a certain type of drug in the storage of the ward. Now she has to remember for which task this data is relevant and to select this task – in this case "Management". However, is it really worth changing the context of the current task (the selected patient, entity etc.) just for a small "jump" aside? In this case the task-based interface provides no support, just the other way around! When such a situation arises, users typically try to browse starting from the current entity. However, free browsing in the hypermedia in most of the cases is the most inefficient way to find the needed information (a result valid across a wide range of information retrieval applications – see Rasmussen et al., 1994). Other authors also point out the necessity of combining browsing with other search strategies (Thompson & Croft, 1989), (Dumais et al, 1992). There is a need to provide a mechanism for access corresponding to an alternative strategy, which is task-neutral. Such an alternative provides the original interface of HYNECOS which is based on a semantic classification of the information, a way orthogonal to the task-based way of indexing of the hypermedia entities (see Figure 8).

It is likely that experienced users would be more brave than novices and try to take "shortcuts" or to use alternative search strategies. Their confidence in their ability to cope with the system supports their wish to explore other strategies of obtaining information in order to minimize the amount of clicks or cognitive load. In the example, the problem is that using the task-based strategy requires a bigger cognitive load (remembering the name of the task that provides access to the needed entity) and possibly, bigger ergonomic effort (more clicking). Results of empirical studies in other domains (e.g. design) show that expert users are more inclined to take "shortcuts" than inexperienced users. Instead of following a plan, they tend to act opportunistically, in order to minimize their cognitive load (Visser, 1994).

If the user is experienced in working with the system and knows how the entities are semantically classified, she can organize her search according to the semantic classification of the information space and the current task remains (temporarily or completely) implicit. Knowledge of the alternative access strategy, i.e. of the semantic classification of information is not necessarily related to the experience of the user in working with the system. However, the need for alternative access strategies becomes bigger with the growing experience (practice and confidence) of the user. Our experiments (see Section 8) also showed that users with higher global level of experience (see Figure 7) employ alternative access strategies.

In order to help in learning how to use an alternative access the UM supports a simple teaching facility for novices. It consists of presenting in parallel two alternative interfaces (see Figure 9) corresponding to the two different access strategies: a graphical representation of the task hierarchy where the user can select the task she wants to perform and four hierarchically organized menus corresponding to the semantic classification of entities (compare with the original HYNECOS interface in Figure 2). For a novice user only the task-based interface is available for selection. However, when an entity is selected from the "Selection" (*Germ.* "Auswahl")-window (see Figure 9), the HYNECOS menus in the top part of the screen show how this entity is semantically classified by highlighting the corresponding menu items. Gradually, (in parallel with their increasing level of experience), the users are allowed to use the semantic classification-based interface of HYNECOS. This is explained in more detail in Section 6.

5. Coupling the UM with the hypermedia system

The UM does not modify the underlying structure of the hypermedia links, but just provides views on it. The viewing mechanism is based on additional weighted links from the tasks in the UM to the hypermedia entities. At the same time it ensures task-dependent data-protection.

Unlike the normalized weights of Hyperflex (Kaplan et al., 1993) which denote the strength of association between a goal and a node, we use discrete values:

-2 forbidden for the user entity, display blocked from any task;

-1 "forbidden" for the task entity, display blocked for current task;

0 neutral entity, not related to the task, but accessible through free browsing;

1 connected to the task with "read only" rights of access;

2 connected to the task with "read and write" rights of access.

The two types of viewing are implemented in the following way:

— free browsing with an anchor – all the entities irrelevant for the task are considered by default as connected with links of value 0. They are not included in the task view, but the user can reach them by free browsing following the standard hypermedia links.

— restricted browsing – all entities irrelevant for the task are considered by default as connected with links of value –1. Entities connected with a link of value –1

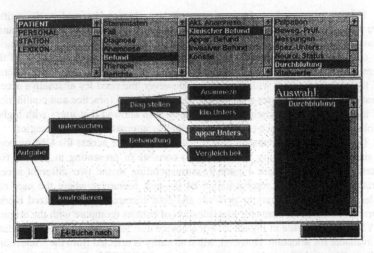

Figure 9. Alternative search strategies offered by the HYNECOSUM interface. The user is a doctor at the ambulance (see in Figure 3c this task hierarchy in English) and a novice at the current task "Instrumental examinations" (*Germ.* "appar.Unters"). The semantic classification menus in the upper part of the screen are not available for selection, but they show how the selected entity from the task-view is classified. Direct search options (button F4 in the lower part of the screen) are currently unavailable (dimmed).

to the current task are not available for browsing and they are "masked", i.e. their display is blocked.

The display of every entity is "filtered" through the current task of the user. If the link between the task and the entity has the value –1, the display is blocked and the user has no way to get this information. If the link has value 0 or 1 and the user has selected the entity, it is displayed (but cannot be changed by the user). If the value is 2, the user can change the contents of the entity.

If a certain entity is forbidden for a particular user or user class, the link between this entity and the root task of this user's (user class) task-hierarchy has the value –2. Even if the user is an expert and gets a view over the entire hypermedia from her root task, or she uses the HYNECOS interface, she will not be able to access this entity, since she is always by default performing the root task.

Straightforward procedures change the read/write rights of a given user-class or individual user. The mechanism for defining a task-view includes two parts:

– assigning values to the links between the Hypermedia entities and the lowest tasks in the hierarchy which need them;
– propagating the values of the links upwards in the hierarchy so that the parent-tasks get access to all entities accessible from their subtasks.

The first part of the mechanism is carried out during the creation of tasks. When a task is created, the entities necessary for completing the task are selected from a list of all hypermedia entities. For each selected entity a link with the assigned value is created between the task and the current entity. Only specially authorized users are allowed to connect tasks to entities with read and write links (i.e. links with value 2), because otherwise the task-dependent write-protection can be violated. Normal users are allowed to create tasks from which they can only read information, i.e. a user is provided only with the "create access link" procedure (links with value "1"). As mentioned before, it is impossible for a non-authorized user to invoke this procedure to change a link from −2 to 1, since she can only operate on entities visible to her (with link 0 to the tasks of her former task-hierarchy) that can be reached through browsing. So, users cannot violate their access rights via the adaptability tool.

The second part consists of propagating the view of the subtasks up to their parent-tasks the task-hierarchy. The "free browsing" type of view-definition is done by creating links from every parent-task to the entities linked to its subtasks with values equal to the maximum value – link to any entity from any of its subtasks. The "restricted browsing" way of viewing is obtained by the same procedure, followed by disabling (assigning a weight of −1) to all entities which are not connected with positive weights to the task.

The procedures for taking away write- or access-rights from a task to a given entity and limiting the access to information for a given user class or for a single user consist of decreasing the values of all links from this entity correspondingly to 1, 0, −1, and −2. The propagation of the weight (−2) goes in the opposite way, from the root to the leaves in the hierarchy. In order to prohibit access to a given entity for a given user, it is not necessary to find out all tasks which potentially require the information, it is enough to set the link from the root task to this entity to −2.

6. Adaptation

Adaptation is a notion referring to the ability of the system to change dynamically according to the changing user's needs in order continually to maintain the appropriate context for interaction (Kühme, 1993). In our case, as in the majority of cases (Norcio & Stanley, 1989), the most important time-dependent factor is the user's experience, therefore the system must have a means for finding out and reacting to the changes in the user's level of experience. One can think of other factors that are time-dependent: for example, the information needs of tasks, or the task-model itself. In our application, however, these factors are not dynamic. The changes of task-structures and information needs normally are regulated and the necessary changes can be conveniently made by the system administrator, if she is provided with the necessary tools. Ensuring adaptivity with respect to these factors would undoubtedly be an interesting research problem, however, it would have been too expensive in the context of our project. Therefore, we provide tools to support adaptability.

6.1. INFERRING THE USER'S EXPERIENCE LEVEL ON A GIVEN TASK

The user's browsing behavior, ability to select correctly and the type of mistakes she makes are taken as evidence of the user's changing level of experience.

A user who works with HYNECOSUM for the first time is considered as a novice at all tasks of her task-hierarchy. If there is evidence that she is able to cope with the browsing space of a certain task, the level of experience on this task is increased. Parent tasks can only increase their level of experience, if the user has demonstrated the higher level of experience on all subtasks of this task. In this way, the level of experience gradually climbs up through the branches of the task-hierarchy. The increase in the experience level starts from the leaf-tasks (i.e. the most specific tasks which can't be decomposed further) since their views are smaller and the user learns faster how to select correctly (see Figures 4 and 7).

Technically the user's experience on a given task is represented as a number, called a task's score, which is calculated as a sum of points. Depending on the task score, the user can fall into one of three possible categories: a Novice, Advanced or Expert on the task.

The user's navigation actions are recorded and if patterns are found which imply that the user's proficiency has increased, points are added to the task's score until a threshold (defined empirically) is reached. Then a flag is set indicating that it seems appropriate to increase the user's level of experience. The patterns of behavior concern the user navigation through the task hierarchy, the time spent on an information item (it is important to be more than a certain threshold to believe that the data was used and not just browsed and considered to be inappropriate), and the correct attempts to select from the semantic classification menus of HYNECOS.

A point is added to the score of a "novice"-task in every case when a sequence of actions defined as a "good" task-navigation behavior is recognized: e.g. selecting a subtask; then selecting one or more entities from a view provided in the "Selection" window; using the provided data (spending more time than a certain threshold); not trying to browse in the hypermedia and being able to come back to the super-task without using the "Help" or "Reset" buttons. At a task with "advanced" level of experience, the increase in the task score happens as a result of correct use of alternative access strategies, for example, using correctly the semantic classification menus or the direct access option to shrink the view provided from the current task.

The same mechanism works in the opposite direction for decreasing the user's level of experience. The user is "punished" for incorrect navigation actions through-out the task hierarchy, in the HYNECOS menus, for asking for "Help", "Info", or using the emergency buttons. For example, when the user selects sibling-tasks one after the other, without selecting any entity from the view provided for the first selected task, this is considered as a sign that the user has selected a wrong task the first time and that she is not familiar enough with the principle of the task-based interface. Therefore, points are subtracted from the user's score on the parent-task. Another significant pattern of behavior is chaotic browsing in the hypermedia from the provided starting points which is terminated with emergency button ("Reset"). A too short time spent on an information entity once it has been selected shows that the entity was wrongly selected. Trying to click on items of the semantic classification menu which are unavailable at the moment, as well as trying to select already selected items; trying to get back to a familiar place by back-tracking (clicking the "≪"-button) – these are all patterns of behavior which lead to "punishing" the user by reducing points from the current task's score. If the threshold to the next lower level of experience is reached, a suggestion of reducing the level of experience for this task is generated by the system.

Strongly adaptive systems, however, threaten the user with a feeling of a loss of control. That is why we decided that the system's adaptation to the user's needs has to be carried out not continuously, but at discrete points in time, and only after the user has given specific permission.

When there is evidence that the user's recorded level of experience can be changed, the system stores this in a list of suggestions together with an explanation of how this will effect the user. The list of suggestions can be read by the user if and when she wishes. For example, the system can be configured to present the list of suggestions at the beginning of every week, or with every second use, or to present it only when requested. If the user decides to accept the suggestion, the system updates the level of experience which comes into effect from this moment. In this way our system follows the strategy of adaptively supported adaptability (Oppermann, 1994a): providing initial adaptive suggestions showing the rationale for the adaptations and the way of performing them, and adapting only after receiving users' consent.

6.2. EFFECTS OF ADAPTATION

The system's adaptation to the user's level of experience concerns the size and type of the task-defined views (the task-based context) and the access strategies which are available for the user.

6.2.1. Adapting the information context to the current task

As explained in Section 4, in our approach appropriate context for information retrieval is obtained by selecting starting points for browsing appropriate for the current task and reducing the size of the browsing space for inexperienced users. By gradually increasing the number of starting points and the freedom of browsing together with the user's growing global experience, the user is always interacting with the system in an appropriate context.

When a user is a novice on a given task she is allowed to browse only within the information entities provided for the task (restricted browsing). If the task is not a leaf-task (i.e. if it has subtasks), the user has to select these subtasks first before being allowed to access the hypermedia entities. When the task score of the current task exceeds the task-threshold for level "Novice" and the user accepts the suggestion of being classified as "Advanced", the system checks whether the level of experience of the user on all sister-tasks is already "Advanced" in order to see whether to propagate the higher level up the task hierarchy. The increased experience level at the task means, that the user can (if she wants) get access to more starting points in the hypermedia (wider view) and to a free browsing type of viewing. In case she gets lost, she can get back to the starting points by clicking on the task-button again.

If all of the sister-tasks have level "Advanced", the system suggests increasing the level of the parent-task. If the user agrees, the system provides the possibility to get a summary view from the parent-task and a free style of browsing (both of the features the user can accept or reject). In this way, by propagating the higher level of experience up to the root task, the user is allowed to browse freely in the Hypermedia and to get wider views (more starting points for navigation) to the Hypermedia without having to specify precisely the task she wants to perform.

The transition from "Advanced" to "Expert" level at a given task doesn't concern the amount of information the user gets for the task. It concerns only the freedom of the user to use alternative access strategies. This will be discussed in the next section.

6.2.2. *Adaptation to the user's access strategy*

Two interfaces are incorporated in the system corresponding to the different access strategies (the task-based one and the semantic-classification one). There is also an option for direct access which is available at any time for the expert user by pressing a function key (button F4 in Figure 9 below) – a window appears where she can write a query. The task-based interface is orthogonal to the semantic classification interface (see Figure 8): it reflects a different cognitive access strategy. The user can apply either of them or a combination or both. For a user who is searching for certain information outside the context of the specified task, it is more appropriate to use direct access or the original HYNECOS interface. For a user who approaches with a specific task, it is more efficient to use the task-based interface.

In order to create an image of the system consistent for all users and to support the learning of the more difficult semantic classification interface, the HYNECOS-menus (in the upper part of the screen), the task buttons (in the central part), as well as the button for direct access (below), are all displayed (see Figure 9). If the user is a novice on the currently selected task, the HYNECOS menus and the direct access button are not yet available for selection – she can only use the "Selection"-menu where the relevant entities for the selected task are presented. When the user chooses an item from this menu, the items which correspond to the semantic classes containing this entity in the inactive HYNECOS menus on the top of the screen are highlighted to show the user how this entity is semantically classified. In this way she sees what selections she would had to make, if the menus were active, in order to find this entity.

If the user becomes "Advanced" at a given task, the HYNECOS menus are enabled for selection, but the user is still restricted to select only among the items from the view provided from the current user's task. In this way the user is stimulated to use the HYNECOS menus to find the information related to the task, in case she gets lost in her free browsing. Other ways to get back are to select again the current task from the task hierarchy or to use the "backtrack" option of the hypermedia system. However, they lead to reduction of points from the task's score, while using the HYNECOS menus is rewarded by increasing the task score.

If the user becomes "Advanced" on a task that is located higher in the task-hierarchy, she will get a wider view composed of the views of the subtasks, i.e. a bigger choice of entities in the "Selection"-menu. This makes the access to the data easier since all the entities are directly accessible from the higher order task. However, in some cases this can be inconvenient since the "Selection"-window has a fixed size and if the task-view it too wide, one has to scroll to select the needed entity. Thus the user is stimulated to use the semantic classification menus since she can additionally reduce the choice by selecting the logical type of the entity from the standard HYNECOS menus on the top of the screen which have now been enabled (this is awarded by adding points to the current task-score). Of course, the user can shrink the "Selection" menu also by selecting one of the subtasks, but for this is she will be punished by subtracting points from the task score.

So, at every time the user can select either as before directly from the "Selection" menu, or by using the menus corresponding to the logical classification of the entities, or by selecting a subtask as before. During the field-test interviews, this redundancy was commented on by most of the users as an advantage, since they were confident that there are several ways to achieve the same effect, if they have difficulties with either of the options.

If the user becomes an expert on a given task, she is provided with a summary view of the views of all subtasks, with a free style of browsing and the possibility of using the HYNECOS interface freely to search through all the hypermedia. In addition, the user is allowed to search directly by name or keyword for the needed data.

In summary, with the growing experience of the user, the system provides her with a wider spectrum of search strategies.

7. Adaptability

User-adaptable systems support users in modifying systems according to their own needs (Fischer, 1992). Our architecture for user modeling allows the user to adapt her individual model. A set of tools are provided for this purpose: a *task-editor*, allowing the user to graphically create task-structures and define the information needs of tasks (views of the hypermedia); a *user-class editor* which allows her to define new user class-stereotypes (i.e. to name task hierarchies, to grant or restrict rights of access to information), and an *individual model editor* (allowing the user to change the level of experience and the type of viewing of every task and to enable or disable alternative access strategies: direct keyword search, task-based search, or the HYNECOS menus).

7.1. DEFINITION AND MODIFICATION OF THE TASK-HIERARCHIES

We have developed a graphical task editor and a library of task-aggregates which allow the user to define a task hierarchy of her own, i.e. to create herself her individual model. This graphical tool supports the creation of new task-hierarchies and the modification of existing ones. The user can define her own tasks and add them to the library of task aggregates. The task-editor allows her to select information entities and to link them ("read-only") to the task, which she wants to create. During the modification of the task-hierarchy and creation of new tasks, the rights of access to information of the user can't be changed, since the "forbidden" entities are specified in her user class and are therefore invisible for the user. However, she can extend the number of starting points for browsing and modify her task hierarchy to make it more convenient for search according to her own preferences.

7.2. CREATING NEW USER CLASSES

The user class editor supports creating stereotype models for groups of users. It takes as input a task-decomposition created with the graphical task editor which is going to be shared by all representatives of the class/group. It allows assigning different read/write rights for every task, banning access to certain information entities or providing access from a task to additional entities. This editor can only be used by specially authorized users.

7.3. CHANGING THE PARAMETERS OF THE INDIVIDUAL USER MODEL

The user can modify her task hierarchy with the task-editor tool. In addition she is provided with an "individual UM editor", which allows:

- Changing the recorded level of experience on a task. This can be done directly by the user without waiting for the adaptation mechanism to suggest a change in the level.
- Selecting the type of viewing. The user can select the "free browsing with an anchor" type or the task-restricted browsing. In this way if she is a novice on a given task, she can still change to a browsing style of viewing, if she feels uncomfortable with the restrictive view.
- Enabling or disabling alternative access strategies. The user can "switch-off" the HYNECOS menus or the option for direct access, if she doesn't want to

use them; or, alternatively, she can "switch-off" the task-based interface and work only with the HYNECOS interface and the direct search option.
- Enabling/disabling access to specific entities which are forbidden/allowed to other members of the user class. This is a privileged option which can be only performed by authorized users.

One consequence of having adaptability tools is that it becomes possible for the users to build highly individualized personal versions of the information system. This is, however, not always desirable. Once control is given to the user, one has to take care that she will use it for her own good and will not, intentionally or not, cause damage or violation of access restrictions. This question has not been addressed in our application. In fact, as the tests showed, our users did not strive to a high degree of individualization. However, we believe that it is important to provide these tools for eventual changes that might occur in the task models.

Another possible application of the adaptability tools is the creation of "team models". A too high individualization could become counter-productive to the team nature of the work in the hospital. In this sense, the information system sometimes serves communicative functions. For example, it can be used on the same computer at the ward by two or three doctors and several nurses. In order not to confuse and impair the communication among them, the system can be adjusted to appear in the same way to users performing the same tasks. That is why the design of the UM should provide for creation and adaptation by a group of users, usually from different user-classes, who are going to work together in a team. In other words, the system should be able to support collaborative work by means of a "team model". The original semantic classification interface of HYNECOS is well suited for this purpose, since it is user-neutral. However, it alone does not provide any help on how to find the needed information entity. If a group UM is going to be created, the group has to reach an agreement about the team task hierarchy, the style of viewing, the level of experience and the type of presentation and then create a group UM using the adaptation tools.

8. Tests

The testing of the system involved 13 users from different classes and with different levels of experience with the system. We posed three main questions which the tests had to answer:

1) Does the task-based interface (i.e. the UM-supported task-based context for information retrieval) provide better support for novice users than the semantic classification interface? Does the system support relevant tasks?
2) Does HYNECOSUM support the user's learning of the semantic classification interface?
3) Does the UM-supported shift among different access strategies really correspond to the changing needs of users with growing level of experience?
4) Is the adaptive capability of the system comprehensible?

Table I. Comparison of the work of two participant-groups with the task-based (TB) and the semantic-classification based (SCB) interfaces. Times are given in min. (') and sec. ("").

Results	Attempts							
	TB	SCB	TB	SCB	TB	SCB	TB	SCB
Average total time of task completion	13.3' (n=4)	> max	11.2' (n=5)	15.0' (n=1)	9.8'	12.2' (n=2)	8.0'	9.3' (n=2)
Number of subjects that succeeded on task	4	0	5	1	5	2	5	2
Average time for finding a task-related entity	16"	12.8'	11"	10.4'	8"	7.8'	6"	7.2'

The following methods were used to gather data about the user's performance during the experiments performed with HYNECOSUM:

- questionnaires;
- on-line logging of all dialogue events (mouse clicks, selections, typing);
- direct observation and protocols;
- interviews.

In this way some redundancy was achieved which offered the possibility of checking what users did against what they said they did.

8.1. TESTING THE TASK-BASED INTERFACE

In order to answer the first question we performed the following experiment.

Experiment 1. The goal was to test whether the task-based interface of HYNECOSUM provides a better learning environment for the novice user than the semantic classification-based interface of HYNECOS. For this purpose we assigned a certain task to two groups each including five novice participants of the same class. All the participants have had some experience with computers in general, and they were familiar with some applications, e.g. text processors. The first group used HYNECOSUM with the task-based interface and the other group used HYNECOS with the semantic classification interface. We selected the user class "nurse at the ward" (see Figure 3b) who had to perform the task "Nursing". This task is performed relatively frequently and follows a well established routine. It contains two subtasks "Treatment" and "Measurements. The first subtask requires access to seven entities and the second one to four entities. Figure 8 shows how the access to the needed entities can be organized via the two orthogonal interfaces.

The participants of each group had to perform the task four times (the results are shown in the columns in Table I framed with thicker line), with data prepared in advance (e.g. measurements have been made in advance and written on paper for typing into the computer), so that they could perform the task entirely on the computer. Time for accomplishing the task was limited to 15 minutes. There was no possibility of using external help or manuals.

An observer sat with every participant during the completion of the task taking detailed notes, including timing of actions and the outcomes. Overall time and success data (see Table I) showed that the task-based interface of HYNECOSUM provided a better environment for novices. Four out of the five HYNECOSUM participants managed to complete the task in the assigned time in the second, third and fourth sessions. Only one participant failed to complete the task in the first session and the reason was that she took too long working on the contents of the entities once she had accessed them! In contrast, no one from the five participants working with the semantic classification interface was able to perform the task in the first two attempts and only two participants were able to complete the task in the third and fourth session. These two participants turned out to be extraordinarily good learners since they were able to achieve an average task completion time similar to the one of the first group. However, they spent far longer finding the task-relevant entities than the first group and comparatively less time in actually working with the entities, i.e. reading and writing data. The third row of the table shows that the time to access the task-relevant entities (across all participants and attempts) differs dramatically in the two groups: while the participants of the task-based interface needed seconds (from 16 down to 6), the participants of the semantic classification-based interface needed minutes (from 13 down to 7)! This can be explained by the more complex cognitive task which the participants of the semantic classification interface have to cope with: they have not only to find their way through the different classes of entities, but also to remember which entities are relevant for completing the task.

In summary, the experiments showed that the task-based interface ensures a higher effectiveness (speed of finding the needed information) than the semantic classification interface.

8.2. TESTING HYNECOSUM TRAINING CAPABILITY

Experiment 2. In order to evaluate the teaching capability of HYNECOSUM we decided to compare the performance with the semantic classification (HYNECOS) interface of a group of participants who have been working during a certain period of time with HYNECOSUM (and, therefore, have been trained to use the HYNECOS menus by seeing how the selected items are classified semantically – see Figure 9) with a group of participants who have been working the same period of time only with the semantic classification interface of HYNECOS and with a third group of participants who have not worked with the system at all before.

The three groups were as follows: one group of six participants who have been working over a course of a week with HYNECOSUM and had increased their global level of experience from novice to advanced or expert on more than 70% of their tasks (we call it the HYNECOSUM group); another group of six participants who

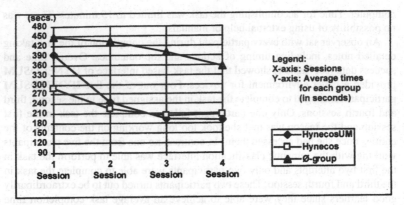

Figure 10. Average times for task-related entity-access with the HYNECOS interface.

have been working approximately one week (the same number of sessions) with HYNECOS (HYNECOS-group) and a third group of three participants who have not been working with HYNECOS or with HYNECOSUM at all (the Ø-group). During the experiment all groups had to work only with the semantic-classification (HYNECOS) interface. In a course of four sessions (half a day) we observed the work of the groups and measured the change in the average times needed for entity-retrieval for the same tasks.

The results can be seen in Figure 10. One can see that in the first session the average time for the HYNECOSUM group is higher than the average time of the untrained HYNECOS group (an effect of the change of interface), but lower than that of the Ø-group. However, the speed of performance increases faster in the HYNECOSUM-group than that of the Ø-group and from the second session on it is close to the HYNECOS group.

8.2.1. *Testing the alternative access strategies*

In order to test whether the different access strategies were really used and whether they satisfied the anticipated user needs, we performed an experiment with a group of subjects who could select freely among different strategies. Their UMs indicated that they were already experts at some tasks, advanced in various regions of their task hierarchies and still beginners in other regions.

Experiment 3. The experiment took place in the course of one day and involved seven experienced participants (with global level of experience more than 70% advanced or expert) from different user classes. Their actions were monitored and recorded. At every information access, the user's current task was either automatically recorded (when the participant was working with the task-based interface)

Table II. The usage of different access strategies (in % of all entity accesses) at tasks with a certain level of experience. (Abbreviations used: RB – Restricted browsing view type; FB – Free browsing.)

Interface used	Task-based		Semantic Classif.	Direct Query	Task-based + Semantic Classif.		Semantic Classif. + Direct Query	Task-based + Direct Query		Task-based + Semantic Classif. + Direct Query	
Experience at task:	RB	FB			RB	FB		RB	FB	RB	FB
Advanced	87%		–	–	12%		–		–		1%	
	62%	25%			8%	4%				–	1%
Expert	29%		10%	5%	23%		8%		7%		18%	
	10%	19%			1%	22%			–	7%	–	18%

Table III. Reasons for selecting a given strategy. (presented in % of all the cases when a certain strategy was selected, abbreviations used: TB – task-based, SC – semantic classification based, DQ – direct query).

Explanation/use interface	TB	SC	DQ	TB + SC	SC + DQ	TB + DQ	TB + SC + DQ
"since I know how to do it"	72%	39%	8%	26%	22%	27%	8%
"to save time/mouse clicks"	23%	43%	89%	37%	70%	52%	66%
"to see what happens"	2%	13%	–	43%	12%	19%	22%
other	3%	5%	3%	4%	6%	2%	4%

or the participant had to say aloud what she was doing. At the end the participants were shown their protocols and asked to explain why they used an alternative access strategy. The average (across tasks) usage of different access strategies and their combinations with respect to the user's level of experience on the task are shown in Table II.

The results about tasks where the user is "advanced" showed, as expected, that most popular was still the task-based access strategy. The reason is that the semantic classification interface and direct query strategies are only available in the context of the current task, so the user has first to select a task, in whose context to search using the HYNECOS menus. The results show that advanced participants preferred (in 62% against 25% of the cases) to keep to the restrictive-browsing. The results in the second row of the table show that the users still prefer to perform task-based access (29%) even from tasks where they are experts. However, nearly as often the participants were combining the task-based access with the semantic classification-based (23%) access and direct queries (18%). A significant number of participants were applying the semantic classification and the direct query strategies in their "pure" form.

We wanted to let the participants explain why they used a given strategy. First we interviewed the participants to get an idea of the possible motives and then asked them to fill in a questionnaire allowing the participants to evaluate in a scale form (Pearlman, 1989) their preferences to different answers. The results are presented in Table III.

The results show that in most (72%) of the cases the participants select the task-based strategy since they were used to it and felt confident that they will find the relevant information, while the use of a different strategy was in most of the cases motivated by the wish to save time or mouse clicks. Most of the participants (63%) who motivated their choice "since I know how to do it" had a lower global level of experience in the task-hierarchy, while the participants motivating their choices with the wish to save time/clicks and to see what happens had a higher level of experience (77%). These results confirmed our assumptions about the influence of the individual level of experience of the user on the preference for different access strategies (see Section 4). The conclusion is that experienced users do not distinguish formally among strategies, but perceive them as alternative options or routes for any type of information need. Each strategy option was designed to be an optimal way of satisfying different needs. Expert users were inventive and used the flexibility of the system by creating individual shortcuts to satisfy their needs.

8.3. TESTING THE UNDERSTANDABILITY OF THE SYSTEM

In order to evaluate the understandability of the system and especially with respect to adaptivity we interviewed all the 13 subjects participating in the tests (to get as much qualitative data as possible) and afterwards asked them to answer questionnaires. The interviews with participants were targeted at finding out if the users recognize the difference between the opportunities provided by the system at different stages of their experience progress and if they feel disturbed by this. 93% (12) of the users who participated in the tests liked working with the system and preferred it to any other information system they had used before. An additional effect, which was pointed out by participants was that the task-based interface allowed them to concentrate more on their tasks instead of information searching and that the visual decomposition of tasks into subtasks helps them organize their work better and reminds them about filling in or checking documents that were needed and which they might have otherwise forgotten.

It turned out that the metaphor which we used to explain the adaptation when we first introduced the system to the users, was accepted and used by most of them as a basis on which they had built their cognitive model of the system. When explaining why the views from higher level tasks are wider, we compared the task hierarchies with peaks in a mountain: the more one climbs up, the more one sees around, therefore, one also sees more possible ways (access strategies) to get to a given place in the valley below. By "climbing up in the mountain" we meant increasing the global level of experience. During the interviews, as well as while giving explanations of their protocols, the subjects spontaneously used this metaphor. Several of them explained that they were using a "different route to that spot" meaning that they were using the HYNECOS interface, and many used the words "from here I can already jump/glide" to the entity in question. Some of the subjects even developed further the metaphor in order to explain themselves the difference between the access options available for novice and advance users on one task.* Once during the interviews, a user got stuck explaining the difference, and another user offered help, saying: "But you haven't been often enough on this peak to take a new route alone – you should study the map first!" The differences between the access options available for advanced and expert users were better understood: "The experts are allowed to jump and flounder all around; they won't get lost even if they get into new territory".

The subjects have been quite reluctant to use the adaptability tools. During the last experiment we provided them with access to the adaptation tools and explained to them how to make adaptations themselves. Only one subject tried to use the adaptation tool – "to see how it works". Two other ones expressed a wish to change their task hierarchy, but instead of trying to do this themselves they consulted the "guru". Their wish for the change was not so much driven by the need to include some particular personal preferences, as by the worry that something is wrong with their system, because it is different. We interpreted this as evidence that probably team UMs would be appropriate after the initial learning stage is over. It also supports Norcio & Stanley's (1989) and Oppermann's (1994b) suggestion that individualized systems are of biggest importance for supporting a beginner in the learning phase and their importance fades when the user is able to apply the full range of options provided by the system.

9. Comparison with other work

Tasks are often used for representing context in office systems. Several systems providing task support for office systems exist. Croft (1984) describes two adaptive systems: an adaptive office assistant (POISE) and an adaptive document retrieval system. POISE is able to identify the user's current task and to provide assistance in selecting the necessary tool (word processor, e-mailer etc.) and assigning the appropriate parameters for the tool invocation. The Adaptive Document Retrieval System is able to represent the user's needs, query, and the history of the current search in an Associative Search Net.** Croft suggests also combining these two approaches in a system for task-based document retrieval in the office. However, we are not aware of the existence of an implementation of this idea so far. In addition the original proposal does not concern hypermedia documentation systems, but

---

* This was the only point which was not self-evident to the users – i.e. why a novice can only see how a task-related entity is semantically classified, but cannot use the classification menus for selection and the direct access options.

** A similar structure for indexing hypermedia entities with respect to the user's goals and preferences appears later in (Kaplan et al., 1993) and in (Mathé & Chen, 1996).

standard information retrieval systems using Boolean- and full text-search, where the problems are essentially different.

Different approaches exist for making hypermedia adaptive. The most common way is to adapt the presentation of the hypermedia nodes to the needs of the user by, for example, increasing the amount of details or changing the level of explanation (Boyle & Encarnacion, 1994; Beaumont, 1994; Hohl et al., 1996). Educational hypertexts *restrict the user's browsing* within small portions of the hyperspace which are focused on a certain topic (lesson) and in this way reduce the risk that the user gets lost (Brusilovsky, 1992). In the context of educational hypertext it has been proposed (Böcker et al., 1990; Hohl et al., 1996; Brusilovsky et al., 1993) to *provide appropriate starting points* for navigation, and local orientation by suggesting links from the current node which will be appropriate to follow (having in mind a specific goal node). More general approaches record a user's typical patterns of navigation and adapt to them by changing the links between the entities to reflect paths that are likely to be traversed having in mind the user's current goal (Kibby & Maes, 1989; Monk, 1989).

Our approach falls in this educational category of Hypermedia by providing task-relevant starting points in the hypermedia and by restricting browsing to smaller subspaces for inexperienced users. This is not surprising, since the possibility of getting lost in the hypermedia system is small for experienced users of office documentation systems and far bigger for novice users. In this sense our system has an educational function.

The problem of finding out which are the relevant starting points and information subspaces for a given goal (task) is very important, but not well investigated in the field of adaptive hypermedia. More relevant work on this problem exists in the field of adaptive information retrieval. The semantic indexing of information with respect to the individual user's interests, goals or tasks has been extensively investigated (Belew, 1986; Belkin et al., 1987; Kok, 1991). Though using different approaches and representation schemes: blackboard architecture with cooperating experts (Belkin et al., 1987), rule based expert systems (Brajnik et al., 1990), first order logic (Kok, 1991), connectionist schemes (Belew, 1986; Biennier et al., 1990; Crouch et al., 1994), relevance networks (Mathé and Chen, 1996), or agent-based architectures (Thomas & Fischer, 1996), these approaches share one feature: users' feedback is taken as an information source for updating the semantic indexing scheme. Like any machine learning system, a UM utilizing such an individualized semantic indexing scheme works in two regimes:

- learning – modifying/extending the task model on the basis of any kind of feedback from the users about the information suggested by the system, and
- applying – inferring the user's current task and recommending information according to the task model.

In most approaches (Thompson & Croft, 1989; Kok, 1991; Brajnik et al., 1990; Bennier et al., 1990; Crouch et al., 1994; Mathé & Chen, 1996;) the user is asked directly to estimate the relevance of every unit that is retrieved. Some approaches, however, employ other sources of evidence about the user in the learning phase to index the information to the current task /goal of the user. For example, (Kaplan et al., 1993) assume that the more time the user spends on a unit, the more interesting it is, i.e. more relevant to the current goal. Maes (1994) proposes apart from user feedback, three types of evidence about the user that could be used for learning about her goals (tasks or interests): observing her behavior, e.g. what she does with the retrieved documents, direct training of the system by the user by giving examples, communication and sharing knowledge about the user with other UMs ("agents" in Maes' terminology).

The most common approach – direct user feedback – has inherent disadvantages. First, the user is not always a reliable source of evaluation about the relevance of the information to her goal or task (especially when she is inexperienced), and second, it poses an additional burden on the user and might distract her from her goals. For example, in our application it is absolutely impossible to expect direct user feedback on the relevance of information to tasks in everyday work. It would have been possible to apply this approach in the knowledge acquisition phase, as an exception, only for a short time. However, we would have needed users who are confident working with the system and who give reliable feedback. Novice users are not good teachers for a machine learning system.

Other ways of getting feedback, for example, using the assumption that the more time is spent on an unit, the more interesting it is (Kaplan et al., 1993), can also be unreliable, since it is not clear what the user is actually doing in this time. Of course, if she spends too little time, not enough even to read the information, this is a sort of evidence that the user was not interested in it. However, still the question remains whether the reason is that she considers this irrelevant to the goal (indexing has to be changed) or that she has changed her goal in the meantime (a new goal has to be recognized). Still, user feedback is the only possibility for learning approaches aiming at adaptive semantic indexing when the information space is very large, as in library applications (Crouch et al., 1994; Mathé & Chen, 1996) and the set of possible user goals is virtually endless. In our case, the information space is comparatively smaller and the number of user tasks is not too big. Also the relevance of information to tasks is stable and does not depend on the individual user. That is why a learning approach in our case is not justified. It is possible to index the information explicitly to the tasks in advance. This has two advantages: first, it is more reliable than automatic learning "which is nothing more than a guess" (Kay, 1994), and second, it does not require any feedback from the users at runtime. We suspect that this is the case with most of the office documentation system applications.

In most approaches (Thompson & Croft, 1989; Brajnik et al., 1990; Kok, 1991; Hoppe, 1992; Kaplan et al., 1993; Mathé & Chen, 1996) the information obtained from the user (or the observation of her behavior) is used also to change the structure of the goals, tasks, interests contained in the UM. Our approach does not learn about the user's task-model. In principle this is possible. For example, Mathé &

Chen build a hierarchical relevance network which starts from goals and keywords and builds up combinations called "compound nodes" whose information needs are derived from the needs of their sub-nodes. One could think of the relevance network as a dynamic task hierarchy where the nodes represent combinations of keywords, information descriptors, tasks/goals, and interests, instead of task-names. The weights of relevance among the nodes in the network are updated based on the user's feedback and in this way a dynamic model of user's interests with respect to tasks can be built. In a similar way, the systems described in (Biennier et al., 1990; Kaplan et al., 1993) learns about the weights of the links among different goals from the user's feedback.

However, this was not necessary in our case. The comparatively smaller number and dynamics of the tasks performed by users distinguishes the domain of our application from other information retrieval applications. In office documentation systems or "institutional hypermedia" (Brusilovsky, 1996), typically the organiza-tion of work assumes well defined tasks associated with actors performing them.

Another aspect according to which we can compare our approach to other approaches concerns the representation of the user model. The approaches aim-ing at a dynamic representation of the user's goals, beliefs, and interests employ rule-based systems (Brajnik et al., 1990), logic-based representations (Kok, 1989; Kobsa & Pohl, 1994b), connectionist schemes (Belew, 1986), or relevance net-works (Kaplan et al., 1993; Mathé & Chen, 1996). As already mentioned, our user model's representation is a combination of stereotype (ensuring the appropriate context of information access) and an overlay model (ensuring the adaptation to the user's level of experience). Stereotype approaches are in practice the most popular user modeling approaches (Kay, 1994) and overlay models are the most practical student modeling approaches for intelligent tutoring systems (Wenger, 1987). Such a combination has been considered by many authors (Kobsa & Pohl, 1994a) as a good basis for user modeling.

Once a UM has acquired and represented some knowledge about the user, it has to apply it in order to diagnose the current situation (task, goal etc.) and to suggest relevant information. In our approach, unlike (Hoppe, 1992) and (Oppermann, 1994b) there is no inferring of the current user's task – the user assigns it explicitly herself. With respect to this feature our approach is similar to (Kaplan et al., 1993), (Mathé & Chen, 1996) and (Höök et al., 1996), where the user interacts with the system by designating her current task. The parallel with the Glass-box model (Höök et al., 1996), can be drawn further since the user in fact sees her model all the time on the screen and manipulates it directly during her interaction with the system. The advantages of this approach are summarized by (Höök et al., 1996) and we do not need to repeat them here. The disadvantages are that the if the tasks are too many, it might become difficult for the user to select or to predict what an alteration of the task will result in. However, unlike Höök, who solves this problem by combining a small set of pre-defined tasks with task/plan-inference, we do it by providing the user with alternative, task-independent search strategies and with a simple teaching facility showing how to use them.

With respect to the ability of our system to support the user's learning of the system, the idea of our approach is somewhat similar to Carroll's idea of "training wheels" (Carroll & Carrithers, 1984) which consists of disabling from the interface for inexperienced users the more complex options of the system and then gradually increasing the amount of available options along with the increasing level of experience of the users. Experimental studies show that this approach provides a very good support in the stage of user learning to work with complex applications, e.g. word-processing programs. However, the idea that the user's level of experience influences not only the amount of information (options) which she is able to cope with but also her search strategy seems not to be investigated elsewhere in the field of information retrieval.

Finally, task-based interfaces to software systems have proven to be very effective (Rasmussen et al., 1994; Fischer, 1995). Our tests also confirmed this result not only for novice users but for experienced users, who turned out to prefer the task-based interface even when they had the freedom to choose among different interfaces. There is a notable tendency in the development of man-machine interfaces, summarized by Fischer: "... *the emphasis in human-computer interaction should be concentrated on the humans and their tasks – not on computers, interfaces and tools*"(Fischer, 1995).

10. Conclusions

This paper describes how user modeling has been applied to ensure task-specific context and adaptation to the individual user's level of experience in a hypermedia-based hospital documentation system. Stereotype models of user classes characterized with specific tasks have been defined. These task-models serve as a kernel of every individual model. This model is transparent to the user and she interacts with the system by means of selecting the task she wants to perform. Every task provides a specific "view" of the hypermedia consisting of the documents which are needed for completing the task. They serve as starting points for browsing in the hypermedia. The individual UM is an overlay on the user's task hierarchy (it can be the user-class task hierarchy or a modification of it) where the user's level of experience is recorded at each task. The level of experience is diagnosed by the system by observing the behavior of the user: the way she selects entities, the mistakes she makes and the way she browses through the hypermedia. The user's level of experience influences the number of starting points, the size of the browsing space and the access strategy to the information. Three different strategies have been provided: direct search (by keywords), and two strategies corresponding to different ways of indexing the information: a semantic classification and a task-based classification. The task-based access is provided for users with lower levels of experience together with a teaching option showing how the selected information is semantically classified. For advanced and expert users, the other search strategies are gradually enabled, together with the possibility of free browsing in the hypermedia. The adaptation takes place at discrete points of time and only after obtaining the user's consent. Adaptability tools are available, allowing the users to change nearly all parameters of their UMs and the organization of the interface.

The testing of the system showed that the tasks models represented in the system correspond to the real tasks performed by the users, and that the task-based interface provides a better support for novice users than the semantic classification interface. HYNECOSUM proved to support a faster learning of the semantic classification interface. The UM-supported shift among different access strategies really corresponds to the changing needs of users with growing level of experience. The users seemed to understand well the adaptive capability of the system and to be able to explain its behavior.

In summary, the UM in the hospital documentation system ensures the following features:

- increases the operational speed and efficiency of task performance;
- provides a task-based context for information access;
- supports novice users by ensuring access to all of the documents needed for a task, while providing experienced users with appropriate starting points for browsing and alternative strategies for information access;
- provides a simple teaching facility to help novice users learn alternative strategies;
- supports adaptivity to the user's level of experience at discrete points in time and after asking the user;
- provides a transparent, directly manipulable model, an integral part of the user's interface and an understandable metaphor for the adaptation;
- provides adaptability tools allowing the creation of group UMs supporting team work.

We believe this approach to user modeling can be applied to achieve adaptivity and -user support in many office information and documentation systems. The requirements are to have comparatively stable, well-defined task structures associated with specific user roles in the working situation which can help in defining user classes. Another requirement is that the tasks themselves should have relatively stable information needs. If any of these conditions is not present, this approach needs to be extended with learning capabilities, like those described in Section 9, so that the UM could acquire automatically from observing the user's behavior the indexing of relevant information to the tasks and/or the task-structures itself.

Acknowledgments

I would like to thank my student, Thomas Stoyke who implemented entirely the -UM part of HYNECOSUM; to Karin Hertwig, Dirk Langkafel and Jack Shiff from SIEMENS ZFE who developed HYNECOS and helped with their experience and advice in the requirement analysis and knowledge acquisition; to the staff of the University Orthopedics Clinic of Heidelberg, to Ralph Deters, Peter Brusilovsky, to three anonymous reviewers who gave valuable comments on previous drafts of this paper, and especially to one of them who helped a lot with the English.

This research has been partly supported by Projects 644 "Documentation" with Siemens ZFE and I-406 with the Bulgarian Ministry of Science and Higher Education.

References

Anderson, J.: 1985, 'Cognitive Psychology and its Implications'. In G. Atkinson, R. Lindzey, and R. Thompson (eds.): *A Series of Books in Psychology*. New York: W.H. Freeman & Co.

Beaumont, I. and P. Brusilovsky: 1995, 'Adaptive Educational Hypermedia: Form Ideas to Real Systems'. *Third International Conference on Educational Multimedia and Hypermedia ED-MEDIA'95*, Graz, Charlottesville: AACE, pp. 93–98.

Beaumont, I.: 1994, 'User Modeling in the Interactive Anatomy Tutoring System ANATOM-TUTOR'. *User Modeling and User Adapted Interaction* 4(1), 21–45 (reprinted in this volume, pp. 91–115).

Begoray, J.: 1990, 'An Introduction to Hypermedia Issues, Systems, and Application Areas'. *Int. J. Man-Machine Studies* 33. 121–147.

Belew, R.K.: 1986, 'Adaptive Information Retrieval: Machine Learning in Associative Networks'. Ph.D. Thesis, Dept. of Computer & Communication Sciences, University of Michigan: Ann Arbour.

Belkin N.J. et al.: 1987, 'Distributed Expert Based Information Systems: An Interdisciplinary Approach'. *Informat. Process. Management* 23(5).

Biennier, F., M. Guivarch, and J.-M. Pinon: 1990, 'Browsing in Hyperdocuments with the Assistance of a Neural Network'. In: Rizk, A., N. Streitz, and J. André (eds.): *Hypertext: Concepts, Systems and Applications*. Cambridge: Cambridge University Press.

Böcker H.-D., H. Hohl, and T. Schwab: 1990, 'HYPADAPTER – Individualizing Hypertext'. In: Diaper D. et al. (eds.) *INTERACT'90 Proceedings of the 3rd International Conference of Human Computer Interaction*, North-Holland: Amsterdam, pp. 931–936.

Boyle, C. and A. Encarnacion: 1994, 'MetaDoc: An Adaptive Hypertext Reading System'. *User Modeling and User Adapted Interaction* 4(1), 1–19 (reprinted in this volume, pp. 71–89).

Brajnik G., G. Guida, and C. Tasso: 1990, 'User Modeling in Expert Man-Machine Interfaces: A Case Study in Intelligent Information Retrieval'. *IEEE Transactions on Systems, Man, and Cybernetics* 20(1), 166–185.

Brusilovsky, P.: 1992, 'Intelligent Tutor, Environment and Manual for Introductory Programming'. *Educational and Training Technology International* 29(1), 26–34.

Brusilovsky, P., L. Pesin, and M. Zyryanov: 1993, 'Towards an Adaptive Hypermedia Component for an Intelligent Learning Environment'. In Bass L., J. Gornostaev, and C. Unger (eds.): *Human Computer Interaction*. Lecture Notes in Computer Science No. 753, Berlin: Springer-Verlag, pp. 348–358.

Brusilovsky, P.: 1996, 'Methods and Techniques of Adaptive Hypermedia'. *User Modeling and User-Adapted Interaction* 6(2-3), 87–129 (reprinted in this volume, pp. 1–43).

Carroll J.M. and C. Carrithers: 1984, 'Training Wheels in a User Interface'. *Communications of the ACM* 27(8), 800–806.

Conklin, J.: 1987, 'Hypertext: An Introduction and Survey'. *IEEE Computer* 20, 17–41.

Croft, B.: 1984, 'The Role of Content and Adaptation in User Interfaces'. *International Journal of Man-Machine Studies* 21, 283–292.

Crouch, C., D. Crouch, and K. Nareddy: 1994, 'Associative and Adaptive Retrieval in a Connectionist System'. *International Journal of Expert Systems* 7(2), 193–202.

Dumais, S., G. Furnas, T. Landauer, S. Deerwester, and R. Harshman: 1988, 'Using Latent Semantic Analysis to Improve Access to Textual Information'. *Proceedings CHI'88*, New York: ACM, pp. 281–285.

Fischer, G.: 1992, 'Shared Knowledge in Cooperative Problem Solving Systems: Integrating Adaptive and Adaptable Systems'. *Proceedings UM'92: Third Int. Conference on User Modeling*, Dagstuhl, pp. 148–161.

Fischer, G.: 1995, 'New Perspectives on Working, Learning and Collaborating and Computational Artifacts in Their Support'. In H.-D. Böcker (ed.): *Proceedings Software-Ergonomie'95*, Stuttgart: Teuber Verlag.

Grazotto, F., P. Paolini, and D. Schwabe: 1991, 'HDM – A Model for the Design of Hypertext Applications'. *Proceedings Hypertext'91*, ACM Press, pp. 313–328.

Hohl, H., H.-D. Böcker, and R. Gunzenhäuser: 1996, 'Hypadapter: An Adaptive Hypertext System for Exploratory Learning and Programming'. *User Modeling and User-Adapted Interaction* 6(2-3), 131–156 (reprinted in this volume, pp. 117–142).

Höök, K., J. Karlgren, A. Wærn, N. Dahlbäck, C. G. Jansson, K. Karlgren, and B. Lemaire: 1996, 'A Glass Box Approach to Adaptive Hypermedia'. *User Modeling and User-Adapted Interaction* 6(2-3), 157–184 (reprinted in this volume, pp. 143–170).

Hoppe, H.: 1992, 'Towards Task Models for Embedded Information Retrieval'. *in Proceedings CHI'92*, New York: ACM, pp. 173–180.

Kaplan, C., J. Fenwick, and J. Chen: 1993, 'Adaptive Hypertext Navigation Based on User Goals and Context'. *User Modeling and User-Adapted Interaction* 3(3), 193–220 (reprinted in this volume, pp. 45–69).

Kay J.: 1994, 'Lies, Damned Lies and Stereotypes: Pragmatic Approximations Of Users'. *Proceedings of UM'94, 4th Int. Conference on User Modeling*, Hyannis, MA, pp. 175–184.

Kibby M. and P. Maes: 1989, 'Towards Intelligent Hypertext'. In: McAleese (ed.): *Hypertext Theory into Practice*, Ablex, pp. 164–172.

Kobsa, A. and W. Pohl: 1994a, 'Workshop on Adaptivity and User Modeling in Interactive Software Systems'. *User Modeling and User-Adapted Interaction* 3(4), 359–367.

Kobsa, A. and W. Pohl: 1994b, 'The User Modeling Shell System BGP-MS'. *User Modeling and User-Adapted Interaction* 4(2), 59–106.

Kok, A.: 1991, 'A Formal Approach to User Modeling in Data-Retrieval'. *Int. J. Man-Machine Studies* 35, 675–693.

Kühme T.: 1993, 'User-Centered Approach To Adaptive Interfaces'. *Knowledge-Based Systems* 6(4).

Maes, P.: 1994, 'Agents that Reduce Work and Information Overload'. *Communications of the ACM* 37(7): 31–40.

Mathé, N. and J. Chen: 1996, 'User-Centered Indexing for Adaptive Information Access'. *User Modeling and User-Adapted Interaction* 6(2-3), 225–261 (reprinted in this volume, pp. 171–207).

Monk A.: 1989, 'The Personal Browser: A Tool For Directed Navigation In Hypertext Systems'. *Interacting with Computers* 1(2), 190–196.

Norcio, A. and J. Stanley: 1989, 'Adaptive HCI: A Literature Survey and Perspectives'. *IEEE Trans. on Systems, Man and Cybernetics* 19(2), 399–408.

Oppermann, R.: 1994a, 'Adaptively Supported Adaptability'. *Int. J. Human-Computer Studies.* 40, 455–472.

Oppermann, R.: 1994b, *Adaptive User Support*. Hillsdale, NJ: Lawrence Erlbaum Assoc.

Pearlman G.: 1989, 'Evaluating How Your User Interfaces Are Used'. *IEEE Software*, January 1989, 112–113.

Rasmussen, J., A. Pejtersen, and L. Goodstein: 1994, *Cognitive Systems Engineering*. New York: John Wiley & Sons.

Schwabe, D., B. Feijó, and W. Krause: 1990, 'Intelligent Hypertext for Normative Knowledge in Engineering'. In: Rizk, A., N. Streitz, and J. André (eds.): *Hypertext: Concepts, Systems and Applications*. Cambridge: Cambridge University Press.

Thomas, Ch. and G. Fischer: 1996, 'Using Agents to Improve the Usability and Usefulness of the World-Wide Web'. *Proceedings UM'96, 5th Int. Conference on User Modeling*, Hawaii, pp. 5–13.

Thompson R.H. and W.B. Croft: 1989, 'Support for Browsing in an Intelligent Text Retrieval System'. *Int. J. Man-Machine Studies* **30**, 639–668.
Tyler, S.W. and S. Treu: 1989, 'An Interface Architecture to Provide Adaptive Task-Specific Context for the User'. *Int. J. Man-Machine Studies* **30**, 303–327.
Vassileva, J.: 1994, 'A Practical Architecture for User Modeling in a Hypermedia-Based Information System'. *Proceedings UM'94, 4th Int. Conference on User Modeling*, Hyannis, pp. 115–120.
Visser, W.: 1994, 'Organisation of Design Activities: Opportunistic, with Hierarchical Episodes'. *Interacting with Computers* **6**(3), 239–274.
Wenger, E.: 1987, *Artificial Intelligence and Tutoring Systems*, Los Altos: Morgan Kaufmann.

Author's vita

Dr. Julita Vassileva
Institute for Technical Computer Science, Federal Armed Forces University Munich, 85577 Neubiberg, Germany

Dr. Julita Vassileva received her master degree in Mathematics in 1986 from the University of Sofia, Bulgaria, and her Ph.D. in Computer Science in 1991 from the same university in the field of Intelligent Tutoring Systems. Since 1992 she works as a research assistant at the Technical Computer Science Institute at the University of the Federal Armed Forces in Munich, Germany. Dr. Vassileva has worked in several areas in AI concerning the development of user-adaptive systems: intelligent tutoring systems, user and student modeling, knowledge representation, planning, machine learning, pedagogical psychology. Her contribution is based on experiences gained in an industrial project for creating an adaptive hypermedia-based office documentation system.

Index